THEORY AND

TABLA

Sadanand Naimpalli

THEORY AND PRACTICE OF

TABLA

Sadanand Naimpalli

Popular
prakashan

Published by Harsha Bhatkal for
Popular Prakashan Pvt. Ltd.
301, Mahalaxmi Chambers
22 Bhulabhai Desai Road
Mumbai 400026
www.popularprakashan.com

First Published 2005
First Reprint March 2006
Second Reprint 2007
Third Reprint 2011
Fourth Reprint 2016

ISBN 978-81-7991-149-5
(3897)

Typeset & Designed by
Vans Information

Printed in India by
Rama Printers
4743/23, Ansari Road, Darya Ganj
New Delhi-110002

Pandit Taranath Rao Hattiangadi
(15-03-1915 to 10-01-1991)

When I came to you as a toddler, you held my little hand, taught me Tabla and led me through a maze of worldly experiences. Even today, in times of crises, I can feel your presence by me, guiding me, egging me on when I am about to give up. Whenever I sit for my Riyaaz or participate in concerts, I can feel your strong vibrations course through my being. For me, meeting you and being under your loving care and tutelage was by itself the greatest fulfillment of my life. That in the process, I got to learn the art of Tabla-playing has been a bonus.

I am trying my level best to repay my debt of gratitude to you by teaching my young *shishyas* the Tabla you so lovingly handed down to me. I can feel the shortcomings in me – painfully. But then, I take solace from the fact you were the Fountainhead and me but a drop of that water.

With deepest humility, as a token of my unabashed admiration for you and unstinted devotion to your ideals, I dedicate this book to your hallowed memory and pray to God – nay to Thee, to inspire me to continue on the path you have shown.

JAI GURU!

FOREWORD

One of the main concerns I have is about the lack of unification in the standardization of the teachings of tabla. Tabla is one of the youngest instruments in the field of North Indian Classical music and is still in the development stage. But the repertoire that is played on tabla is a mix of the pakhawaj compositions of the old tradition and compositions that have been recently written for tabla. By recent, I mean the last 150 odd years. The Ustads of the old times were illiterate and believed in the oral tradition of passing on the knowledge, because of that, most of the repertoire that was passed on went through subtle changes from generation to generation, both in its execution and its definition. This led to many interpretations of the repertoire creating confusion amongst the students. It is this confusion that Sadanand Naimpalli has very ably addressed in this book. He has not tried to take sides or offer his own opinion as the final one. Instead he has magnified and pointed to a suggestion that although the definitions of the syllabus differ, the basic execution of the compositions remain the same.

Mr. Naimpalli received his training from one of the great educators of tabla, Pandit Taranath Rao. Taranathji's analysis of the repertoire of tabla was based in logic and practicality and this approach is clearly evident in Sadanand Naimpalli's book. Sadanand Bhai is one of the finest tabla maestros of our country. I have heard him do solo recitals of tabla and was very impressed with the way he handled the repertoire of this great tradition. Considering, that this may be the first step towards the way we look at tabla in the future, I wish him well and thank him for giving me the honour of being a part of this endeavour.

(Zakir Hussain)

PREFACE

About the Book

When I decided to take up Tabla playing again after a lapse of twenty years with my late Guruji's blessings, I realized that I could not sit to play the Tabla for more than five minutes at a stretch. I was hopelessly out of touch. Neither did I have the train of thoughts nor the stamina. When I learnt my Tabla, Guruji just would not allow me to take down the lessons. He made me listen to his recitation of a bol with all the attention that I could muster and try to reproduce it first orally and then on the Tabla. It came to such a stage that I could immediately grasp whatever was taught and reproduce it on the Tabla. Thus, when I needed some sort of reference to start my new innings with the Tabla, I was like a lost kid groping for ideas.

At this stage I took a momentous decision. I decided that the best way to get back the forgotten legacy was to start teaching youngsters the same way that I, along with several of my colleagues were taught by Guruji. As I went about doing this, I slowly began remembering all the lessons. Not only did I teach them but I practiced them along with my students.

After a few years I realized that I should start writing these lessons for posterity. Once the decision was made, page upon page of written Tabla compositions began piling up. Only last year did I feel that it was time I put these things in print. This is the first of my books and is meant primarily for those students who have a strong desire to pursue Tabla as a profession.

Being a convent educated person, I found it easier to put my ideas down in English. Also, there were not many books in this language that could be used as a guide by the younger generation. Moreover, the popularity of Tabla has transcended our shores and today, mainly due to the unstinted efforts of my Guruji Pandit Taranathji, Ustad Allarakha Khan, Ustad Zakir Hussein and a host of prominent Gurus, Ustads and popular percussionists, Tabla enjoys a pre-eminent position among all Indian musical instruments both in India and abroad.

Tabla has developed as a solo instrument only lately. Even today, many musicians are reluctant to consider it as a musical instrument. Neither are they inclined to learn more about it, preferring to make themselves aware of only those Taals and Thekas that are useful to them. Tabla has its own language— grammar, aesthetics, prose, poetry, in fact everything that is associated with any language. Only, the mode of expression is different. Why is Tabla considered the most popular accompanying instrument today? Obviously, because of the wide range of pleasant sounds and its ability to blend with the vocalist's or instrumentalist's idiom. Be that as it may, the scope of this book is to present Tabla as a Solo instrument.

The language of Tabla has developed from that of its more ancient predecessor, Pakhawaj. However, there is a wider range of sounds and bols, mainly because of the separation of the Bass and Treble i.e. Dugga (Baayaan) and Tabla. Also, the Tabla lends itself efficatiously to a range of styles of singing and instrumental accompaniment.

Tabla, as is the case with all musical arts, is mainly a "Gurumukhi - Vidya" i.e. knowledge passed to a Shishya from the mouth of a Guru. Even today, there are some discrepancies in definitions and presentation of compositions depending on which "Gharana" or school of Tabla one represents. Seminars and Conferences are held at regular intervals to discuss and narrow the differences and bring about a concensus so that a uniform methodology is evolved for future dissemination of knowledge of Tabla.

It has been my effort to present as comprehensive a view of Tabla in all its diversity in so far as various "Gharanas" are concerned. The material given should cater to any student, from a rank beginner to a Tabla player who is already trained to some extent. Besides "Dadra", which is mainly for beginners, nine more Taals have been dealt with, such that each can be presented in a Solo of about half an hour. Of-course, TeenTaal has been dealt with in greater detail. There is enough scope for an enterprising student to try and make his own permutations and combinations of various Kaidas Relas etc.

I intend to bring out a sequel shortly, wherein the Taals covered here are dealt with in greater detail and some more Taals are added to a performer's repertoire.

Sadanand Naimpalli

ACKNOWLEDGEMENTS

My deepest gratitude to

1) **His Holiness Srimad Parijnanashram Swamiji III of hallowed memory:** At the time when I was about to venture into my second innings as a Tabla player, I went to seek Swamiji's blessings. The moment He set eyes upon me, He called out "Come in, Tabalji !" I was dumbfounded and just nodded my thanks. This only reinforced my belief that I was going in the right direction.

2) **My dear Mother, my biggest fan:** For having faith in me and instilling in me a sense of confidence that whatever decisions I took, I was destined to be successful.

3) **My dear spouse Aruna:** Without her encouragement and unstinted support, I would not have dared to close my Foundry business and attempted a comeback to Tabla.

4) **Ustad Zakir Hussein:** My association with Zakir-ji goes back to the days when both of us were in short pants. Our paths took different directions when I went in for Engineering studies, service and Business, thereafter and Zakir Hussein set about conquering the musical world with his charm and incredible musicality, added of course to his "Out-of-this-world" Tabla playing. Recently, I sent feelers to Zakir-ji through his shishya, young and upcoming Tabla player, Aditya Kalyanpur, with a request that he do me the honour of writing a Foreword for my forthcoming book on Tabla. He agreed to my request at once without even asking to see the script. The world knows the greatness of Ustad Zakir Hussein as a percussionist par excellence. But not many have been privileged to have known him for his deep sense of humility and down-to-earth nature.

5) **Pandit Nityanand Haldipur:** For strongly supporting me during those difficult days of transition.

6) My son, **Sameer** and disciple, **Hemant Koppikar:** For doing the bulk of computer-related jobs, which, to me were more daunting

than writing the book. Also my shishya, **Shantanu Shukla** for all the art related work.

7) **Shri Ramdas Bhatkal of M/S. Popular Prakashan:** For agreeing to print and publish the book so that it can reach a wider circle of students and afficionados.

8) **Pandit Arvind Mulgaonkar** for going over the script and giving valuable suggestions.

9) **To innumerable people:** Who may have wittingly or unwittingly influenced my career as a Tabla player and inspired me to write this book.

GURU - SHISHYA PARAMPARA

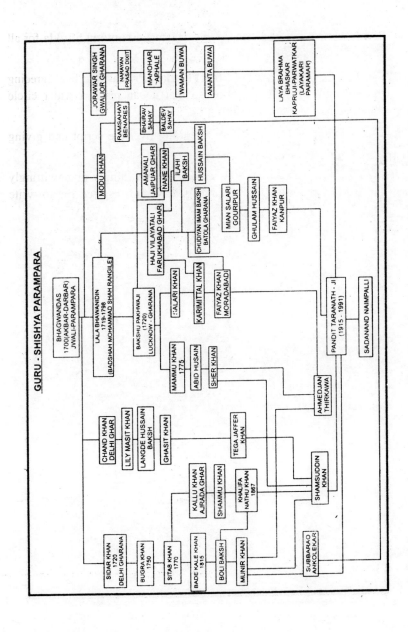

CONTENTS

PART I

PART II

PART - I

Manifestation of Laya

Nature has endowed man with the twin blessings of intellect and the power to think. Unlike other animals who do not possess the benefit of these qualities, man has been able to make his life happier and more fulfilling. He first started directing his efforts in improving the basic necessities of life i.e. Food, Shelter and Clothing. Once these needs were fulfilled, his mind automatically veered to the idea of entertainment and improvement in the quality of life-both socially and culturally. In this aspect, his ability to take in sounds and rhythms from nature around him, contributed to the concept of musicality in him. He gradually developed in himself the sense to discriminate good sounds from bad ones (noise), to use these sounds to express himself in any emotional state. He learnt to recognize basic rhythms to which he began to sway and dance when in a mood for enjoyment on happy occasions. He also learnt to duplicate them by creating various basic instruments out of those things that were available around him.

As human life developed in its manifold spheres, concepts such as God, Country, Society, Language, Religion, Culture and Collective or Co-operative Living took root. Man, putting to use the elementary knowledge of rhythm and melodic sounds must have started singing the praises of the powerful super-natural being, to whom he felt thankful and indebted for showering upon him the bounties of Nature and looking after him in times of distress. This may have led him to form small groups of like-minded co-humans consequently leading to the formation of Clans and Society. With this development, ideas of forming enlarged groups over vast tracts of land must have led to formation of Countries. Alienation of communities because of distances, different behavioural patterns and thought processes must have resulted in the birth of different Religions. Also, along with these advancements, came Literature and the ability to systematize knowledge, which is what Science is.

"Laya" manifests itself in phenomena that occur routinely in nature viz. Rotation of the Earth about its axis, as also its revolution round the Sun, the cycle of the Seasons, the tides of the Sea, the continuous beating of the human heart, the pulse beat, the activity of breathing etc. Phenomena, which produce Rhythmic/Musical sounds in nature, are also a manifestation of "Laya" eg... Pitter-Patter of Rain drops, Drip-Drip of water drops falling from the roof gutters, Swirling sounds created by leaves of trees, the cooing of the nightingales, the crowing of the cock, the sound of a horse's hooves, the rhythmic rattle of the wheels of a running train, as also sounds created while talking, singing etc. When man became aware of the sounds & phenomena around him, he also must have realized that they occur at regular intervals for specific periods & keep repeating in the same order. All the instances given above show a break, a gap & periodicity. In short, to know or feel the pulse of anything that is moving, we should know the periodicity or repetitiveness, its breaks or stoppages at regular intervals.

Man must have got the inspiration to formulate the speed or movement, having observed the occurrence of natural phenomena eg...day/night; cycle of seasons; tides of the sea etc. He must have first set about to measure the time intervals & the longevity or otherwise of the above-mentioned natural phenomena. Having done that, he came down to splitting these time intervals into smaller & smaller units eg: days, to hours, to minutes, to seconds & so on.

The collective or net result (or experience) of categorizing any progressive (or moving) activity into well-defined time intervals, stops or repetitions in the same cycles is what is termed as "Laya".

Music is now an inseparable part of human life, having been with man both as an experience and a tradition going back into thousands of years. This relationship between the human race and music will continue to exist and even flourish as long as human life and civilization exists.

A man devoid of musical or literary qualities is the personification of a beast without a tail and horns.- Translation of a Sanskrit Shloka (couplet).

The Evolution Of Rhythmic Instruments

Rhythmic Instruments must have started appearing quite early in man's life. In fact they may be presumed to be as old as mankind itself. Musical notes and their awareness or knowledge came much later. Early man found that Rhythm was not only a part of himself or his being, but also in his surroundings, as in "Nature". It could be said that the "Clap" of the hands was the first rhythmic instrument. Man may have experienced rhythm when he stamped his feet on the ground, in glee or even anger, at regular intervals. Beating his chest or abdomen or slapping his thighs at regular intervals could have also given him the same experience. This could have happened even before he realized that he could produce sounds orally to duplicate the pleasant sounds he heard around himself. In due course he must have utilized his resourcefulness and intelligence to create instruments that produced more enjoyable sounds.

The earliest instruments had to be rhythmic in nature, made out of things that man could lay his hands on anywhere, such as bones, stones, rocks, coconut-shells, gourds (extracted after drying or eating the inner flesh).

Some of the earliest rhythmic instruments are as follows :

1) **Rattle** : Putting small solid objects such as pebbles or grains in a thin walled hollow body such as emptied out and dried shells of small coconuts or round fruits / gourds. This instrument in its modified version is used even today eg : "*Maraccas*".

2) **Scrapers** : These are instruments using **"Friction"** caused between two rough surfaced objects, as a means of giving rhythmic sounds. Instruments such as a bone with serrated surface and a plectrum like object have been found in Stone Age cave sites.

3) **Stampers** : Instruments using stamping by feet. A pit would be dug in the ground and covered by rough planks or wood or bark of trees. Men would dance or stamp their feet on these surfaces to get rhythmic sounds.

Later on, these planks could have been replaced by animal hides stretched out over the dug out pit – to get a deeper sound. This was the precursor of the *"Bhoomi-Dundubhi"*.

4) **Clappers** : Jaw bones of slain animals or **cymbal-like** objects made of bones – hitting one with the other

5) **Slit Drums** : In this category fall instruments that were made by carving out wooden portions of trees. Variations of this type are found even today. Of course, there have been changes in shapes and sizes, the smallest found to date has been a drum of about 6 inches long and made up of a hollow bamboo of 3 inches diameter.

6) **Dhol** : This name implies an instrument using Animal hides i.e.: stretching out a skin across the hollowed out portion of an object. Initially, it used to be played by hands but later on, sticks were used. Earlier, skins of serpents, lizards or even fish were used. In course of time, these were replaced by skins of deer, sheep or cattle. The development of this genre of instruments was considered to be a landmark development of rhythmic instruments.

Further classification of the **Dhol** group :

a) Using the ground / earth **(Ground / Slit Drums)** eg : *"Bhoomi Dundubhi"*.

b) Using Clay **(Clay Drums)** – Initially patterned by hand, the invention of the Wheel popularized the form of *Drum Shells*. The *Shells* were then covered with stretched skin. Even today, Pakhawaj is sometimes referred to as *Mridang* i.e: one whose body is made up of Clay.

c) Examples of **Wooden drums** are in use even today.

d) **Metallic drums** – are also popular today.

The *Dhols* of prehistoric times were huge. It is presumed that they were over ten feet tall and were kept tilted against a cliff or tree and then played.

Clay drums came into existence with the introduction of the art of moulding clay. These displaced the instruments carved out of wood to some extent.

Thus, the stages in the development of Rhythmic Instruments can be broadly classified as follows:

Musical Instruments

Ghana Vadya	Avanadha Vadya	Sushir Vadya	Tanta Vadya

A) **Ghana Vadya**: Any solid object which, when struck by another object produces a sound. Such instruments are called *Ghana Vadya* eg: Cymbals, Bell, Metal triangle, *Ghungroos*, Rattles etc. or even clapping of hands.

B) **Avanadha Vadya**: Instruments made by capping or topping an empty vessel with a stretched skin are called *Avanadha Vadya* or "*Percussion Instruments*". These instruments are played by means of sticks (strikers) or bare hands eg : *Nagara, Dhol, Taasha, Duff, Dholak, Dholki, Mridangam, Pakhawaj, Tabla-Dugga*.

C) **Sushir Vadya**: Instruments that need "*Air*" to pass through to produce sound are called *Sushir Vadya* eg ; Conch, Horn, *Tutaari*, Flute, *Sundri, Shehnai*, Bugle, *Harmonium*, Clarinet, Saxophone, etc.

D) **Tanta Vadya**: Instruments using metallic strings to produce sound fall in this category. This category must have originated from the "Bow" (and arrow). These are further divided in "*T't Vadya*" i.e. : Plucking Instruments and "*Vi-T't Vadya*" i.e. : Bowing Instruments. Examples of *T't Vadya* are *Ek Taari, Taanpura, Veena, Sitar, Sarod, Santoor*, etc. Examples of *Vi-T't Vadya* are *Sarangi, Violin, Dilruba, Taar-Shehnai*, etc.

DIFFERENCES BETWEEN GHANA AND AVANADHA VADYA

It is apparent that *Ghana Vadya* must have preceded the *Avanadha Vadya* instruments. A clap with bare hands or rapping ones thighs with the hand are the first indications of *Ghana Vadya*. This must have been followed by striking of one object by another eg. bones, sticks, etc. Consequently, through the various ages must have been born instruments such as *Tipris*, cymbals, etc.

The evolution of *Avanadha Vadya* came about in more interesting circumstances. Man had to hunt down animals to satisfy his hunger. After the feast following the killing, the bones and skin had no use for man. But curiosity and the spirit of adventure – the reason for man's advancement from Barbarism to Civilised Society, made him experiment with these. He stretched dried skin parchments on hollow bones and found that on striking the skin, he could get deeper and baser sounds. Thus began a process of experimentation, where he even covered big pits dug into the ground with the dried skins and then started dancing on them or striking them with bones or wooden sticks, to produce booming sounds. Thus was born the *"Bhoomi Dundubhi"* – *Bhoomi* means Earth or ground and *Dundubhi* means a loud and deep sounding percussion instrument.

STAGES IN THE DEVELOPMENT OF *AVANADH A VADYA*.

Percussion Instruments developed in stages :-

i) *"Bhoomi Dundubhi"* was the first stage, where the leather parchment is stretched over a dug out pit.

ii) Blocks of wood from trees, carved out into hollow pots and covered on one or both sides with skin parchment eg : *Duff* or *Dhol.*

iii) Clay pots whose openings were covered with skin eg : *Ghumat.*

iv) Metal pots or frames covered on the top or sides respectively with skin parchment eg : *Taasha, Nagara, Tambourine.*

"Oordhvak", "Aankik" and *"Aalingya"* are three percussion instruments mentioned in Ancient Texts. Besides being topped by stretched skins, they also had layers of very fine clay applied in stages at the center of the skin tops to get appropriate Tonal quality.

7

Oordhvak was to be played by keeping it standing in front of the person playing the instrument. *Aankik* was to be played by taking the instrument on the body or laps of the player. *Aalingya* was to be played with the player holding the instrument in the position of an embrace i.e. : holding it between the arm and the body. These three, together were also called "*Tri-Pushkar*" i.e. ; an instrument with three heads.

7) **Mridang**: A "*Mridang*" is so named, because its body was made of clay ("*Mrith*" meaning clay and "*Ang*" meaning body – in Sanskrit.) Both sides of this hollow body were covered with skin tops, which were held tightly by ropes. Both the tops were given application of layers of fine clay in the center. The "*Mridangam*" and "*Pakhawaj*" are refined or improved versions of the "*Mridang*" of olden times.

8) **Damaru**: This is the drum that was used by Lord *Shiva* at the time of His Celestial Dance or "*Taandav-Nritya*".

The instrument is generally around 6 to 12 inches in length, having 3½ to 5 inches diameter sides covered with skin. The shape of this instrument is like an hour-glass. The skins are held in place by strong strings which can be pressed and released by hand to vary the tone of the instrument. The striking on the skin tops is done by a long string which has a hard head on either side. Mythology gives us to believe that the *Damaru* was the first and original rhythmic percussion instrument and was used by Lord *Shiva* at the time of the "*Taandava Nritya*". This phenomenon is considered to be fountain-head of all Arts, Languages, etc.

The *Atharva Ved* mentions the "*Dundubhi*", probably "*Bhoomi Dundubhi*", which was used during the *Vedic* recitations. The *Vedas/Upanishads* are not the creation of one person but different *Rishis* or Sages have periodically contributed to them and hence, as per the period of the contribution, various instruments find a place in the *Vedic* writings.

9) **Tabla**: The most popular percussion instrument in recent times, Tabla is a combination of two instruments, viz :- "*Tabla*" or "*Daayaan*" and

"*Dugga*" or "*Baayaan*". The *Daayaan* i.e. : right hand instrument is made up of a hollow tapered cylindrical block of wood. The bottom is solid and tapered in the reverse direction. The open top is mounted by a skin-head or "*Pudi*", made of goat-skin, having a black layered application of "*Shaayee*" in the center, quite similar to that in the Pakhawaj. This *Pudi* is woven around the "*Khod*" or the wooden vessel by means of straps of hide called "*Vaadi*". The *Vaadi* straps are interspersed with wooden blocks called "*Guttas*" all around the outer diameter of the *Khod*. The *Guttas* are used for rough tuning of the Tabla. The finer tuning is carried out closer to the "*Pudi*". The *Gajara* is the outer diameter of the *Pudi* and is got by the twining or weaving of the ends of the Goat-skin with thinner straps of the *Vaadi*.

The *Dugga* is an inverted dome-shaped pot made of copper, brass or clay, whose open and wider top is mounted by the *Pudi* just as in the Tabla. However, the *Pudi* mounted on the *Dugga* has the *Shaayee* applied eccentrically, generally at a distance of about the thickness of four fingers from one side.

The *Dugga* provides the "*Bass*" and the Tabla provides the "*Treble*".

NOTE : *Please refer diagram on page no.11 for details of construction.*

The Genesis Of Tabla

Tabla must have been in existence in India for many many years – at least during the reign of Allaudin Khilji (1296 to 1316). It is believed that Tabla is the contribution of the Mughals to our Music. This is a contentious issue, as we know that the *Pushkar* was in existence long before even the Pakhawaj. It is quite likely that an instrument resembling the Tabla was in existence even before the Mughal invasion. But it is definite that the use of the Tabla was accentuated during the Mughal rule, when *Dhruv-pad* (**Dhrupad**) tradition of singing gradually gave way to *Khayal* singing. The *Dhruv-pads* were songs, all in praise of the pantheon of Hindu Gods. These were replaced by *Khayal* singing in which the compositions sung were mainly in praise of the King and were not robust as *Dhrupad* singing. This entailed a softer and subtler accompaniment. This is where the Tabla got its importance.

The word Tabla has come from the Arabic word "*Tabl*" which is the equivalent name for percussion instruments. Hence, we have varieties of instruments having names like "*Tabl-Balaadi*", "*Tabl-Turky*", "*Tabl-Jung*", "*Tabl-Saami*", "*Tabl-Mirgi*", etc.

Tabla must have come into greater use during the period 1210 to 1247, which also happens to be the period in which the "*Sangeet Ratnakar*" was written by **Sharang Dev**, the son of a Minister in the Kingdom of *Devgiri*.

In the period before 400 A.D. there was a uniform system of music across the length and breadth of India. From the treatises of Sage *Bharat-Muni* (*Natya Shastra*) and Shaarang Dev (*Sangeet Ratnakar*), it seems that this was the case till 1290 A.D. In this period, "*Swar*" and "*Laya*" i.e. : Melody and Rhythm, were accorded equal importance. Thus, any musician was equally comfortable in both – which, sadly is not the case today. Although in the *Carnatic* Tradition and to some extent in the *Dhrupad* Tradition, Vocalists and Instrumentalists are quite aware – infact very much so – of the Taals involved and being played during their performances. *Khayal* singing, laid too much emphasis on the "*Swar*" development, to the detriment of the "*Taal*" aspect.

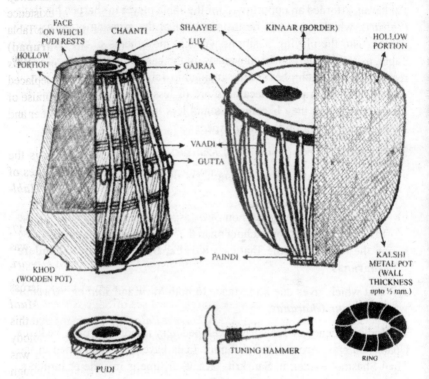

TABLA (DAAYAAN)

FACE ON WHICH PUDI RESTS

CHAANTI

SHAAYEE

LUV

GAJRAA

HOLLOW PORTION

VAADI

GUTTA

KHOD (WOODEN POT)

PAINDI

DUGGA (BAAYAAN)

KINAAR (BORDER)

HOLLOW PORTION

KALSHI METAL POT (WALL THICKNESS upto ½ mm.)

PUDI

TUNING HAMMER

RING

11

The popularity of the *Khayal* singing was the downfall of the Pakhawaj. Just as the deeply resonant, profound and forceful accompaniment of Pakhawaj was suitable for *Dhrupad* Tradition, it would have proved ruinous for the soft and subtle forms of *Khayal* singing. The soft, restrained and at times forceful (when necessary) sounds of the Tabla and the Dugga, proved an ideal accompaniment for the *Khayal* singing. The style adopted for playing the Tabla i.e. using fingers as against the palm being used for the Pakhawaj, afforded an opportunity for the Tabla player to sharpen his skills (*Taiyari*), which proved to be instrumental in the growing popularity of Tabla. Also, the playing positions, vertical movements of the hands for Tabla, as against horizontal movement in the case of Pakhawaj – are also responsible for the higher speeds attained in Tabla playing. Over a period of time, the Tabla player became more or less a human metronome for *Khayal* singers as they became less and less involved in *Taal* and *Laya*, while concentrating on the *Swar* aspect.

There are three types of singing of *Khayals*:

a) That which gives greater emphasis on *Laya* and *Taal* eg : **Agra Gharana**.

b) That which gives emphasis on *Swar* aspect while almost ignoring the Taal aspect, except for latching on to the "*Mukhada*" or the catch phrase on the last beat of the Taal eg : **Kirana, Bhendi Bazar** and **Indore Gharanas**.

c) That which gives due importance to both *Swar* and *Taal* eg : *Gwalior* and *Jaipur Gharanas*.

The Indian Science of Taals has developed very rapidly since the Vedic or Upanishad eras. Around 360 different Taals have been mentioned in the "Taal-Shastra" written in Sanskrit. "Kaal" or time is infinite or limitless. Hence, we can have any number of Taals or cycles of Matras (beats).

Tabla, as also Pakhawaj have their own distinct language which is mainly of consonants. The vowels serving as gaps or "Aakaars". These consonants are pronounced a little differently in various regions of India eg : **Gi** or **Ghi** in Maharashtra and Goa, it will be **Ge** or **Ghe** in Purab, Farrukhabad,

12

Benares, Ajrada. N' in Delhi is a softer form of N' in Punjab etc. (the alphabet 'N' represents its phonetic sound).

Differences Between Pakhawaj And Tabla

Pakhawaj   Tabla

A) USAGE:

Pakhawaj:

Accompanying instrument for Dhrupad Gayaki, Rudra Veena (also Dhrupad style) and Solo playing.

Tabla:

Accompanying instrument for Khayal Gayaki, Instruments such as Sitar, Sarod (played in the Gayaki/G'th Styles and Solo playing.

B) CONSTRUCTION:

Pakhawaj:

One-piece body made of wood. Hollow cylindrical body, blown up on the middle and tapering towards both ends. Both ends are capped by "Pudis" woven tightly by means of "Vaadi". Wooden Blocks (Gutta) are provided for tuning of the instrument.

On the Treble (Chaanti) side there is an application of "Shaayee"* in layers. On the "Dhumma" or Base side there is no Shaayee but, while performing, an application of moistened wheat flour is made at the centre.

Tabla:

This is a two piece instrument. The "Chaanti" or the Tabla is a wooden body two-thirds hollowed out. The Dugga or Base is a metallic pot (Brass or Copper) about 9¼ inches in diameter, bulging in the middle and

This will be explained in detail at a later stage.

tapering towards the end to about 4 inches in diameter. Both Tabla and Dugga are covered by pudis as in the Pakhawaj.

But the pudi on the Dugga has an eccentric application of Shaayee in layers as done on the Tabla. The pudi is tightened on top of the metal pot (at the larger diameter end) by a leather strap called Vaadi and Wooden Blocks (Guttas) are provided in the case of the Tabla for rough tuning of the instrument.

C) POSITION:

Pakhawaj:

The Pakhawaj is placed on the ground horizontally and played by striking the Pudis at the ends with open palms. The sounds produced are highly resonant and forceful. For some bols fingers joined together are also used.

Tabla:

The Tabla and Dugga are placed on rings, standing up, with the Chaanti pointing towards the listeners or away from the performer. They are played by means of fingers mainly and sometimes by the palm. The sounds produced are both soft and forceful, but not as much as the Pakhawaj.

D) PLAYING TECHNIQUES:

Pakhawaj:

The use of palms, and heavy striking for production of open or sonorous sounds means that the speed of playing is limited. But because of this Pakhawaj creates a very serene and profound atmosphere.

Tabla:

The use of fingers enables very high speeds to be achieved while playing most bols. Thus, softness, sweetness and beauty of sound are characteristics of Tabla playing.

E) REPERTOIRE:

Pakhawaj:

Generally the Taals played are Dhrupad (Choutaal) Dhamaar, Farodust, Surphaak, Tevraa, etc. The concept of Khaali* is not there in Pakhawaj.

Tabla:

Taals played are Keharwa, Dadra, Jhaptal, Ektaal, Teentaal, Tilwadaa, Jhumraa, Roopak, etc. The concept of Khaali – Bhari* is quintessential in Tabla.

Rhythm Instruments from the South

The main accompanying percussion instruments from the South of India (used for Carnatic music) are the Mridangam, Tavil, Ghatam, Khanjira and Morsing

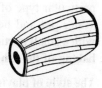
Mridangam

Mridangam: The "Khod" or Body is made from wood of the Jackfruit or Lime Trees or Sheeshum. The shape is similar to that of the Pakhawaj, although a little smaller. There are skin pudis on either sides tightened by leather straps. The treble or Chaanti side has an application of Shaayee in layers. But the Kinaar or border is not cut as much as in a Tabla or Pakhawaj. There is a gap of about 1 mm between the outer diameter of the Shyaaee and the inner diameter of the Kinaar. The skin used for the pudis is thicker than that used for the Tabla and Pakhawaj pudis. On the base side, there is no Shaayee but an application of moistened rice or wheat flour is made everytime the Mridangam is to be played.

The instrument is placed on the laps when seated and played with both palms and fingers – as in a Pakhawaj. The bols are very different from those heard on the Tabla and Pakhawaj eg :- **Dh'Laanku, T'k'Dhiku, T'DinGin'Tom, Thai, Jhunu, Dimi, ThRiKuKu,** etc.

Tavil

Tavil: This is similar to the **Mridangam** though a little smaller in width. But it is bigger in the middle and sides. The *pudi* diameters are about 20 to 21 cms and the diameter at the center is about 35 cms.

The *pudi* is constructed by tightly stretching skins on a round frame made by thick leather straps or thin

* These will be explained in detail at a later stage.

Bamboo strips. These *pudis* are then woven around the **Tavil** ends by means of leather straps. Because the *pudis* are already fully stretched, the **Tavil** does not need to be tuned everytime it is being used for playing. One has to only see that the tightness is uniform throughout. The fingers are covered by caps formed out of paper and rice flour coating which are hardened. The Base is played by means of a thick and short stick. The **Tavil** is used both for Folk and Classical music accompaniment – especially with *Nagaswarams*.

Ghatam: This is an instrument made out of a particular type of clay. It is shaped in the form of a Water pot and hence the name. The clay is mixed with a small portion of iron powder. The making and baking of the **Ghatam** is done with great care.

Ghatam

The style of playing on the **Ghatam** is different from that adopted for other percussion instruments. The artist sits cross-legged on the floor and holds the **Ghatam** close to his body with the opening near the abdomen. The Base effect is got by pressing and releasing the **Ghatam** to the abdomen and striking the body of the **Ghatam** by the lower parts of the wrists. For Treble sounds, fingers are used to strike the **Ghatam** at different parts to get different sounds. The *bols* are the same as for **Mridangam**. The **Ghatam** is used together with the **Mridangam** in concerts. Other instruments used in the accompaniment ensemble are **Khanjira and Moorchang** (Morsing) – which is actually a metallic stringed instrument. In this case the instrument is held to the lips and when the string is plucked, the lips and tongue are used to get different sounds. The mouth is used as a resonator. The **Khanjira** is a small instrument made by stretching Lizard skin on one side of a round wooden frame. The instrument is held in one hand which also controls the changes in the pitch, while the other hand is used to play the various strokes.

NOTE : Please refer diagram on page no. 17 (Khanjiri)

Folk Drums

Folk music has to be given a special place in the Indian music scenario. India, because of the sheer diversity of religions, people, natural characteristics and multifarious lores and mores has a lot to offer in the Folk music genre. Indeed our entire Classical music has come down from Folk music. This being the case, there has to be a large number of percussion instruments that have been used for accompanying or even embellishing these Folk songs. Each state has its own distinct form of Folk music which is connected to the culture and life styles of the region, which we can witness even today.

Some of the percussion instruments used in Folk music are as follows :

1) **Damaru**: Shaped like the hour-glass, the top and bottom of this wooden body are covered with stretched skins on both the faces, woven by means of a strong string. It is around 22 cms. in height. It has two strings tied at the center, which is the thinnest part of the hour-glass figure and these strings have their tips hardened into small balls, which, when the instrument is shaken, hit the skin tops to produce a sound. The strings that go around the pudis can also be pressed at the center of the instrument where it is narrow to provide variation in tone.

Damaru

2) **Khanjiri**: A skin is stretched tightly on one face of a wooden circular frame. The smallest in this kind of percussion instrument is called **Dimdi**. The next in size is the **Khanjiri** and larger than this is the **Duff** or **Halgi**. For the **Halgi** sometimes a frame made of metal sheet is used. The frame is held in one hand and the other hand is used for striking on the pudi. While playing the **Halgi**, a small wooden stick is also used. The **Dimdi** is more used for Folk dances, *Bhajans*, devotional music singing. The **Khanjiri** is used for group songs or for *Shahiri-Powada* singing. The **Halgi** is used for *Lazim* or Group dances. *Powadas* are songs

Khanjiri

17

in Marathi, the predominant language spoken in Maharashtra, extolling the bravery and virtues of Folk Heroes. *Lazim* is an accessory used in a form of group dance and is in the form of a stout wooden rod about 15 inches long, having an iron chain loosely attached to it. This chain is interspersed with pairs of metallic discs at regular spaces to give a metallic tone when the *Lazim* is jerked rhythmically while dancing.

3) **Ghumat**: This instrument is made from baked Clay. It is long and shaped like a dome and has two faces. The right face is broad and is covered by a skin stretched across it. The left face is narrow and left open. The instrument is played by striking the skin on the right (broad) face by fingers or palm. The left (narrow) face is covered by the palm of the other hand to control the pressure of the air inside the **Ghumat**. By varying this pressure, we can get different sounds on striking the right face. There are two versions of the Ghumat. One is longish, in the shape of a Pakhawaj, popular in the areas of North Karnataka and the other type is shaped like a Baayaan (Dugga) and is popular in Goa.

Ghumat

4) **Taasha**: The pot for this instrument is made from Copper or Brass. The pot is rounded and not very deep (like a compressed *Baayaan*). The skin is tightly stretched across the top and held in place by a metallic band and keys that can be tightened or loosened. It is played by means of thin bamboo sticks.

5) **Dhol**: The body is hollow, wooden, shaped like a drum and has two faces. Sometimes, it is also

Taasha

made of sheet metal. The skins are tightened by means of a thickish rope (1/8th inch to 1/4th inch) and has metal rings to tighten or loosen the tension of the *pudis*. The skin on one side is thicker than the other and gives a base sound. This side is played by a stick while the other side (treble) is played with the fingers or palm. It is normally used as an accompanying instrument of the *Taasha*. The combination of these two instruments can give different patterns of *Layakari- ie. :Syncopations.*

Dhol

6) **Nagara**: Ancient texts refer to this instrument as *Dundubhi* and is also known as *Bheri*. The pot of the **Nagara** is very big, round and deep, shaped like a *Baayaan*, and made of Copper or Brass. The skin is stretched across the broad face and held by a band and woven around the pot by ropes. Nowadays, the band is made of steel and the pudi is held by keys around the band that can also be used for loosening or tightening the pudi. The **Nagara** is played by two sticks. This is generally found at temples, religious places and is used at the time of *Aartis, Bhajans,* etc.

Nagara

7) **Choughada**: This is made of two instruments shaped like the **Nagara**, but much smaller, though, one is bigger than the other. The pots are made of Copper or Brass. The skins are stretched tightly across the broader faces by means of thin ropes. The smaller of the two has a sharp tone. Generally played along with the *Shehnai* or *Sundri*. This, along with the *Shehnai* is considered an auspicious instrument and is often used for marriages, thread-ceremonies and in temples.

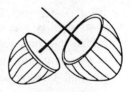

Choughada

8) **Samel** or **Sambal**: These are pairs of wooden instruments, one bigger than the other. Both these instruments are broad at the top and narrowing down to the bottom. The skin is

Samel

19

tightened around a band and the band is tightened on top of the broad face by means of thin ropes (⅛ᵗʰ inch thick). The base **Sambal** has an application of *Shyaaee* on the top. For playing the instruments, the two are tied together and by means of a strap, hung around one's neck. The striking is done by means of thin wooden sticks that are bent round at the striking ends.

9) **Khol**: Shaped like the *Mridang* and made of wood but the diameters on both the faces are much smaller than those of the *Mridang*. Sometimes the **Khol** body is also made of baked clay. The skin tops are firmly fixed on the openings and held tight by leather straps. Played by both hands and fingers just as the *Mridang*. The Khol is used a lot in *Manipuri* Dances and also for *Bhajans*, *Kirtans*, etc. mostly in the North-Eastern regions of India.

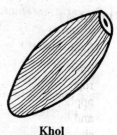
Khol

10) **Naal**: This too is shaped like the *Mridang* and played by means of hands and fingers. But the treble pitch is very high. Usually, for playing the instrument, two such instruments are used. One is placed horizontally on a wooden stand and the base or *Dhumma* of this is played. The *Chaanti* or treble is used in an upright position. Used generally for *Bhajans* and group singing.

Naal

11) **Dholki**: This instrument also belongs to the *Pakhawaj* or *Mridang* family i.e. wooden body, hollow, broad at one end and narrowing down to the other end. The broader end is the base (bass) which has an application of a *Masala* (something like molasses) from the inside i.e. : the inner face of this *pudi*. The narrower face also has a skin top, tightly stretched and having application of *Shaayee*, but on the outside. The two *pudis* are held tight by means of a thin rope. To increase the tension on the *pudis*, small wooden pegs are introduced in the ropes and twisted. These

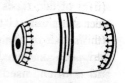
Dholki

days the *pudis* are mostly held in place by steel keys that can be tightened or loosened by means of a spanner. The treble is at a high pitched note. Usually played by hanging it around the neck when used in *Marathi* Folk Dances (*Tamasha)* or played by placing it on ones lap when seated cross-legged on the floor. Mainly used for *Marathi* Folk songs (*Laavni*) or dances (*Tamasha*), devotional music, Film music, etc.

12) **Dholak:** Two-faced, wooden instrument, like a smallish **Dhol**. The skin is fixed on round bands made of leather straps and then placed on the two open sides and held together by means of a thin rope. One side has a thicker skin with a *Masala* application on its inner face, just as in a **Dholki**

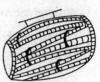

Dholak

and the other side has a tightly stretched thin parchment which gives a sharper tone that can be adjusted by means of metal rings or small wooden pegs inserted between the ropes holding the *pudis*. It is placed horizontally on one's laps and played with both hands and fingers. Used mainly for light music, *Qawallis*, film-music, etc.

13) **Ghana-Vadya**: Instruments for Folk music that have to be used by striking one with the other to provide the base rhythm for songs and dances.

(i) *Tipris*: Rounded sticks, approximately a little over one foot long a little narrow at one end – such as those used in *Garba* dance, a dance form associated with the region of Gujarat.

Tipris

(ii) *Chiplis*: About a span of the hand in length, identically shaped wooden strips, having metal discs (thin) placed between them. The outer side of the strips are fitted with hooks to hold them by the fingers mainly thumb and middle finger on each hand.

(iii) *Zanjh*: Made from Brass, Bronze or Copper. They are two identically shaped discs which are

Chiplis

dimpled in the center having a hole, through which passes a string/rope that can be held from the outside (non-striking end of the *Zanjh*). They are played by striking one on the other. The smaller version of this is called *Manjiri*. Thicker and deeper varieties are called *Taal*.

Zaanjh

(iv) *Ghanta* (Bell): Made of Brass or Bronze having a hook at the top for holding or hanging. Metallic pendulum which is heavy and thick at the bottom hangs through a hook inside it – for striking the sides.

Ghanta (Bell)

(v) *Ghunghroo* (Anklet): Made from thin sheet of metal. The metal sheet is shaped like petals of flowers and then bent into half rounds and joined at one end with a hook after placing a small metallic sphere between them. When shaken, the metallic sphere stikes the walls and produces a sound characteristic of them. They can also be used in bunches where the *Ghunghroos* also strike one another to produce rhythmic sounds – generally associated with dancing.

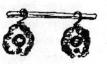

Ghungroo

Some Stringed Instruments used in Folk Music.

1) **Tuntune:** This has a wooden / metal vessel open at both ends. One end has a tightly stretched skin across the face. The other end is open. The outside wall of the vessel is fitted to a long stick to which is attached a wooden peg. A metallic string is passed through a small orifice in the center of the skin parchment and knotted so as not to pass through the hole when once fixed. The other end of the string is taken through the open face and tied to the wooden

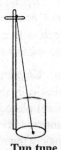

Tun tune

peg which can be turned to tighten or loosen the string. The string can then be plucked to produce sounds. Also, the wooden stick can, in some cases be drawn back and forth to change the tension on the skin, thereby adding to the variety of the notes. (In Tuntune the 'U'

22

should be pronounce as in 'put' and the 'E' should be pronounce as in 'prey'.)

2) **Ektaari**: As the name suggests, this is an instrument that has only one string. A very small and pristine version of the *Taanpura*. It is made by sticking a skin parchment on the open end of a *Gourd*. A bamboo stick is passed through the *Gourd*, which passes under the skin from inside. At the lower, smaller end, a metallic string is held tightly and is

Ektaari

passed over a wooden bridge placed on the stretched skin and attached to a wooden peg passing through the bamboo stick at the other end. The peg can be used to slacken or tighten the string.

The Alphabets And Language
Of Tabla

The sounds created by striking with the fingers on different locations on the Tabla are called *"Varnas"* or Alphabets or Syllables. These *Varnas* join to form words or phrases. Various words or phrases then combine to form a statement. Just as in any other language known to mankind, Tabla has its own language with Alphabets, words, phrases, sentences, paragraphs, chapters, prose, poetry, etc.

The syllables of *Tabla* and *Dugga* can be classified according to their resonance or lack of it.

> Resonating syllables are *NA, TA, DHA, TIN, DHIN, TUN, GE* or *GHE*, etc.

> Non-resonating syllables are *Ti, T', T'th, Ki, K'th, Dhit*, etc.

> Then there are small words which are formed by joining 2 or 3 syllables eg:

> *DHAGE, DHINNA, TINNA, DHAGENA*, etc.

There are combinations or words which are characteristics of compositions such as *Kaidas, Peshkaar* and *Relas* eg: *DHINAGINA, DHADHADHINNA, DHAGEDHINNAGINA*, etc.

Tabla is an instrument of one tone or mono tone. There are different sounds that can be produced at different places on the Tabla by means of fingers. Some of these are resonant and some are not. These sounds are mixed or combined to form various phrases that sound attractive.

In a Solo Tabla recital we hear so many compositions such as *Peshkaar, Kaida, Rela, G'th, Paran, Tukda, Mukhda, Mohra, Tihaai, Chakradaar,*

24

etc. If we study the nature of these compositions, we find that they can be divided into two broad categories:

1) Those in which the concept of *Khali-Bhari* is used.

In this there are two categories; ones which use the *Khali-Bhari* concept in a pre-planned manner eg : like in a *Kaida* and the others in which *Khali-Bhari* is not used eg : as in a *Paran*.

2) Those which can be expanded and others that are not.

In the first category are compositions such as *Peshkaar, Kaida, Rela,* whose prime quality is that they lend themselves to permutations and combinations. The other category constitutes those compositions such as *G'ths* and *Parans* which are fixed compositions and do not brook any changes.

Generally, it is found that those compositions which fall under *Khali-Bhari* form are also those that lend themselves to elaboration. There are some *G'ths* that have *Khali-Bhari* in them, but are not expandable.

Characteristics of expandable compositions are as follows:

1) These compositions have the impressions of the *Taal* or *Theka*.

2) *Khali-Bhari* is used in a pre-planned manner in them.

3) The elaboration of these is generally done in one *Jaati*, though this is not compulsory. The concept of *Jaati* is explained later in **Dasha Praan** chapter.

4) The length of such compositions is generally of shorter duration.

5) These compositions start from **Sum** or first beat of the *Taal* and end on the last *matra*, only to start again on the following **sum**. For this reason, it is easy to elaborate these compositions. Examples of these are – *Peshkaar, Kaida, Rela, Raon, Laggi, Ladi,* etc.

Compositions such as *Paran, Tukda, G'th, Chakradaar, Mukhda, Mohra* are those that are complete in all respects such as language (phraseology), mathematics, *Layakari*, etc. Hence, there can be no changes to be made. Compositions such as these are characteristic of their creators and hence cannot be changed by anyone.

Tuning:

The Tabla or *Daayaan* is tuned to a predetermined pitch or note in the octave and the *Dugga* or *Baayaan* is tuned to the same note, but of the lower octave. If this is not possible, then the *Dugga* should be tuned to the lower octave "*Pancham*" or "*Madhyam*" *swar*, depending on which of the two are prominent in the melody.

To achieve the above mentioned ends in tuning, use is made of a tuning hammer, (refer diagram on page no. 11) which is generally 300 to 500 grams in weight. In case of the Tabla, the *Guttas* or wooden blocks are tightened or loosened by pushing them down or up by means of the hammer. This is done for rough tuning. For finer tuning, the *Gajraa* or the outer border of the *Pudi* (skin-top) is manipulated. The *Gajraa* is given a downward rap of the hammer if the sound is to be made sharper and an upward rap of the hammer if the sound is already sharp and needs to be made flatter. If the sound is only marginally sharp, sometimes even exerting a little pressure on the skin-top with the palm brings it to the desired level of tuning. Similar procedures are adopted in case of the *Dugga*. One must give maximum scope for the Tabla to resonate while playing and also be able to get matching notes on the *Dugga* by exerting pressure on the skin below the *Shaayee*, with the wrist. This can also be done by rubbing the *Shaayee* with the base of the wrist – as done in the **Benares Gharana** and to some extent in the **Ajrada Gharana**.

Construction of the Tabla and *Dugga*. (refer diagram on page no. 11)

The body of the Tabla is of wood and the following varieties of wood are generally in use :- "*Khair*"(Latin name:- ACACIA ATECHU), "*Sheeshum*" (TILA, SEASUM INDICUM LINN); "*Cheench*" (TAMARIND); "*Bijasaar*" or "*Bibhla*" (Latin name:- PTEROCARPUS MARSUPIUM or INDIAN KINO); "*Saag*"(TEAK).

The body or *Khod*, as it is known, is a tapered cylindrical body, approximately 10 inches to 11 inches in height. The diameter at the top end determines the pitch at which it is likely to give the best tone. A rough guide for the same is as follows :

Diameter	Pitch
7 inches	W – 1 to B – 1 (lower octave pitch)
6 ¼ to 6 ½ inches	B – 2, W – 3 (lower octave pitch)
6 to 6 ¼ inches	W – 4 (lower octave pitch)
5 ¾ to 6 inches	B – 4, B – 5
5 ½ inches	B – 1 (high pitch)
5 ¼ inches	B – 2, W. – 3 (high pitch)
5 inches	B – 4, B – 5 (high pitch)

NOTE : In the above Table 'B' and 'W' represent the black and white keys on the Harmonium.

The tapered cylinder is hollowed out to about 2/3 of the height of the cylinder from the top i.e. where the skin head will be mounted. The wall thickness of the hollow portion should be between 3/8 inches to ½ inch. The lower 1/3 portion of the cylinder is given a sharper reverse inclination, terminating in a projection of approximately 4 inches in diameter and ¾ inches in thickness.

The pot or "Kalshi" as it is known, in case of the Dugga is made of clay, brass or copper sheet metals. The weight of this ranges from 1 ½ kgs to 3 ½ kgs, depending on the thickness of the sheet metal used. The shape is generally like an inverted dome, flattened at the bottom. The diameter at the open end is generally between 9 inches to 9 ½ inches and the height is around 11 inches. The heavier the Dugga, the better it is for sound production and stability during playing.

Pudi: (Top or head) (refer diagram on page no. 11)

These are generally made of goat-skin by weaving the ends of the skin parchment through "Gajraa" – the outer border. This pudi is then fixed on to the open end of the Tabla or Dugga by means of leather (hide) straps called *"Vaadi"* or *"Baddi"*. At the center of the *pudi*, in case of the Tabla and slightly eccentrically in case of the *Dugga*, is an application of the *"Shaayee"*. The *"Shaayee"* is 2 ½ to 3 inches in diameter and is applied in layers of reducing diameter. The outermost diameter is 2 ½ to 3 inches, as mentioned and the final layer of the *Shyaaee* is ½ to ¾ inches in diameter. The height of the *Shyaaee* is about 1/8 inches higher at the center than at the outer edges.

The making of the *Pudi*

The skin selected for the *Pudi* is goat skin – generally from the back of the goat, as it is uniform in thickness and texture and also, a larger area is available. The skin is cut in circular pieces. Four* pieces are placed one on top of the other. The diameters of these pieces should be larger than that of the *Tabla* or *Dugga* for which the *pudi* is to be made. The skin which is second from the top is the main skin for the *pudi*. The four skins placed as mentioned above are then pierced to make holes around the outer diameter, with a spacing of 1 inch to 1 ½ inch between two holes. The holes so made should be either 8 or 16 in numbers. This assembly is then placed on the *Tabla* or the *Dugga* and tightly woven around the *Khod / Kalshi* by means of a thickish rope, around 1/8 inches thick. The skins are moistened to soften them and thus, sit tightly around the top. The rope is repeatedly tightened as the skins dry up. After this, a *"Gajraa"* is fabricated around the *pudi*. This is made of leather straps made of Buffalo or Ox hide. In fact, they are thinner versions of the *"Vaadi"*. In order to make the *Gajraa* more eye catching, strips of goat-skin, taken from the abdominal part, are inter-woven with the hide straps. The use of the *Gajraa* is to enable the weaving of the *pudi* (i.e. fixing it on the top) by means of the *Vaadi*. The bottom of the *Tabla / Dugga* is fitted with a ring made of the Buffalo hide. The *Vaadi* goes up and down around this ring called *"Paindi"* and the *Gajraa* alternately.

*(NOTE : *sometimes three or five pieces are used)*

Once the *Gajraa* with the skin assembly, is fitted on the *Khod / Kalshi*, it is kept in the open for drying (by natural heat i.e. : sunlight). Then, the ropes or cords are removed. Thereafter, the bottom two layers of the 4-skin assembly are cut off in a circular fashion, about 1 inch away from the outer

28

diameter. This should be done without inflicting damage on the top two layers of the skin – especially the second layer. This done, the *Pudi* is moistened once again and fitted on top of the *Khod / Kalshi* and, this time woven around by means of the *Vaadi,* through the *Gajraa* on the top and the *Paindi* at the bottom. The *Pudi* is then sun-dried and after that, the central part of the topmost layer of the skins is cut off, leaving a width of about 2 inches from the *Gajraa*. A coating of an adhesive is applied at the center (cut out portion). This is where the *Shaayee* will be applied.

The *Shaayee* is made of a mixture of very fine particles of pig-iron or cast-iron, coal-dust and a binder made of steamed rice or fine wheat flour. A bit of Copper-Sulphate is added. The ingredients are mixed in the right proportion and applied in stages on the part of the second layer of skin that has been exposed after a central portion of the top layer has been cut off. In case of the *Dugga*, the *Shaayee* application is done eccentrically such that the outer diameter of the *Shaayee* is at a distance of approximately 2 ¼ inches to 3 inches from any one point on the outer diameter of the *Dugga Kalshi* (pot). After every application of the *Shyaaee*, it is vigorously rubbed by a black stone. Due to friction between the iron particles and the stone, heat is generated and this helps in drying the layer. This process goes on till the right pitch and tone are obtained.

The *Vaadi* or leather straps are then fitted with eight small, cylindrically shaped wooden blocks (1 ½ inches in diameter and 3 inches long). These provide additional tension on the *Pudi* and are used for rough tuning of the Tabla. The topmost layer of the skin is now further cut circularly, leaving a width of approximately 1 to 1 ¼ inch from the *Gajraa*. This is the "*Kinaar*" (Border) or "*Chaanti*". A thin thread is then inserted between the *Chaanti* and the main skin (second layer) of the *pudi*. This provides a partition between the two skins and hence allows better scope for vibration of the skin when it is struck. The *Shaayee* provides a weight on the skin that will help to control the vibrations of the skin. The metallic particles are the ones which give the tone to the Tabla.

Taal Shaastra And Time Management

According to "*Natya Shastra*" written by Sage Bharata Muni, there used to be a uniform tradition of Music all over India. This must have continued until atleast 1210 to 1247 i.e. : at the time of writing of the "*Sangeet Ratnakar*" by Shaarang Dev. The Science or the Grammar of *Taals* and their measurement as obtained then, gradually got lost with the waning popularity of Sanskrit language. A lot of "*Praakrit*" words i.e. : the layman's dialect of those days, found their way in these texts. This was even more diluted during the Mughal rule, only to remain as a base – not to be really understood, but taken for granted. Hence, in today's Tabla Solo Recitals, the definitions and terms used in *Taal Shaastra* are not so much in evidence. Also, terms and definitions as known today and those from old texts are difficult to correlate or compare. Some theoreticians notably, Acharya Brihaspati, have tried to establish a connection. But lack of understanding of the Sanskrit language has prevented this from being spread among the average musical fraternity.

Taal has a premier position in Music. *Taal* is taken as the standard of measurement of "*Kaal*" or Time (***Taalah Kaalakriyaamaanam***). The genesis of the word *Taal* has a few explanations eg : ***Hara nrityasya Taandavam / Gowryaa nrityasya Laasyam Itisangyaa/ Taandavasya aadyaaksharen "Taa"/ Laasyasya aadyaaksharen "Laa" Ubhow Militvaa Itisangyaajaataa //***

The above couplet in Sanskrit translates as follows :

The word *Taal* has come from the "*Taandava*" the celestial dance of Lord Shiva and "*Laasya*" the effeminate grace of His consort Gauri also known as Paarvati. The word *Taal* has been coined from the "*Ta*" of "*Taandava*" and "*La*" of "*Laasya*".

Another explanation comes from the word "*T'l*" meaning palm of the hand. Hence the striking of one palm by the other is called "*Taal*" or "*Taali*" i.e. : clap.

Taalchakra

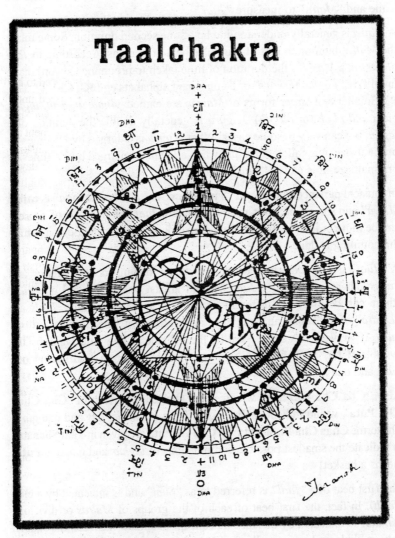

The above diagram is representative of the cycle of Taals and is the art work of Pandit Taranathji.

A *"matra"* is a unit to measure a *"Taal"*. So, we have *"Taal"* to measure Time and *"Matra"* to measure *"Taal"*.

A *matra* is generally understood to be of one second duration. Some relate the *Matra* duration to that of the Pulse beat of humans. According to *Taal Shaastra*, a *Matra* is the duration of time taken to pronounce a word made up of five *"Laghu Akshars"* or 5 consonant alphabets eg : **K', Ch', T', Th', P'.** Smaller and larger forms of *Matras* are named *Anudrut, drut, laghu, guru and pluth* (or *plooth*). A *guru* is generally double the duration of a *laghu*, but can vary in some cases. When a *guru* is enlarged by 1½ times its original size, it is called *pluth* and when a *laghu* is enlarged by 1½ times its original size, it is called *"Chith-pluth"*.

In musical parlance, the rate of "Time-flow" or *"Kaala-Pravaha"* is called *"Laya"* and since a *matra* is used to measure *Taal*, the duration of a *matra* can be more or less, as the situation demands i.e. : as per the *Laya* in which the counting is done.

A *"Taal"* is a predetermined cycle of beats, having its own *laghus* and *gurus*. There cannot be a *Taal* without atleast one *laghu* and one *guru* (there can be more for different *Taals)*. The most elementary *Taals* are *"Dadra"* of one *laghu* and one *guru* and *"Teen Taal"* of 2 *laghus* and one *guru*. If we were to denote *guru* by the syllable **'Chaa'** and *laghu* by the syllable **'Cha,'** then, **Chaa Cha Puta** would indicate a Taal having one *guru* and one *laghu*.

Also, **'Cha Cha ChPuta',** which is the shortened version of **'Cha Chaa Cha Puta',** would indicate a Taal comprising of two *laghus* and one *guru*. The terms **Chaa Cha Puta** and **Cha Cha ChPuta** are given in **Taal Shaastra** to indicate the smallest possible combinations of *laghus* and *gurus*. (**'Puta'** means a basket)

The first beat of a *"Taal"* is referred to as *"Sum"* and is indicated by a clap *(Taali)*. In fact, the first beat of each of the groups of *Matras* or divisions *(Khand)* is indicated by a clap. The concept of *Khaali* has been introduced only in Tabla and is generally the midpoint of a long *guru*. The *Khaali* is indicated by a wave of the hand with the palm pointing **upwards**. The rest of the *Matras* are counted on the fingers. Thus the actions of providing *Taali*, *Khaali* and counting of *matras* are called "*Kriya*" and two of its forms are called "*Sashabda*" *kriya* and *Nihshabda kriya* i.e. : actions having sound and no sound respectively.

Those portions of the *Taal* that fall in the sections shown by a *Taali* are called "*Bhari*" and those portions that fall under the *Khaali* part are called "*Khaali*". The "*Khaali-Bhari*" concept is an important one in Tabla playing and is generally followed by most performers. The *Bhari* part of the *Taal* is replete with strong or stressed *bols* i.e.: those which have both Tabla and *Dugga* sounds (**Ghe**). The *Khaali* part of the *Taal* has only unstressed *bols* i.e.: bols that do not have the base *Dugga* sounds of **Ghe**.

Definitions of "*Taal*".

1) *Taal* is a cycle of beats (*matras*) in which a musical composition or Dance sequence is set or performed.

2) The demonstration or maintaining of a "*Taal* cycle" by various pre-defined actions is called "*Taal*".

3) *Taal* is a device that measures the length or the duration of a Vocal / Instrumental / Dance composition.

4) A unique and well-constructed composition which is used to measure the "Time-flow" in music is called "*Taal*".

5) That composition in time which is characterized by well defined groups of *Matras*, indicated by sound producing (clap or *taali*) and silent (*khaali* or counting of *Matras* by fingers) actions and used to establish the rigidity of the compositions (Vocal, Instrumental or Dance) in Time, is called a "*Taal*".

Theka:

In order to show or demonstrate a Taal on a percussion instrument, one has to compose a sequence of sounds produced by striking the concerned instrument by fingers / palms of the hands at different locations on the instrument. These sounds are termed as "*Bols*" or "*Varnas*". Bols are of two kinds viz : "*Bhari*" i.e. : Stressed and "*Khaali*" i.e.: unstressed strokes. (also called "*Varnas*").

33

Thus, a **Theka** is a predetermined and widely accepted composition, made up of a collection of *Bols / Varnas* of Tabla / Pakhawaj, representing different divisions (*Khand*) of the *Taal* for which it is composed.

Hence, *Taal* is an abstract form and **Theka** is its concrete or audible form. A *Taal* remains unchanged whereas it can have more than one **Theka**.

A **Theka** can thus be considered as the first "*Bandish*" or composition of a *Taal*. It is one entity that is heard non-stop or continually during a musical presentation. A *Theka* has all the characteristics of a *Taal*. In addition, there are other considerations that are noteworthy. These are:

    (a) Selection of appropriate *bols*,

    (b) "*Khaali-Bhari*",

    (c) Selection of *Laya*.

(a) **Selection of Bols**: While doing this, one must consider the character of the musical composition which is to be provided accompaniment. Emotions such as peace, pathos, love, bravery, anger or devotion can be expressed through different *bols* of Tabla and Pakhawaj. For serious musical expressions such as *Dhrupad / Dhamaar*, traditional *Thekas* have been composed with forceful and sonorous *bols* using open-handed style of playing or "*Khula Baaz*". However, for softer emotions such as peace, pathos, love, softer *bols* are preferred using the "*Chaanti*" and others produced by finger tips i.e. : the "*B'nd Baaz*" or the compact-handed style. In such cases, the *Taal* cycles are also smaller eg: *Keharwa, Dadra, Roopak*, etc.

(b) **Khaali-Bhari**: This concept is unique to Tabla and has a great deal of importance in the formation of a *Theka*. The "*Bhari*" or stressed bols are used to represent those parts which fall under the *Taali* and are generally **Dha, Dhin**, etc. "*Khaali*" or unstressed bols are mainly for the *Khaali* parts of a *Taal,* using bols such as **Na, Ta, Tin**, etc.

(c) **Selection of Laya**: Selection of an appropriate *Laya* for a composition is very essential in order to bring the right emotions to the fore. For example, slow tempo is used for songs expressing pathos or beatific or peaceful moods. These kinds of *thekas* should have as few *bols* as possible. Buoyant moods are conveyed by faster tempo with more *bols* in the *Theka*. Also *Thekas* for such songs are played more loudly than for those that are used for songs of peace and pathos.

The contribution of Taal to the upliftment of Music.

Music is an overall combination of "*Sur*" i.e. : purity of the note and "*Taal*" i.e. : Rhythm or "*Laya*". These two features are comparable to the *Warp* and *Weft* i.e: criss-crossing of threads in the weaving of cloth. Some musicians are of the opinion that *Taal* and *Laya* act as a sort of limitation to the free expression of melodic ideas. If, at the end of an "*Alaap*" or a "*Taan*", the musician is unable to latch on to the "*Mukhda*" or the starting phrase of the song, on the appropriate *Matra*, the effectiveness of the *Taan* is lost. This is the reason why many musicians find *Taal* to be uncomfortable and thus lack confidence in their presenataion. Their contention is that Melody alone has the ability to convey the feelings or the moods and does not need the restrictive influence of *Taal* i.e. : *Taal* is irrelevant to the presentation and all that it does is put obstacles in their imaginative exposition of a *Raga*. Some in fact say thus "*Taal gayaa to Baal gayaa, lekin Sur gayaa to S'r gayaa*" which translates thus :- If *Taal* is lost, a hair is lost but if *Sur* is lost, the head is lost.

This attitude is comparable to a Tennis player saying that if it had not been for the net and the boundaries of the court, he could easily have won any match. Can one appreciate the true beauty of a painting if it is not properly framed and mounted? Imagine the catastrophe that would befall mankind if the celestial bodies were to say "To hell with the laws of gravitation! Let us all go our own way!"

One can only say that if vocal music is the "Heart", Instrumental music the "Lungs", then, verily, Rhythm is the "Breath". Rhythm is the medium that brings life to any recital, a sort of discipline to a musical presentation.

"Dasha Praan" or 10 salient features of *Taal*

Kaalo Maargah Kriyaangaani Graho Jaatih KalaaLayah/

Yatih Prastaara Kashcheti TaalaPraana Dashasmritaha //

The above couplet in Sanskrit mentions the ten vital characteristics of a *Taal*. They are:- *Kaala, Maarga, Kriyaa, Anga, Grah, Jaati, Kalaa, Laya, Yati* and *Prastaar*.

1) **Kaala** (Time): By this, one generally understands the time that is involved in a musical presentation. These time measurements have been made from the shortest duration to larger ones. We know what a *Matra* is, taking its duration as one second, these can be classified as follows:

   (a)   *Truti* --------------------- ⅛ of a *Matra* or second.

   (b)   *Anu Drut* ---------------- ¼ of a *Matra* or second.

   (c)   *Drut* --------------------- ½ of a *Matra* or second.

   (d)   *Laghu* ------------------- 1 *Matra* or second.

   (e)   *Guru* --------------------- 2 *Matras* or seconds.

   (f)   *Kaak P'd* ---------------- 4 *Matras* or seconds.

   (g)   *Hans P'd* ---------------- 8 *Matras* or seconds.

   (h)   *Mahaa Hans P'd* ------- 16 *Matras* or seconds.

According to *Bharata Muni* who is credited with the treatise known as "*Natya Shaastra*", a "*Laghu*" *Kaala* is one *Matra* and that is taken as the time taken to utter five consonants viz : **K', Ch', T', Th', P'** as clearly and as rapidly as possible. The splitting of the *Laghu* into smaller components came about much later with Shaarangdev, the author of "*Sangeet Ratnakar*" and other researchers.

36

In today's musical scenario, *Laghu* and *Guru* are quite well-known and understood. *Drut* and *Anudrut* correlate with faster tempo eg : as in *Drut G'ths* and *Jhaala*. Similarly, *Kaakp'd* is generally seen in *Ati Vilambit* tempo.

2) **Maarga**: The word literally means Road or Way. But in musical parlance it has a deeper meaning.

According to *Bharata Muni* there are three modes of musical presentation, viz : "*Chitra*", which is *drut* or fast, "*Vaartik*", which is *Madhya Laya* or Medium tempo and "*Dakshin*", which is *Vilambit* or slow tempo. Besides these there are three others mentioned by researchers having different "*Kalaas*" or duration of "*Gurus*".

Name of Maarg	Laya / Speed	Number of Matras in Guru
Dakshin	Vilambit / Slow tempo	8
Vaartik	Madhya / Medium tempo	4
Chitra	Drut / Fast tempo	2
Chitra-t'r	*Anudrut / Fast tempo	1
Ati-Chitra-t'r	Anudrut-t'r / Fast tempo	½
Ati-Chitra-t'm	Anudrut-t'm / Fast tempo	¼

*This, i.e.: Anudrut is also referred to as "*Dhruvaa*".

3) **Kriyaa**: When the music is being presented in slower tempi such as *Vaartik* or *Dakshin*, in order to keep the *Laya* stable, various actions of the hand are used. These actions are called "*Nih Shabd Kriyaa*" or silent action and "*Sa-Shabd Kriyaa*" or actions that produce a sound eg : Clap or snapping of fingers. Most of these are not in use today. What we see are only "*Taalis*" (*Sashabd Kriyaa*) and *Khaali* (*Nih Shabd Kriyaa*). However, these *kriyaas* must have been of immense value to maintain the constancy of *Laya* at a time when percussion instruments were not in vogue.

Taal may be played in different "*Layas*" and the *Taal* is itself made up of different "*Angs*" i.e. : parts of divisions. So, it is very essential that when a *Taal* is expressed in different *Layas*, its *Angs* also have to be adequately expressed. Hence, even before the advent of percussion instruments, the *"Hasta Kriya"* or Hand Gestures were formulated so that, a *Taal* and its different *Angs* could be explicitly shown to maintain the desired *Laya*.

Broadly, there are two types of *kriyaas* viz : *"Sa-shabd Kriya"* or sound producing action and *"Nih-Shabd Kriyaa"* or silent action.

Both these are further subdivided in four types each and are as follows:

Sa-Shabd Kriya

"Dhruva"	"Shampaa"	"Taal"	Sannipaat
(snapping of fingers of the right hand)	(clap produced by striking the left hand by the right hand)	(clap produced by striking the right hand by the left hand)	(clapping with both hands together in the front)

Nih-Shabd Kriya

"Avaap"	"Nishkraam"	"Vikshep"	"Pravesh"
(holding together fingers of the uplifted right hand)	(Separation of the fingers of the left hand which is placed down and palm facing up)	(Taking the right hand towards one's right side of the back, before striking the upturned left hand for a clap)	(keeping the left hand ready for the right hand to come down and strike)

4) *Ang*: The divisions of a *Taal* are called *"Ang"*. Just as a body is identified by its various parts such as arms, legs, torso, face, etc; similarly can a *Taal* be identified. Even two or more *Taals* having the same number of *Matras* have different identities – as they have different *Angs*. *Angs* are groups of *Matras* known as *"Laghu"*, *"Guru"*, *"Plutha"*, etc. For measurement of *Angs* we take *"Anudrut"*

38

as the smallest constituent. Various *Angs* with their symbols and *matra* duration are given below.

Ang	Symbol	Matra duration
(i) Anudrut	∨	1 (alphabet)
(ii) Drut	O	2
(iii) Laghu			4
(iv) Guru	S	8
(v) Plutha	⃛	12
(vi) Kaakpad	+	16

"*Khand*" and "*Ang*" are synonymous ; these are indicated by "*Taalis*" and "*Khaalis*".

5) **Grah:** A specific point in a *Taal* from where a musical composition begins is called *Grah*. It is also referred to as "*Paani*".

Most of the time, a song begins at the starting point of a *Taal*. But sometimes, maybe to achieve a special effect or to emphasise the meaning of a rendition or also for the musician to exhibit his skill in *Taal*, the beginning of a song was deliberately shifted to a different point i.e. : other than the "*Sum*" – either before or after the "*Sum*."

Any composition that starts at the beginning of a *Taal*-cycle i.e. : its first beat is called "*Sama-Grah*" or "*Sama-Paani*".

If the composition starts before or after the first beat, it is called "*Vishama-Grah*".

There are two types of "*Vishama-Grah*" viz : "*Ateet*", in which the composition has its end after the first beat of the *Taal* cycle and "*Anaaghaat*", in which the composition ends just before the first beat (Sum) of the *Taal* cycle. Here, the stroke of the first beat is left open and not played. Hence the term "*Anaghaat*" which literally means no stroke. It is also referred to as "*Aasum*" or "*akaal*".

6) **Jaati**: *Jaati* literally means types or categories. But, as applied to *Taals*, these classifications are based on the number of *Laghu* counts

between two successive *matras*. Thus, we have *"Chaturasra"* (Chatushra) *Jaati*, where the gap between two successive *matras* is filled with counts in multiples of four i.e. : 2, 4, 8, 16. *"Tryasra"* (Tishra) *Jaati* is one in which the counts are in multiples of three i.e. : 1 ½, 3, 6, 9, 12, 24, etc. Then there is *"Khanda" Jaati* with counts in multiples of five i.e. : 1 ¼, 2 ½, 5, 10, etc. *"Mishra" Jaati* is one where the counts are multiples of seven i.e. : 1 ¾, 3 ½, 7, 14, etc. Lastly, there is *"Sankeerna" Jaati* which has counts in multiples of nine i.e. : 1 ⅛, 2 ¼, 4 ½, 9, 18, etc. Originally there were only two Jaatis *Chaturasra* and *Tryasra*. These emanted from the basic concepts of the *Taal* structure with *Laghus* and *Gurus*. Thus we has **"Chaa-Cha" puta** i.e. : a set with one *Guru* and one *Laghu* or a total count of three, (2 + 1), as the *Guru* is twice a *Laghu* count and **"Cha-Cha-Ch" puta** or **"Cha-Chaa-Cha" puta** i.e. : a set of *Laghu, Guru, Laghu* or a total count of four (1 + 2 + 1). These were also called *"Yathakshar" Taals*. The permutations and combination of these basic *Jaatis* led to *Khanda, Mishra* and *Sankeerna Jaatis*.

NOTE : *Chaturasra* and *Tryasra* are also referred to as *Chatushra* and *Tishra*.

7) **Kalaa**: Broadly, *Kalaa* refers to the artistry in presentation of a Tabla / Pakhawaj recital. This includes various facets such as how to perform, position of the hands while striking, spreading of fingers, movement of the body parts whilst playing, etc. Sharangdev, in his *Sangeet Ratnakar* mentions *"Pancha Sanchaa"*, or five body parts that can move viz : shoulders, thumb, wrists, elbows and left leg. For a good *Mridang* player, thumbs and wrists are all that move.

Kalaa also has another meaning in *Taal Shastra*. The time span of a *Guru* Syllable is also known as *Kalaa*. The doubling or quadrupling of a *Guru* which is known as *"Dugun"* and *"Chougun"* is also known as *"Dwee kalaa"* and *"Chatush kalaa"* respectively.

8) **Laya**: In *Taal Shaastra*, the uniform movement of any part of a "Time-phase" is called *"Laya"*. Also the regular interval between *Kriyaas* or actions over a period of time is also called *Laya*. There are five *Layas* in vogue today viz : *Atee-Vilambit* (very slow), *Vilambit* (Slow), *Madhya*

(Medium), *Drut* (Fast), *Atee-Drut* (Very Fast). These are generally referred to as such with the *Chaturasra Jaati* in mind. There are also other *Layas* which are not so often played or heard. These are:

Kuwaadi - 1¼ times the *Laya* as obtained in *Madhya / Vilambit*

Aadi - 1½ times the *Laya* as obtained in *Madhya / Vilambit*

Biyaadi - 1¾ times the *Laya* as obtained in *Madhya / Vilambit*

Nowhere is the standard of measurement of *Laya* in terms of Time. But it is generally taken for granted that *Madhya Laya* is close to the human pulse rate or even the speed of the second hand of a clock. The other *Layas* are established in relation to this. Thus, *Vilambit* is half of *Madhya* and *Drut* is double of *Madhya*.

9) **Yati**: "*Layah Pravruttir niyamo Yatir iti abhidheeyate*" i.e.: The movement or Flow of *Laya* is **Yati**. There are five basic *Yatis*:

Yati				
"Samaa" (Uniform movement through-out)	**"Strotaagataa"** (indicative of water-flow— from stored or static water to its flow, gathering momentum and then cascading)	**"Gopuchcha"** (Like the tail of a cow, thin to begin with, flaring in the middle and then narrowing down at the end)	**"Mridangaa"** (Like the shape of a Mridang or a Pakhawaj i.e.: narrow to begin, flaring at the center and then again narrowing a little bit)	**"Pipeelika"** (Like the movement of Ants, small clusters and and quick movement)

10) **Prastaar**: The imaginative presentation of the various *Angs* of different *Taals* in multifarious forms is what **Prastaar** essentially is. In other words, like an Algebraic equation, it is just simplification. By this means, not only can we create variation of *Kaidas*,*Relas*,etc., but can also create new *Taals* by varying their *Gurus* and *Pluthas*. Thus, **Prastaar** means making different smaller froms of one basic form.

41

Gharanas

Indian Classical music is tradition based. Information Technology being a recent phenomenon, this art has been preserved and propagated by person to person contact and teaching. This is what is called *"Guru-mukhi Vidya"* i.e. : knowledge through the mouth of a *Guru* or *Ustad*. Thus it was that the art was passed on from a *Guru* to his sons or disciples, who in turn passed it on their progeny and disciples, thereby establishing their identity or stamp on the style of playing and / or the compositions that were passed on. Since this was on the lines of a "Family Tree" it was referred to as *"Gharana"* which is the Hindi equivalent of Family or Lineage.

Most of the disciples of a *Guru* definitely follow the tradition laid down by him. But, once in a way, there comes one disciple who, besides following his *Guru's* tradition, takes a few bold steps outside the path laid by his mentor. He lets his imagination wander a bit and experiments some. Within a span of a few years, his students and later their students are seen and heard to be playing the same compositions a little differently or, playing suitably amended compositions.

Art is not static and keeps evolving because it comes from the heart and soul of a performer. Every artist has the priviledge of putting forth his expression of a composition. Hence, any composition need not sound the same when presented by two or more artists.

By common consent, Delhi *Gharana* is considered as the parent *Gharana*, as it was in Delhi that Tabla first took roots under the *Mughals* in their courts. Although Tabla is believed to have come into existence in the period 1200 to 1300 A.D., its *Gharanas* came about much later. Solo Tabla playing may have begun in the late 15th or early 16th century in Delhi. During *Amir Khusro's* period i.e. : 1196 to 1316 A.D., Tabla was mainly used to accompany *"Khayal"* style of Vocal musical compositions. But side by side it evolved independently and reached a stage where it could be played as a solo instrument and heard and appreciated as well. It was after this that various *Gharanas* such as *"Ajrada"*, *"Farrukhabad"*, etc. developed.

The development of Tabla and *Khayal* singing went on almost at the same time. Hence, we find that Tabla solo recitals are presented in almost the same format as that of *Khayal* singing.

The term *"Baaz"* comes from the Hindi / Urdu word *"Bajaanaa"* – to play (an instrument) or *"Baajaa"* which means instrument. There are two distinct styles of playing Tabla viz : *"Khula Baaz"* and *"B'nd Baaz"*.

"B'nd Baaz":

In this style of playing, the sound produced from the Tabla and Dugga have a limited resonance. One of the important aspects of Tabla playing is that lesser the resonating time, greater is the speed of playing and vice-versa. When one stroke has been played, before its resonance dies down, another is played. In this style of playing the hand on the Tabla must have a compact look with fingers close together. Kaidas and Relas are two important compositions that can be played at high speeds with skillful co-ordination of the fingers of the Tabla and Dugga. In the B'nd Baaz strokes on the "Chaanti" and the "Luv" of the Tabla and the "Luv" or "Maidaan" of the Dugga are prominent.

"Khulaa Baaz":

In this style, exactly the opposite holds good. *Khulaa* means open-handed, the fingers are spread out and the hands never rest on the Tabla or *Dugga*, giving enough scope for them to reverberate to the fullest after a stroke has been played. One finds the influence of the Pakhawaj on this style of playing. As against the *B'nd Baaz*, in this, the full palm is used and sounds are produced more by fingers joined together rather than single fingers. As a result, the speed of playing is reduced, giving more scope for the *"Aas"* or resonance. In this style, compositions such as *G'ths*, *G'th Parans*, *Gth Todaas*, *Parans* and *Chakradhaars* abound and not much of a repertoire of *Kaidas* and *Relas*. The *B'nd Baaz* is associated with *Delhi* and *Ajrada Gharanas* and the *Khula Baaz* with *Lucknow (Poorab) Gharana*, *Farrukhabad* and *Benares Gharanas*.

43

Delhi Gharana:

Among the *Gharanas* prevalent tody, *Delhi Gharana* is considered to be the oldest or the first one. **Delhi**, being the highest seat of the *Mughal* Emperors, having great wealth and musicians of the calibre of *Amir Khusro* and *Miyan Tansen*, became an attraction for musicians from all over India. They came and settled there trying to catch the eyes and ears of the influential courtiers and also earn a living. Hence, the beginning and the initial advancement of Tabla took place in **Delhi**, especially during the reign of Emperor *Akbar*.

At about this time, *Khayal* singing started gaining in popularity as *Dhrupad-Dhamaar* style started declining. The accompaniment for *Khayal* singing was done using the Tabla, because of its softer tones.

Delhi *Gharana's* style of playing is called the *Delhi Baaz* or the *Chaanti Baaz* and also the *"Do-Ungli"* (In *Do* the 'O' to be pronounced as in NO) or two-finger *Baaz*. In this *Gharana* there is a surfeit of *Peshkaars, Kaidas* and *Relas*. The phrases mostly used are **DI-T', TI-T', KI-T', DHA, TA, DHA-GE, TA-GE, DHA GE NA, TA GE NA, DHIN NA, GI NA, DIRI DIRI** (with 2 fingers on the *Shaayee*). Most of the compositions are in *Chaturasra Jaati*.

Sidaar Khan Daadhi is acknowledged as the founder of the **Delhi** *Gharana*. Some of the other stalwarts of this *Gharana* are *Ustad Chaand Khan*, younger brother of *Sidaar Khan, Bugraa Khan, Ghasit Khan* and a third one (name unknown), who later founded the **Lucknow** *Gharana* – (all sons of *Sidaar Khan), Kallu Khan*, who later founded **Ajrada** *Gharana*, *Ustad Gaami Khan* and his son *Ustad Inam Ali Khan, Ustads Boli Baksh* and his son *Nathu Khan*. Besides these there are also others who have contributed to the propagation of this *Gharana* and some others who have had an undeniable influence of this *Gharana* on their playing.

Lucknow Gharana:

This is also known as the ***Poorab*** *Gharana* and the style of playing is known as *Poorab Baaz* or *Khulaa Baaz*.

Within about a hundred years of the birth of the **Delhi** *Gharana*, the **Lucknow** *Gharana* came into being. The *Nawaabs* of **Lucknow** were well-known for their interest in the Arts, especially Music and Dance. They patronized *Kathak* Dancers and hence this dance form became quite popular in a short time. The Pakhawaj was earlier used to accompany this dance. But the **T'th kaars**, which are rhythmic variations in a fast speed could not be reproduced on the Pakhawaj with clarity. Thus its place was gradually taken by the Tabla, whose softer tones also were found to be of immense value in the lilting tunes and matching steps and expressions of the dance form. The Pakhawaj was relegated to the second position. But it always proved superior where sound quality and resonance were concerned.

The **Lucknow** Tabla players tried to combine the outstanding characteristics of the Pakhawaj with those of the Tabla, thereby giving rise to the *Khulaa Baaz* or the *Poorab Baaz*. With this evolution in the playing style, Tabla totally dominated the Pakhawaj so far as Dance accompaniment was concerned.

The **Lucknow** style of playing is also known as the "*Thapiya*" *Baaz* because the full palm and four fingers (no thumb) was used to strike the "*Thaap*". In course of time the open-handed striking of the *Dugga*, as done in the Pakhawaj got lesser and lesser, consequently adding to the sweetness of the playing. The resonance of the stroke on the *Luv* of the Tabla, such as **TIN** or **TA** lasts longer than the stroke on the *Chaanti*. Also, the **TA** played on the *Luv* is more rounded in sound and hence more aesthetic. Because, striking **TA** on the *Luv* and the other syllables such as **T'th, DI T'** etc. involves playing with fingers joined and lifting of the hands, this *Baaz* is not conducive to playing at very high speeds.

Bols or phrases used in the **Lucknow** *Gharana* are **DI T' DI T', KD'DHE-TIT', K'th TA K'thTA, DHET DHET, TA GE S N', DHAD' S N'**, etc.

The eminent stalwarts of this *Gharana* are *Ustads Modu Khan* and *Bakshu Khan, Ustad Abid Hussein Khan, Ustad Wajid Hussein Khan* and his son *Ustad Afaq Hussein Khan* and *Ustad Jehangir Khan* of Indore, a direct disciple of *Ustad Abid Hussein Khan*. Two other prominent Stalwarts of this *Gharana* were *Pandit Ram Sahay*, a disciple of *Ustad Modu Khan* and *Pandit Biroo Mishra*, a disciple of *Ustad Abid Hussein Khan*. These two later laid the foundation of the **Benares** *Gharana*.

Ajrada Gharana:

This *Gharana* is also recognized as the *"Shagird"* *Gharana* of **Delhi** *Gharana*. This is so because the founder of this *Gharana*, *Kallu Khan,* was a student of **Delhi** *Gharana*. It is named after a small village in the *Meerut* District of Uttar Pradesh, barely 50 km. from Delhi. Broadly speaking, there is not much of a difference in the playing styles of **Delhi** and **Ajrada** *Gharanas*. Just to make its own impact, to show something different from **Delhi** *Gharana*, most of the *Kaidas* were made in *Tishra Jaati*. In those days, composing and playing a *Tishra Jaati Kaida* was something out of the usual and hence it contributed largely to the popularity of the **Ajrada** *Gharana*. Also, the protagonists of this *Gharana* have made a few changes in the playing style to enable their *Kaidas* to be played at a much faster speed than similar sounding *Kaidas* of the Delhi *Gharana*. They also tried to increase the sweetness of the compositions by introducing such phrases where resonance or *"Aas"* of the Tabla coupled with variations on the *Dugga* added to the beauty. Examples of some phrases are:-

DHASS   GET'K   DHING'DHIN   NAGEN'   GET'K
GET'K   DHING'DHIN   NAGEN'

The variations of the *Dugga* were made by rubbing of the *"Shaayee"* with the wrist. Later on the **G'th Todas** of the *Poorab* style also made their impact on this *Gharana*.

Some of the prominent personalities to have left their mark are *Ustad Bugra Khan* and *Ustad Sitab Khan*, (son and grandson respectively of *Ustad Sidhar Khan Dadhi), Ustad Kallu Khan, Ustad Chaand Khan, Ustad Habib-ud-din Khan* and *Pandit Sudhir Kumar Saxena.*

Farrukhabad Gharana:

This *Gharana* came into existence around the same time as the **Ajrada** *Gharana* i.e. : 1700 to 1750 A.D. The main feature of this *Gharana* is its adaptation of the Pakhawaj style of playing, as in the ***Poorab*** *Gharana.*

46

Eminently suited to play compositions such as *G'ths, G'th Parans* and *G'th Todas*, the **Farrukhabad** *Gharana* has also introduced in its repertoire *Peshkaar, Kaidas* and *Relas*. This was initially absent in the **Lucknow** tradition – *Relas* were rarely played.

Lucknow compositions have come into this *Gharana* as hereditary handouts. These have been further enriched by the Stalwarts of **Farrukhabad** *Gharana* by introducing their own characteristic phrases. Individual alphabets such as **NA, TA, T'th, TIN** and **THAE** form the backbone of most of the phrases used in **Farrukhabad** style of playing. Some of these phrases are as follows :

DIN-G'-DHINNA-GINA, DHIN N'T'K DHIN N'T'K, DINGNAGT'K, TRK DHET TAGE SN, DHA-G'-ST'KIT', DIRIDIRI KIT' T'K T'KIT'DHA, etc.

The founder of this *Gharana* is *Ustad Haji Vilayat Ali Khan*, also known as "*Haji Saheb*" as he had gone on the *Haj* pilgrimage seven times. The story goes that the then *Khalifa** of the **Lucknow** *Gharana, Ustad Bakshu Khan* gave his daughter in marriage to *Ustad Vilayat Ali Khan* and presented 1000 *Poorab G'ths* as part of the marriage dowry. This daughter of *Ustad Bakshu Khan* was also well-versed in Tabla and later on initiated *Ustad Choodiya Imam Bux* into this *Gharana*, by putting her own bangle on his hand instead of tying the traditional "*Gandaa*" or sacred coloured thread. (* *Khalifa* means Chief).

Some of the other prominent Stalwarts of this *Gharana* are *Ustad Salari Khan, Ustad Munir Khan, Ustad Masit Khan*, his son *Ustad Karamat Khan* and grandson *Ustad Sabir Khan, Ustad Ahmedjaan Thirakwa, Ustad Shamsuddin Khan*, his disciple *Pandit Taranathji, Pandit Ravi Bellare, Pandit Shashi Bellare, Ustad Amir Hussein Khan, Pandit Subbarao Ankolekar* and *Pandit Gyan Prakash Ghosh* who had learnt under *Ustad Masit Khan* and later, under *Ustad Karamat Khan*.

Benares Gharana:

This is a *Gharana* in which both the *B'nd Baaz* and the *Khula Baaz* are in evidence. Tabla players of this *Gharana* play *Kaidas, Relas, Peshkaars* of

Delhi and **Ajrada** *Gharana*. But the influence of their neighbour **Lucknow** *Gharana* is evident in their style of playing. Most of the **Benares** *Gharana* Tabla players prefer to keep the *Shaayee* of the *Dugga* facing towards themselves and the *Maidaan* away i.e. : towards the audiences. This facilitates their style of playing on the *Dugga* which involves rubbing of the *Shaayee* with their wrists (lower part of the palm). Also, their preference for the high-pitched, small diameter Tablas is quite well-known. Many of the Tabla players of this *Gharana* are adept at accompanying Instrumental musicians and dancers. Due to the presence of outstanding compositions, their solo recitals of Tabla are also of a high order. There is also an opinion among some experts that the *"Chowghada"*, the percussion instruments used to accompany the *"Shehnai"* has influenced the **Benares** *Gharana*. Super-fast playing of *Teen-Taal* with one finger (fore-finger) on the Tabla is a hallmark of this *Gharana* and so also is the **DIRI-DIRI**, both with palm and fingers.

Eminent Tabla players of the **Benares** *Gharana* are its founder *Pandit Ram Sahay-ji*, a disciple of *Ustad Modu Khan* of Lucknow, *Pandit Bhairav Sahay-ji*, *Pandit Pratap Maharaj-ji*, *Pandit Baldev Sahay-ji*, *Pandit Biru Mishra*, *Pandit Anokhelal*, *Pandit Kanthe Maharaj*, *Pandit Kishen Maharaj*, *Pandit Samta Prasad* (*Gudai Maharaj*) and *Pandit Sharada Sahay*.

Punjab Gharana:

The originator of this *Gharana* was the son of a noted *Pakhawaji*. He was born at a time when the *Pakhawaji* father was at an advanced age. Before the father passed away, he left his young son in the care of two of his senior disciples, to train him as a *Pakhawaji*. However, the youngster, as he grew up, felt that he was not getting the respect due to him as the *"Khalifa"* or Chief of that family. He thus decided to change course and with whatever knowledge of Pakhawaj he had, coupled with his own skill and imagination decided to wield the Tabla. He created new compositions and achieved such name and fame that even his father's disciples, who had earlier refused to recognize him as their *"Khalifa"*, now did so. Thus it is that one finds the influence of Pakhawaj on the style of Tabla playing in the **Punjab** *Gharana*.

Peshkars and *Kaidas* are recent occurrences in this **Gharana**. One finds more of *G'ths, G'th Parans, Todas* and *Relas*.

Some prominent Tabla players of this *Gharana* are *Lala Bhavani Das Pakhawaji*, the originator, his disciple *Ustad Qadir Bux, Pandit Baldev Sahay* of **Benaras** *Gharana, Ustad Shaukat Ali Khan, Ustad AllahDitta Khan, Ustad Allarakha Khan* and his son *Ustad Zakir Hussein Khan*.

Gandaa Bandhan:

In *Hindustani* Musical Tradition, the *"Guru-Shishya Parampara"* or the traditional bonding between the *Guru* and his disciple is of great significance. The *"Deeksha" Ceremony* is an ancient event signifying a bond between the Guru and the Shishya to preserve the knowledge of a tradition. The ritual of *"Gandaa Bandhan"* is one that adds its own stamp of validity to the *Guru-Shishya Parampara*. This is quite an old tradition and is followed more reiigiously by the *Muslims* than *Hindus*. The underlying significance of this ritual is to make an announcement before an invited audience comprising among others, well-wishers of both the *Guru* and the *Shishya* and a host of lesser and better known names in the musical world.

The *Guru* ties a five-coloured stringed rope to the wrist of the disciple after having prayed to the Almighty and the souls of the great musicians of the past, particularly those belonging to his own *Gharana*. Blessings are also sought from those present among the august gathering by having them touch the sacred thread. The *Ganda* represents the connection to a lineage of teachers and the tradition embodied by the *Guru*. The atmosphere is reminiscent of a *"puja"* or *"havan"* with insence being burnt and prayers being recited.

The *Guru* swears in the name of his art by placing his hands on the instrument placed before him, that he will impart knowledge to the disciple without holding anything back and strive to make him attain a position of eminence whence he will bring glory to the *Gharana*.

After this, the *Guru* feeds the *Shishya* with a helping of *Chanaa* (Roasted Gram) mixed with Jaggery. This is done to signify that the *Shishya* is now like his own son and that he shall bring him up with the same love and affection and also impart knowledge as he would to his own son.

The *Shishya* follows suit with a similar act, which is to show that he in turn shall be deligent and honest to his chosen field and *Guru* and that he shall look after his *Guru* in his old age in the same way as a son would.

This ceremony over, the *Guru* teaches the *Shishya* a small composition to culminate the proceedings. This is followed by a musical soiree in which the *Shishya* as well as the *Guru* present their art and so do some invited artists.

The *Shishya* presents the *Guru* with a "*Guru-Dakshina*" which consists of mainly cash and also gift articles such as clothes, etc.

The system of *Guru Shishya Parampara* is a time honoured tradition in India for bestowing knowledge of an Art form. It recognizes the need for extended contact and interaction between the Teacher and student, unlike that which is usually available in academic settings. Study of Arts is considered a spiritual discipline, since the origin of the performing and visual arts is revealed through the wisdom contained in the *Vedas*, the *Upanishads* and the *Bhagavad Geeta*.

Riyaaz

This is an *Urdu* word which means practice. It is most essential that proper *riyaaz* patterns are followed to achieve the desired results. As in any other faculty, Tabla also demands full devotion of its votaries. It is unthinkable for any individual to assume that he can master the art in a matter of four to five years. Getting a grip on the medium needs as much, or in some cases, even more of assiduous *riyaaz* than one would put in one's academic pursuit. Here too, one must take care to avoid thoughtless and devotionless practice. *Riyaaz* has to be done after giving due thought to all aspects of the art and with a lot of patience and understanding.

Due emphasis has to be given to see that melodic aspects of Tabla are not ignored at the cost of speed. Speed cr the ability to play faster is always desirable. What is most important though, is the clarity with which the phrases are played and also the spirit of the *bols*, its character and the impact that it is expected to have on the listeners. For this reason, *riyaaz* has always to be done in the initial stages under the supervision or the watchful eye of the *Guru* or *Ustad*. Besides the routine *riyaaz* of polishing of the strokes, attention must also be paid to the syncopations or mathematical variations of phrases.

Riyaaz is a personal matter and different artists may adopt their own methods. But as long as the ultimate aim – that of perfecting the art is achieved, it matters little which route one has followed. However it has been seen that the most popular and result oriented system of *riyaaz* is known as "*Chilla*". This is mostly followed by *Muslim* proponents of music. It involves patience, persistence and sincerity – qualities that are rare in today's students due to the circumstances prevailing. Most of today's Tabla students are school-going children. They hardly have the time for even going over the lessons learnt from their *Guru* – leave alone *riyaaz*.

A *Chilla* when undertaken, lasts for 40 days and involves 10 to 12 hours of assiduous *riyaaz* everyday. In some cases, undertaking a *Chilla* is made into a sort of public function wherein, the elders of the locality make an announcement that such and such person has decided to take up a *Chilla* and that it is the duty of all concerned people to see to it that his family is well looked after, so that he has the time and peace of mind to carry on with his *riyaaz*. For a person who is newly into a *Chilla*, it is advisable to do so under the *Guru*'s or a senior's guidance.

There are different modes of *riyaaz* undertaken in a *Chilla*. The one recommended most is to start out with *Kaidas* in the slow speed giving due stress on bols that need to be perfected and then doubling the speed, maintaining the same stresses. Gradually, one achieves a good speed. But care should be taken to see that clarity, resonance and balance of the *bols* are not sacrificed. After going over a preset number of *Kaidas*, one can turn one's attention to *Relas* and then *G'ths*, *G'th-Parans*, *Tukdas*, etc. The ideal time for *riyaaz* is early morning as it is believed that good spirits are moving about and thus do not bring any hinderances in the sessions.

A form of *riyaaz* undertaken by some Tabla players especially of the **Benares** *Gharana* is to wear heavy bracelets on the hands at the time of *riyaaz*. Some though, feel that this may cause undue stress on the nerves, tendons and muscles of the hands resulting in permanent damage to hands and subsequent disability.

Some patterns (*bols*) for *riyaaz* are given hereunder :

1) DHA DHA   TIT'   DHADHA   TIN NA / TA TA   TIT'   DHA DHA   DHIN NA

2) DHA DHA   TIRI KIT' DHA DHA   TIN NA / TA TA TIRI KIT' DHA DHA   DHIN NA

3) GE GE   TIT'   GE GE   NA NA / KE KE   TIT'   GE GE   NA NA

4) DHIN-N' GI-N' DHA DHA GI-N' / TIN-N' KI-N'   TA TA   KI-N' (N' on shaayee)

5) DHIN-N' DHIN-N' NA GE DHIN N'   NA GE   DHIN-N'   DHIN-N' NA GE
                                                              (N' on shaayee)

6) DHA-TIRI KIT'-TIRI .KIT' DHA   TIRI-KIT' / TA-TIRI KIT' TIRI KIT' DHA TIRI-KIT'

7) GID' NAG' TIT' TIT' GID' NAG   NA GE   TIT' / KID' NAK' TIT' TIT' GID' NAG'
    NA GE TIT'

8) DHA TIT' GID' NAG', DIT' TIT' GID' NAG', DHA TIT' GID' NAG', TIN-NA KID' NAK'
    TA TIT' KID' NAK',   TIT' TIT' KID' NAK', DHA TIT' GID' NAG', DHIN NA GID' NAG'

9) DHA TIRI KIT' T'K', DIRI DIRI KIT' T'K',   DHA TIRI KIT' T'K'   TIN NA KIT'-T'K'
    TA TIRI KIT' T'K',   TIRI TIRI KIT' T'K',   DHA TIRI KIT' T'K',   DHIN NA KIT' T'K'

10) DIRI DIRI   KIT' T'K'   T'thKIT'   DHA,   DIRI DIRI   KIT'T'K'   T'th KIT' DHA
    (DIRI DIRI   KIT' T'K') x 3 T'th KIT' DHA

11) **Teen Taal Theka** played with fore-finger only – in different speeds.

As one goes on progressing, more avenues open up and lead to more phrases that can be practiced. The patterns given above are by no means the ultimate. But they are as good for a seasoned Tabla player as they are for a beginner.

Solo Tabla Recital

If one were to go back into the history of Tabla, it will at once be noticed that its development has been alongside that of *Khayal Gayaki*. Also, subsequently, being used for *Kathak* dance accompaniment, Tabla has been enriched by the repertoire of both these forms.

Solo Tabla Recital was developed quite late – maybe because:

1) Lay people were not prepared to look upon it as a solo instrument – some of them are present even today despite the overwhelming popularity that Tabla has been able to establish for itself.

2) It took some time to generate the repertoire needed for a full solo concert.

   The language of Tabla is like any other literary language in that, we have basic alphabets which are joined to form small and big words (what we call *bols*). These *bols* are used to make sentences or statements like a *Kaida* or *Rela*. Again, development of these forms are like essays or chapters. In *Peshkaar* we have the preface as in any literary book, which is used to introduce the events and characters that will follow. Then, there is also the poetic part of the language, which is mainly found in the *G'ths*, *G'th Parans*, etc. Finally, there is the climax, which ends in a crescendo with the *Parans*. Mathematics is also to be found in doses small and large where *Layakari* is expounded.

A Tabla Solo Recital may be broadly said to be comprising of four parts, viz:

1) *Peshkaar*
2) *Kaidas*
3) *Relas*
4) *G'ths, G'th Parans, Chakradaars, Tihaais and Parans.*

Among these categories, **Peshkaar, Kaidas** and **Relas** are basically set statements, if one could call them that. But they lend themselves to improvisations i.e. : making permutations and combinations of the phrases involved. These are called *"B'ls"* or *"Paltaas"*. However, this is not the case with *G'ths*. The *G'th* is an original and unique composition of a maestro. It has inherent expressions which the composer intended to be played just the way he would have envisaged it. Hence, a *G'th* is generally not subjected to permutations. All that one can do is change its *Tihaai*, if it has one or play the same *G'th* in another *Taal* – *matras* permitting. The *G'th* is a sacrosanct composition just as a poem is in the literature of any language. The *Tihaai* is more of a mathematical statement and hence can be subjected to changes – that too, if done sensibly without upsetting the character of the *G'th*.

Peshkaar:

Literally, *Peshkaar* means presentation before an audience. It is a derivative of the root *"Pesh"* which is to present or put forth. One can broadly compare it to the "Preface" that one reads in literary works, wherein the author sets forth to outline the plot and the characters involved in his novel etc. The *Peshkaar* is also on the lines of the *Alaap* of *Ragas*. In the *Alaap*, the musician explores each and every note, its relation to other notes and combination with them. This is mainly to establish the identity of the *Raga*. Similarly, the *Peshkaar* has *bols* that stem from those of the *Theka* of the *Taal*. The *Peshkaar* is gradually developed in stages with passages which highlight parts of all the compositions that are likely to follow in the Solo Recital. This also includes *Layakari* aspects. This way, just as a musician uses the *Alaap* to make himself comfortable with the *Raga / Swaras* and their combinations, which he will be singing or playing at far greater speeds in the latter part of his recital, so also, a Tabla player gets a feel of all or most of his repertoire that he is going to present after the *Peshkaar*.

To a knowledgeable listener, the *Peshkaar*, if properly presented, gives an insight into the Tabla player, his depth of knowledge, *Taiyaari* or speed with clarity and of course his spontaneity in developing the *Peshkaar*.

Unlike a *Kaida*, *Peshkaar* does not have to abide by stringent conditions. In a *Kaida*, while developing it, one cannot go beyond the parameters set out in the theme i.e. : one cannot introduce extraneous *bols* or *Jaatis* other than those already present in that *Kaida*. Nor can a Tabla player change the style of playing. He has to follow the same style as that of the *Gharana* whose *Kaida* he is playing.

In a *Peshkaar*, upto the *Khaali*, it is developed by using the *bols* inherent in itself. After the *Khaali*, upto the following *Sum*, a different set of *bols* / *jaatis* are used, thereby generating a sense of suspense and pleasant surprise among the listeners. This facility is not available while playing a *Kaida*. *Peshkaar* is generally played in *Madhya Laya* and the most popular among *Peshkaars* and also most aesthetic, is the **Farrukhabad** *Peshkaar*. There is also a *Peshkaar* of **Delhi** *Gharana*. But in this case it is developed on the lines of a *Kaida*.

Kaida:

The word *Kaida* is taken from the Urdu word which means "Rule" or "Law". There was a time, when *Ustads* of **Lucknow / Farrukhabad** in their Solo recitals played more of *Peshkaar*, *Relas*, *G'ths*, *Tihaais*, *Chakradhaars* and *Parans*. The *Kaidas* were used more as a whetstone, to sharpen or polish the phrases so that they could be played with an air of confidence as and when they occurred in *G'ths*, etc. But nowadays, *Kaidas* have come to occupy the most important and also the largest part of a Solo Recital. It would not be incorrect to state that *Kaidas* form the "body" of the performance. In a Solo recital of an hour, one hears at least four to five *Kaidas*. Of course each would be different from the others in terms of phrases, *jaatis*, the style of composition and the way in which they are played – according to the *Gharana* they represent. The *Kaida* is the medium through which an artist can exhibit his command over the Tabla and *Dugga*, and also his power of imagination and aesthetic qualities.

As the name implies, a *Kaida* can be expanded or expounded only along certain guidelines which are as follows :-

1) At no stage of exposition of *Kaida*, should bols other than those obtained in the theme or original be introduced.

2) There should be no attempt to play a *Kaida* of a particular *Gharana* in any style other than that followed by that *Gharana*.

3) **Proper** *Khaali / Bhari* should be shown at every stage of the development.

4) No other *jaati* should be introduced in the *Kaida*.

Most of the *Kaidas* are composed as per the divisions or "*khand*" of the *Taal*. But in rare cases, one comes across compositions which do not adhere to the structure of the *Taal*. All the same, they manage to leave a good impression on the listeners if well-presented. One may say that the variations in a *Kaida* go along the same lines to the "*swara-vistaar*" in *Raga* music. But the parallel ends here. Whereas in a *Kaida*, the *bols* of the theme or original statement are not to be changed, in the *Khayal Gayaki*, once an artist, knows the "*Swars*" of the *Raga* or the notes involved in it, there is no limiting him to any particular fashion of using these notes.

A lot of importance is attached to speed or *Taiyaari* in a *Kaida*. *Kaidas* are composed using such bols that can be played at a considerable speed. The rapid movement of the fingers and the ease and neatness with which the artist plays the *Kaida* in the fourth speed, attracts the applause of the audience. Hence, the *Kaida*, though in many cases less appealing aesthetically than the *G'ths* or *G'th Parans* is appreciated by audiences for the above reason. Composing a *Kaida* is far easier than a *G'th* or *G'th paran*. Thus there are innumerable *Kaidas* in existence today and more are being churned out. Since each *Kaida* has one or two phrases which are to be repeatedly played, these phrases get polished to a high degree. Therefore, it is recommended to practice *Kaidas* regularly.

Generally *Kaidas* are short and limited to one cycle or "*Aavartan*". But there are also some which are longer and extend to two cycles. Most of the *Kaidas* are from **Delhi** and **Ajrada** *Gharanas*. **Lucknow** and **Farrukhabad** *Gharanas* do have *Kaidas*, but the accent is more on *G'ths* and *G'th parans*.

Rela:

This is a composition which is made up of *bols* or phrases that lend themselves to faster playing and form a sort of unbroken chain i.e. : the end of one phrase and the beginning of another are interwoven. This results in continuity and sense of resonance. A *Rela* is generally played in the fourth speed and according to the *Taali-Khaali* of the *Taal*. It is given the same treatment as a *Kaida* for further development.

Raon:

This is like a *Rela*, but generally, it is played as a sequel to a "*Chalan*". A "*Chalan*" is first played and then, keeping the prominent bols of the *Chalan* intact, the spaces are filled with smaller faster *bols* such as **TIRI KIT', DHIN' GIN', DHIN-N' DHIN-N'**, etc. When played thus, it sounds like a *Rela*. The only difference is that the speed of the *Chalan* remains the same as in the *Vilambit*. This form is generally found in **Ajrada** or **Farrukhabad** *Gharanas*.

L'di:

This is a form that is employed in *Kaidas, Relas* and to a large extent in "*Laggis*". Literally, *L'di* means a thin round rope which is used to lace or tie a garment around the waist. The comparison to a Tabla *bol* comes from the fact that, the *L'di* composition is smooth and well-rounded and the "end" *bol* merges with the "sum" *bol* in such a manner that, after sometime it becomes difficult to latch on to the sum (i.e. : for the listener).

Another version stems from the derivation of "*L'd*" which means "fight". Some compositions which do not go according to the *Theka*, but go against it are referred to as *L'di G'ths*.

G'th:

This is an important component in the format of a Solo Tabla Recital. *G'ths* in most *Gharanas* have come as heirlooms, handed down by their "*Buzurgs*" or elders i.e. : *Gurus* or *Ustads*. Most of the *G'ths* in existence today are compositions of great masters of the past. A *G'th* is like a poetic composition i.e. : it has both Rhyme and Rhythm. It is a composition in which each phrase has a matching phrase with a mix of soft and loud sounds, short and long phrases and also involving different *Layas* and *Jaatis*. Because of all these characteristics, *G'ths* are classified as "*Bandish*" i.e. : sacrosanct compositions. Each *G'th* reflects the personality of the composer and hence, a *G'th* is not subjected to permutations and combinations, as is done for a *Kaida* or *Rela*.

There are speciality *G'ths* also that have some special characteristics about them. They are as follows :

1) **Baraabari G'th** or a straight forward composition without twists and turns in *laya* etc. In this variety, the phrases are organised in Madhya Laya and Samaa Gati or uniform tempo. Such G'ths are also called Samaa G'ths and they are more to be found in Pakhawaj playing.

2) **Rela G'th** : As the name suggests, in this type of *G'th*, a *Rela* is generally attached to it at the end.

3) **Manjhdaar G'th** : A composition that is comparable to the flow of water in a river. When the river runs down-stream, the speed of the flow of water and its impacting the rocks and stones with force at some points are portrayed in this type of *G'th*.

4) *Tiyedaar G'th* : As the name suggests, these *G'ths* end with a *Tihaai*. Most of the G'ths come to Sum. But there are some special ones which end in Anaaghaat ie. a fraction of a matra before Sum. There are also G'ths in this variety which are wholly Akaal or off beat.

   (a) **Akaal Tihaai G'th** – In this variety, the *Tihaai* of the *G'th* ends in *Anaaghaat*.

   (b) **Sab Akaal Tihaai G'th** – As the name suggests, the entire *G'th*, including the *Tihaai* is off-beat.

   G'ths of both varieties are also called *Anaaghaat G'ths*. Another variety is also known as *L'pet*, in which the last phrase of the previous *matra* is repeated at the beginning of the next *matra*. *L'pet* literally means winding as in the case of a thread.

5) *Ti-palli G'th* : This *G'th* is in three different stages of *Layas* e.g.:

DIN S G'	DIN S G'	T'th KIT'	T'th KIT'	in Tishra Jaati
DHA TIRI KIT'	DHI KIT'	K'th TA GE	DIN GIN'	

59

DHA TIRI KIT'DHI   KIT' K'th TA   GE S DIN S   GIN' DHA S --------- in Chatushra Jaati

DINSG'DINSG'   T'thKIT'T'thKIT'   DHATIRIKIT'DHIKIT'   K'thTAGE DINGIN'.

The last line is in Dugun of Tishra Jaati

6) **Du-Mukhi G'th**: A **G'th** which has the same *bols* in the beginning and at the end.

DHE S KD'DHIN   DHA S GID'N'G'   TIRI KIT'T'K'   T'th G'DAN S ------- (in Tishra)

DHASSS   DIRI DIRI KIT'T'K'   DIRIDIRI KIT'T'K'   TAKI TIRI KIT'T'K'

T'K' TIRI   KIT'T'K'   T'th KIT'DHA   DHIN S TA S --------(both 2ⁿᵈ & 3ʳᵈ lines in Chatushra)

DHE S KD'DHIN   DHA S GID'N'G'   TIRI KIT'T'K'   T'th G'DA S N S

The 1st and 4th lines are identical and in Tishra

7) **F'rd G'th**: The word **F'rd** is Persian in origin and it means unique or only one of its kind. The characteristic of this **G'th** is that unlike in a normal **G'th**, this does not have matching phrases. In fact they may even seem to be unconnected with each other. Also, this **G'th** comes to Sum most unexpectedly and with a short, fast phrase. There are also **G'ths** in different *Jaatis* such as *Khanda* and *Mishra*. There are also *G'ths* composed on Natural phenomena such as Thunder and Lightning, Behaviour-patterns of animals, sounds of Conch, Flute, percussion instruments, **G'ja Parans** and some based on *Sanskrit Shlokas* in praise of Gods, **Manje Ki G'th**, etc.

G'th Paran:

Paran is a commoner's version of the Sanskrit word "*Parn*" which means "Leaf". Just as in a leaf, where the main vein divides the leaf symmetrically into two halves and the halves get further subdivided by smaller branching veins on both sides of the main vein, similarly a **G'th Paran**, when it ends on *Khaali*, it gets duplicated, showing the same branching in its structure.

Both the **G'th** and **G'th Paran**, because of their character of interplay between *Laya* and *Matras* are attractive and pleasant to listen to. Moreover, the sweet sounds of both *Tabla* and *Dugga*, singly and jointly, add to the attraction.

There is a bit of similarity between **G'th Paran** and *Kaida*. Just as there is *Khaali-Bhari* in a *Kaida,* so also we find them in a **G'th Paran**. Thus, a

G'th Paran can also be given the same treatment as a *Kaida*, expanding it and making *paltas, tihaai*, etc. But, the phrases of a *G'th Paran* are more complex and difficult to play and make permutations. Hence, expanding of a *G'th Paran* is rarely done.

In drut *Teen Taal*, we generally have Tabla players playing a series of small but forceful compositions which are called "*Tukdas*". These are mainly **Poorab** *Gharana* compositions and are pieces gleaned out of large *Parans* of Pakhawaj. *Tukdas* are by that token, small in length generally extend 2 to 4 *Aavartans* of Drut *Teen Taal*.

Then there are *Chakradaars* which, as the name suggests mean that the same composition is repeated thrice either with a gap between the three repetitions in case of a *D'm Daar Chakradaar* or without gap in case of a *Be-D'm Chakradaar*.

The composition which is played three times over is in itself a complete one containing a stretch of *bols* or phrases followed by a *tihaai*. At the end of the composition, **DHA** is played followed by a preset gap (or no gap, as the case may be). The whole process is followed three times and the last time that **DHA** is played, it should fall on *Sum*.

Lastly, the solo performance ends with a series of *Parans*, which are forceful *bol* compositions, played in the Khula Baaz.

61

Accompaniment

All Percussion Instruments have been made primarily for providing rhythmic accompaniment to different kinds of music and Tabla is no exception. However, with a lot of thought going into the development of the language of Tabla and because of the vast number of compositions created by great masters of the medium, Tabla Solo recitals gradually took the fancy of the listeners. Indeed today, Tabla Solo recitals are looked forward to by audiences the world over.

Music as a whole has attained great heights and with it, the standard of Tabla accompaniment. In fact an accompanist can elevate the level of the performance of a musician by his skillful accompaniment. The Hindi term used for accompaniment – "*Saath Sangat*" only highlights the importance of the accompanist. If one were to term the playing of Tabla as an Art, then accompaniment is indeed the essence of this Art. The accompanist in demand nowadays is not only a skilled Tabla player, but also a sort of an alter – ego of the musician. He is able to read the musician's thought process and complement it with his own timely contributions. Gone are the days of providing Thekas like a metronome. Today's accompanist has to be able to embellish his Thekas with appropriate soft sounding bols, without in anyway distracting the main artist. There have been any number of instances where listeners have flocked to a musical soiree to hear the Tabla accompanist.

For any budding Tabla player, it is of utmost importance to listen and understand musicians and also try and appreciate the Music rather than only play his part of a Tabla player. Only if a Tabla player is able to listen and appreciate the music can his accompaniment be of some essence in the concert taken as a whole. The art of accompaniment has to be developed by a Tabla player on his own, unlike a Solo Recital where, by and large, he plays compositions learnt and perfected by practicing over and over again.

In accompaniment, there is no set pattern to be followed as in a Solo. The accompanist has to be attentive and may play any composition that he feels will be complimentary to the main artist's expositions.

Given below are some of the Thekas of Taals that are used in the accompaniment of Light Music and Light-Classical Music.

I) **Taal Dadra**: Matras 6.   Taali (clap) on 1,   Khaali on 4

	1	2	3	4	5	6
THEKA :	DHA x 1	DHIN	NA	DHA 0	TIN	NA

Some variations played as *laggis* in the *Dugun* are as follows :

	1	2	3	4	5	6
1.	DHA TIN x	TIN TA	DHIN DHIN	DHA TIN 0	TIN TA	DHIN DHIN
2.	DHA TIN'	KIN'TA	DHIN'GIN'	DHA TIN'	KIN'TA	DHIN'GIN'
3.	DHATI	DHA DHA	TINNA	TATI	DHA DHA	DHINNA
4.	DHIT S	DHA DHA	TINNA	T'th S	DHA DHA	DHINNA
5.	DHA S TIT'	GID'NAG'	TIN'KIN'	TA S TIT'	GID'NAG'	DHIN'GIN'
6.	DHATI GINA	DHATI DHAGE	TINNA KINA	TATI KINA	DHATI DHAGE	
	DHINNA GINA					
7.	(DHA DHIN NADA	DHA DHINNA DA	DHA TIN NADA) x 2			

There can be many more variations possible, depending on the speed at which they need to be played.

II) **Taal Keharwa**: Matras 4   Taali on 1,   Khaali on 3

	1	2	3	4
THEKA :	DHAGE x 1	NA TIN	NAKE 0	DHINNA

Variations:

	1	2	3	4
1.	DHA S	S TIN	NAKE	DHIN NA
2.	DHA S	TIN S	NA S	DHIN S
3.	DHA TIN	S TIN	NA NA	DHIN NA
4.	DHATI	T'th TA	TATI	DHIT TA
5.	DHIT TA	TATI	T'th TA	DHA TI
6.	DHA DHIN	NA DA	DHA TIN	NA DA

7.	DHIT S	TA TIN	T'th S	DHA TIN
8.	DHIT TA	S TA	T'th S	DHA DA
9.	, GI D'	NA TIN	S TIN	DHA TIN
10.	DHA S TIT'	TIT'KIT'	TA S DI'T'	TIT'KIT' --------- and so on.

Once again, there is an unlimited scope for creating more laggi patterns – depending on the situation and speed at which they need to be played.

Some light compositions are presented to the accompaniment of Taal **"Dhumaali"**, **"Deepchandi"** **"Bhajan"** Theka or **"Adhdhaa"** in the slower tempo and then the Tabla player plays laggis in **Keharwa** once the singer concludes a verse and takes up the sign line.

The above mentioned Thekas are given below.

Taal DHUMAALI: Matras –8

1	2	3	4	5	6	7	8
DHA	DHIN	NA	TIN	NAK'	DHIN	DHA GE	TIRIKIT'
x				0			
1		2				3	

Taal AADHAA DHUMALI: Matras -8

1	2	3	4	5	6	7	8
DHA	DHIN	DHA DHA	TIN	TÁ	TIN	DHA DHA	DHIN
x	2			0		3	

BHAJAN THEKA:

1	2	3	4	5	6	7	8
DHIN S	NA DHIN	S DHIN	NA S	DHIN S	NA TIN	S TIN	NA S
x		2		0		3	
1							

Taal DEEPCHANDI: Matras -14

1	2	3	4	5	6	7	8	9	10	11	12	13	14
DHA	DHIN	SS	DHA	DHA	TIN	SS	TA	TIN	SS	DHA	DHA	DHIN	SS
x		2					0			3			
1													

ADHDHAA Matras –16. (This is a variation of TeenTaal)

1	2	3	4	5	6	7	8
DHA S	G'DHIN	S G'	DHA S	DHA DHA	G' DHIN	S G'	DHA S
x				2			
1							

9	10	11	12	13	14	15	16	
DHA S	T'th TIN	S N'	TA S	I TA TA	G' DHIN	S G'	DHA	S
0				3				

NOTE : In all the Taals and Thekas given above, the Bhankhande script is followed.

In the accompaniment of pure Classical Vocal Music, the Taals most often in use are Ektaal, Jhumra, Tilwada, Teentaal, Jhaptaal and Roopak.

To establish the Tempo, the rule of thumb generally adopted is that the average range of heart beats / pulse rate is taken as the *Madhya Laya* or Medium Tempo. Half this rate is taken as *Vilambit Laya* or Slow Tempo and Quarter of the rate is taken as *Ati Vilambit Laya* or Very Slow Tempo. Double of the *Madhya Laya* is known as *Drut Laya* or Fast Tempo. Four times the *Madhya Laya* is *Ati Drut Laya* or Very Fast speed. Of course, all these above mentioned Tempi extend over a range. For the sake of convenience the *Madhya Laya* is also taken as one Matra per second

Given below are the above mentioned Taals as they need to be played in *Vilambit* or *Ati Vilambit Layas* ; i.e.Slow Tempo or very slow Tempo.

By far, the most popular Taal, so far as accompaniment of Vocal Music is concerned, is **Ektaal**. If one were to consider a pulse rate of 1 matra per second for *Madhya Laya*, then, 1 matra per 2 seconds is *Vilambit Laya* and 1 matra per 4 seconds is *Ati Vilambit Laya*.

Taal Ektaal:

Matras 12, Taali on 1, 5, 9, 11. Khaali on 3, 7.

Madhya – Laya (1 matra per second):

1	2	3	4	5	6
DHIN	DHIN	DHAGE	TIRIKIT'	TUN	NA
x		0		2	
1					

7	8	9	10	11	12
T'th	TIN	DHAGE	TIRIKIT'	DHIN	NA
0		3		4	

Vilambit (1 matra per 2 seconds):

```
   1                2                3                      4
DHIN    S  |  DHIN    S  |  DHA    GE  |  TIRI    KIT'  |
x
1                        0


   5                6                7                      8
TUN     S  |  NA      S  |  T'th    S  |  TIN     S  |
2                        0


   9               10               11                    12
DHA    GE  |  TIRI     KIT'|  DHIN    S  |  NA      S  |
3                        4
```

Ati – Vilambit (1 matra per 4 seconds):

```
   1                        2                        3
DHIN  S  S  S  |  DHIN  S  S  S  |  DHA  S  GE  S  |
x
1                                0


   4                        5                        6
TI  RI  KI  T'  |  TUN  S  S  S  |  NA  S  S  S  |
                         2


   7                        8                        9
T'th  S  S  S  |  TIN  S  S  S  |  DHA  S  GE  S  |
0                                              3


  10                       11                       12
TI  RI  KI  T'  |  DHIN  S  S  S  |  NA  S  S  S  |
                         4
```

Now, while accompanying, the Theka is filled up by using appropriate but soft sounding bols per pulse beat of 1 second but only the main Matra strokes are accentuated (as shown in bold italics.) Thus, the Ati – Vilambit Theka can be played as given below :-

```
DHIN  S  DHIN  GEGE |  DHIN   S  DHIN  DHIN  |  DHA  S  DHA  DHAGE |
x
1                                          0


TI   RI   KI   T'  |  TIN  S  TIN   TIN   |  NA   S   NA   NA NA |
                      2


T'th  S  T'th  T'th  |  TIN  S  TIN  TIRIKIT'  |  DHA  S  DHA  DHAGE |
0                                           3
```

66

TI	RI	KI	T'	DHIN	S	DHIN	DHIN	I	*DHA*	S	DHA	DHA	DHA|

4

DHIN
x

In the Theka given above, the last quarter matra ; i.e. DHA DHA can be substituted by a short phrase such as SS TIRIKIT' T'K' T'K' TIRIKIT' or GINA DHAGE TINNA KINA etc. (played in chougun)

Similar treatment can be given to Theka of "JHUMRA" Taal when it has to be played in Ati – Vilambit Laya.

Taal Jhumra:

Matras 14, Taali on 1, 4, 11. Khaali on 8.
Madhya – Laya (1 matra per second)

1	2	3		4	5	6	7	
DHIN	DHA	TIRI KIT'	|	DHIN	DHIN	DHAGE	TIRI KIT'	|
x				2				
1								

8	9	10		11	12	13	14	
TIN	TA	TIRI KIT'	|	DHIN	DHIN	DHAGE	TIRI KIT'	|
0				3				

The Theka given above is modified a bit in many cases where the gaps between 1st and 2nd matras and 8th and 9th matras is 1½ matras.eg :

1	2	3		4	5	6	7	
DHIN S	S DHA	TIRI KIT'	|	DHIN	DHIN	DHAGE	TIRI KIT'	|
x				2				
1								

8	9	10		11	12	13	14	
TIN S	S TA	TIRI KIT'	|	DHIN	DHIN	DHAGE	TIRI KIT'	|
0				3				

Vilambit – Laya (1 matra per 2 seconds) :

1	2	3	4	5	6	7	
DHIN S | S DHA | TIRI KIT'|	DHIN S | DHIN S| DHA GE |	TIRI KIT'|
x			2			
1						

8	9	10	11	12	13	14	
TIN S | S TA | TIRI KIT' |	DHIN S | DHIN S | DHA GE |	TIRI KIT' |
0			3			

Ati Vilambit Laya: (1 matra per 4 seconds)

```
1                        2                              3
DHIN  S   S   GE GE  |  DHIN  S     DHA   GE GE  |  TI  RI  KI  T' |
x
1

4                    5                        6
DHIN  S   S   KD'  |  DHIN  S   DHIN   DHIN  |  DHA   S   DHA   DHA GE |
2

7
TI  RI   KI   T' |

8                    9                        10
TIN  S   S   KD'  |  TIN   S     TA   KE KE  |  TI  RI  KI  T' |
0

11                   12                       13
DHIN  S   S   KD'  |  DHIN  S   DHIN   DHIN  |  DHA   S   DHA   DHA GE |
3

14
TI  RI   KI   T' |
```

Here too, the main bols of the Theka are shown in bold italics print. It may be noticed that an additional DHIN is played softly at the beginning of the second Matra and TIN at the beginning of the 9th Matra. This is done to keep the resonance going.

Taal Tilwada:

Matras 16 Taali on 1,5,13 and Khali on 9.

Madhya Laya: (1 matra per second)

```
1       2       3       4              5      6      7      8
DHA   TIRI KIT'  DHIN   T'thDHIN  |  DHA    DHA    TIN    TIN
x
1

9      10      11      12             13     14     15     16
TA    TIRIKIT'  DHIN   T'thDHIN  |  DHA    DHA    DHIN   DHIN
0                                    3
```

Vilambit Laya: (1 matra per 2 seconds)

```
1       2          3          4
DHA  S  |  TIRI   KIT'  |  DHIN  S  |  T'th   DHIN  |
x
1
```

68

5			6			7			8		
DHA	S	|	DHA	S	|	TIN	S	|	TIN	S	|

2

9			10			11			12		
TA	S	|	TIRI	KIT'	|	DHIN	S	|	T'th	DHIN	|

0

13			14			15			16		
DHA	S	|	DHA	S	|	DHIN	S	|	DHIN	S	|

3

Tilwada is not used much in the Ati Vilambit Laya by vocalists. But if such a situation does arise, it can be played in the Ati Vilambit Laya by giving it the same treatment as done in case of Ati Vilambit Ektaal or Jhumra Taal.

Some useful suggestions regarding accompaniment for budding Tabla players.

1) Be a perfectionist in the matter of tuning of the Tabla to the pitch (*sur*) of the main artist, be it a vocalist or an instrumentalist.

2) Tune the Baayaan to the *Kharj* or the lower *Shadj* (main note) of the pitch to which the Tabla has been tuned. If this is not possible, tune the Baayaan to the Madhyam, Pancham or Gandhaar of the main note, depending on which of these notes is the most important one for the Raga selected. This step will ensure that when both Tabla and Baayaan are struck together as in DHA or DHIN, the singer or instrumentalist will get a sound that is in perfect consonance with his drone.

3) Be very alert and observe every movement or nuance of the main artist. Many a times instructions are conveyed to the accompanist by small gestures of the hands, head or eyes.

4) Provide the artist with a resonant, balanced, and measured Theka in the Laya selected, without sounding like a metronome. Fill up the Theka with appropriate, soft and melodious phrases, only accentuating the main bols of the Theka.

5) Always endeavour to end the Theka with a small phrase or *Tihaai* so as to enhance the *Sum*. This may preferably done once the main artist is seen to be comfortable both with the Theka and the Laya.

6) It takes a great deal of restraint for a *Taiyaar* or a proficient Tabla player to refrain from playing too much while accompanying Vocalists. But this has to be done in the interest of the concert as a whole. An accompanist should always remember that his main task is to elevate the performance of the main artist.

7) While accompanying an instrumentalist, the Tabla player must observe the same restraint while providing Theka to the G'th of the instrumentalist. While doing this he must also pay attention to the patterns that are being played. This will help him to play an appropriate Kaida or Challan which in a way is complimentary to what the main artist has played. Also, one should not be overtly ponderous and try to impress the audience with unnecessary demonstrations of high speed and loud playing.

8) In the Ati Drut phase, which is always a part of an instrumentalist's repertoire the accompanist must give a clean Theka of TeenTaal until the beginning of the final *Tihaai* and then join him to provide a crescendo.

9) Gone are the days when it was presumed that the instrumentalist would take up a G'th in Teen Taal. Nowadays most instrumentalists are proficient in playing G'ths to odd matra Taals. The accompanist must endeavour to perfect this part of his repertoire and be able to play well enough in any Taal.

10) In addition to all the points listed above, the Tabla accompanist must try not to think of himself as an individual but as a partner. He must listen to the artist's delineation and derive maximum pleasure and inspiration from it. Only then can his accompaniment be an apt foil to the main artist's skill and thus lead to a highly satisfying performance both for the performers as well as the listeners.

Scripts used for the Language of Tabla

Taals are written by means of a script. There are two such scripts in *Hindustani* Music, wherein, use is made of set symbols to signify various concepts such as *Taali, Khaali, Sum, Khand* (divisions) and *bols*. The two scripts are:

1) Pandit Vishnu Digambar Paluskar Script

2) Pandit Vishnu Narayan Bhatkhande Script.

Pandit Vishnu Digambar Paluskar Script

In this script, Matras are not indicated by numbers. There are symbols which represent a Matra, its fractions or two Matras. There are symbols for Sum and Khaali also.

Symbol	What it stands for	Symbol	What it stands for
—	1 matra	1	Sum
O	½ matra	+	Khaali
‿	¼ matra	|	sign to signify end of Theka or bols.
⤵	⅛ matra	1, 2, ….. numerals	for Taalis other than Sum eg. :
⬳	⅓ matra		for Teen Taal — 5, 13 & for Jhap Taal – 3, 8, etc.
≋	⅙ matra	S	Gaps.
⁓	2 matra		

71

Given below are *Thekas* of some *Taals*, using the above script :

1) Keharwa:

DHA	GE	NA	TIN	NA	KE	DHIN	NA	
O	O	O	O	O	O	O		
1				+				

2) Jhaptaal:

DHIN	NA	DHIN	DHIN	NA	TIN	NA	DHIN	DHIN	NA	
—	—	—	—	—	—	—	—	—	—	
1		2			+		3			

3) Roopak:

TIN	TIN	NA	DHIN	NA	DHIN	NA	
—	—	—	—	—	—	—	
+			1		2		

4) Ektaal:

DHIN	DHIN	DHA GE	TIRIKIT'	TUN	NA
—	—	O O	〰〰	—	—
1		+		2	

T'th	TIN	DHAGE	TIRIKIT'	DHIN	NA	
—	—	O O	〰〰	—	—	
+		3		4		

5) Teen Taal:

DHA	DHIN	DHIN	DHA	DHA	DHIN	DHIN	DHA
—	—	—	—	—	—	—	—
1				2			

DHA	TIN	TIN	TA	TA	DHIN	DHIN	DHA	
—	—	—	—	—	—	—	—	
+				3				

72

Pandit Vishnu Narayan Bhatkhande Script

The important symbols to note are as follows:

Symbol	What it stands for
Numerals 1, 2, etc. written above bol...	Indication for Matras
X	Indication for Sum (1st beat)
O	Indication for Khaali
|	Indication for Khand (Division)
⌣	Indication for more than one Bol / Matra
S	Gaps
Numerals 1, 2, 3, 4, etc.	Indication for Claps other than Sum and are written below that matra.

Given below are some Thekas using the above Script:

1) Keharwa:

1	2	3	4
DHA GE	NA TIN	NA KE	DHIN NA
x		0	
1			

2) Roopak:

1	2	3	4	5	6	7
TIN	TIN	NA	DHIN	NA	DHIN	NA
0			1		2	

NOTE : For writing Dugun, Tigun or Chougun in this script. Follow the same procedure, but now write 2,3 or 4 bols as the case may be, in each matra and give the symbol "⌣":- to indicate bols more than one per matra e. g. **Jhaptaal** in dugun will be writtern thus:

1	2	3	4	5
DHIN NA	DHIN DHIN	NA TIN	NA DHIN	DHIN NA

x
1   2

6	7	8	9	10
DHIN NA	DHIN DHIN	NA TIN	NA DHIN	DHIN NA

0   3

Teen Taal in Tigun

1	2	3	4
DHADHIN DHIN	DHADHADHIN	DHINDHADHA	TINTINTA

x
1

5	6	7	8
TADHIN DHIN	DHADHADHIN	DHINDHADHA	DHINDHINDHA

2

9	10	11	12
DHATINTIN	TATADHIN	DHINDHADHA	DHINDHINDHA

0

13	14	15	16
DHADHINDHIN	DHADHATIN	TINTATA	DHINDHINDHA

3

Carnatic Taal System

Carnatic Music is known as *"Laghu"* Music whereas *Hindustani* Music is known as *"Guru"* Music. Thus, while in *Hindustani* Music we have *Vilambit* and *Ati Vilambit Layas*, in the *Carnatic* Tradition there is only *Madhya* and *Drut Laya*.

The items presented are mostly poems in the South Indian languages viz :- *Kannada, Tamil* or *Telegu.* There are six different types of songs or items presented viz:- *Varnam, Kriti, Padam, Pallavi, Jaavali, Keertanam.*

The names of the *"Raags"* and *"Thaats"* are different from those in *Hindustani* Tradition. In case of *Raags* having the same names in both styles, the *Carnatic* Raagas have different *swars* or notes. Some *Carnatic* *Raags* like *Kirwaani, Saalagvaraali, Hansdhwani* are now quite popular on the *Hindustani* Concert platform.

The *Taal* system followed in the *Carnatic* Tradition is a little different from that of the *Hindustani* Tradition. But, ancient *Taal-Shaastra* has *Taal*

74

compositions which are quite close to those found in the *Carnatic* Tradition. The *Taal* compositions in the *Carnatic* Tradition are made up of Divisions or "*Angs*" eg :- In a *Taal* of 6 beats there are 2 divisions – one of 2 beats and another of 4 beats.

There are 6 "*Angs*" in all and all the *Taals* are played within the framework of these 6 "*Angs*". The names, symbols and *matra* or *Akshar Kaal* are as under :-

Name of *Ang*	Symbol	Matra (*AksharKaal*)
1) *Anu Drut*	U	1
2) *Drut*	O	2
3) *Laghu*	|	4
4) *Guru*	ς	8
5) *Pluth*	ς	12
6) *Kaak pad*	+	16

The *Laghu Ang* or its symbol is found in every *Taal* and is very important. The *Akshar Kaal* of the *Laghu* changes according to the various *Jaatis*. Accordingly it is reflected in the *Taals*. The various *Akshar Kaals* as per different *Jaatis* is given below :

Name of Jaati	Akshar Kaal of Laghu
1) *Chaturasra Jaati*	4
2) *Tishra Jaati*	3
3) *Khanda Jaati*	5
4) *Mishra Jaati*	7
5) *Sankeerna Jaati*	9

There are seven prominent Taals in the Carnatic Tradition, based on Laghu, Drut, Anudrut Angs. There are some Taals based on Guru, Pluth and Kaakpad, but these are not so popular.

Name of *Taal*	*Ang* Configuration	*Akshar Kaal*	Total *matras* In *Chatushra Jaati*
1) *Dhruv Taal*	|O||	4 + 2 + 4 + 4	14
2) *M'th Taal*	|O|	4 + 2 + 4	10
3) *Roopak Taal*	|O	4 + 2	6
4) *Jhamp Taal*	|UO	4 + 1 + 2	7
5) *Triput Taal*	|OO	4 + 2 + 2	8
6) *A'T' Taal*	||OO	4 + 4 + 2 + 2	12
7) *Ik Taal*	|	4	4.

As mentioned earlier, *Laghu Ang* changes according to the *Jaatis*, thus each of these seven *Taals* has 5 different types. Hence, there are in all 35 *Taals* which are in use in the *Carnatic* Tradition. These 35 *Taals* are further expanded to 175 by varying the speed or "G'ti" of their Laghus. Thus, each of the 35 Taals can be varied in 5 different ways eg. one can have Khanda Jaati M'th Taal in Mishra G'ti or Tishra Jaati Triput Taal in Khanda G'ti.

Differences between *Hindustani* and *Carnatic Taal* System

Hindustani	Carnatic
1) *Taal* Compositions are made mainly on *Matras* and Divisions.	*Taal* Compositions are based on *Laghu Guru Ang* concepts. *Laghu Ang* is important. The value of the *Laghu Ang* changes according to *Jaatis*. Each *Laghu* or *Guru* is considered as a separate division.
2) Measurement of *Taal* starts from "Sum" (1st beat), which is indicated by a Clap (*Taali*).	SAME

3) Every *Bhari* division starts with a *Taali* and *Khaali* is shown by way of upturned hand.

Each *Laghu* or *Guru Ang* is treated as a separate division and the beginning of each division is indicated by a clap. The *'Visarjitam'* (equivalent of *Khaali*), even if it is present in the Taal, is not considered as a separate division.

4) There are 15 to 20 *Taals* which are in regular use. But there are countless *Aprachalit* or lesser known Taals

Main Taals are seven. As per the Jaatis, the value of the *Laghu Ang* changes. Hence there are 7x5=35 *Taals* in regular use. These can be further expanded to 35x5=175, by varying the speed or G'ti of the *Angs*.

5) *Taals* have "*Thekas*" of definite *matras* and *Bols* which do not change. The *Taal* can be expounded only in this framework of *Matras*.

The *Taalas* are expounded on *Laghu Guru Ang* Concept. No definite *Thekas* are involved. The *Taal* is expressed in terms of the *Bols* that signify *Jaatis*.

6) The *Taal* compositions are played on Tabla and Pakhawaj for accompaniment. Also, solo recitals are played on Tabla and Pakhawaj, using these *Taals*.

All the *Taals* are played on *Mridangam*. Instruments like *Khanjira* and *Ghatam* are side-accompaniment instruments. Purely *Mridangam* Solo recitals are rare. But during the accompaniment, enough scope is provided to the Mridangam player by the instrumentalist to show his talent or prowess.

7) The *Taals* or compositions like *G'ths* or *Kaidas* can be written down by scripts like *Pt. Paluskar* or *Pt. Bhatkhande*, with signs, symbols for various divisions, *matras, Taalis* or *Khaalis*.

Symbols for *Laghu, Guru* are used for noting down *Taals*, etc.

Thani Avartanam-A Solo Play

In a Carnatic music concert a percussion accompaniment is indispensable. The Mridangam is the standard percussion instrument. A Ghatam, Khanjira or a Morsing is only employed as a secondary instrument. You will never attend a music concert which does not have a Mridangam accompanist. Towards the end of the concert, a separate time is allocated for a thani or solo play (thani-literally meaning alone). Earlier when concert durations were much longer even two such allotments were given for the solo or thani. When there is an ensemble of three of four percussion instrments, the mridangist takes the lead. Then each instrument is played in the order of importance viz. The Ghatam followed by Khanjira and finally the Morsing. Each instrument is played one by one-each contributing to the development of the rhythmic theme. The theme is gradually developed and then tapered uniformaly. At the end the instruments join together in the finale.

Terminology – Definition, Meaning and Description

It is very essential that terminology used in any field must mean the same for any individual, irrespective of the region to which he belongs. Even in Tabla, whose language is pretty recent and lends itself to various interpretations in different *Gharanas*, names and their meanings have to be standardized. Some of the most common terms one encounters are given hereunder :-

1) *Ang*: In ancient *Sangeet Shaastra*, the divisions or *Khands* were called *Angs*. But in today's music any style of playing is referred to as *Ang*. Eg : *Gaayaki Ang* or *Gatkaari Ang* or *Dedhi Ang* or *Poorab Ang* or *Upaj Ang*, etc.

2) *Akshar* i.e.: syllable or alphabet : The sounds created by striking on the Tabla or *Dugga* surface by various fingers and even palms is referred to as *Akshar*. These combine to form various words or phrases (*Bols*) which ultimately leads to a Tabla language.

3) *Ateet*: A composition that ends a fraction of a *matra* after the Sum i.e.: the 1ˢᵗ beat of the *Taal* is called *Ateet.*

4) *Anaghaat*: A composition which ends suddenly a fraction of a *matra* before the Sum of a *Taal* is called *Anaghaat*.

   Both *Ateet* and *Anaghaat* sound very attractive if the end point of the composition is as close to the Sum as possible.

5) *Aad-Laya*: Eg : *Dedhi* or 1 ½ times of original speed. This is *Tishra-Jaati Laya* i.e. : counting three in two *matras*.

6) *Aavartan* (cycle): This is a complete count of the number of beats in a *Taal* eg. : 16 beats in *Teen Taal*, 10 beats in *Jhaptaal*, 7 in *Roopak*, etc.

   The time taken in a given *Laya* to complete a cycle beginning from one Sum of a *Taal* to its next Sum is called *Aavartan.*

7) **Badhant** (or **Badhat**): Meaning expansion or making variations as in a *Kaida* or *Rela*. In the **Benares** *Gharana*, instead of *Peshkaar*, a *Madhya Laya Teen Taal Chalan* is taken and **Badhant** is made of this.

8) **Baraabari**: i.e.: one to one. When a presentation is made in *Madhya Laya* with one *bol* per *matra,* it is referred to as **Baraabari** *ka Laya.*

9) **B'l**: *Paltaa* or variation as in a *Kaida* or *Rela.*

10) **Baant**: *Paltaas* of *Laggi* are called **Baant**.

11) **Bol**: The words or phrases that occur in the language of Tabla are called **Bols**. **Bol** in Hindi ordinarily means spoken word. Hence, this word is freely used even in Vocal / instrumental music and dance.

12) **Chalan**: This, as the name suggests shows the way in which a *Kaida* or a *Rela* is being played. The **Chalan** incorporates the prominent *bols* of the compositions. The finer and faster *bols* are played once the **Chalan** is established.

13) **Chakradhaar**: This is a longish composition whose latter part is generally a *Tihaai* and the whole composition is played three times over. **Chakradhaars** as a rule, begin on the first beat and also end on the first beat.

14) **Chaant-Thaap**: The border-skin on the Tabla-*pudi* is called "**Chaant**". But the stroke of **NA** or **TA** produced by striking the border with the fore-finger is also called as "**Chaant**". "**Thaap**" is the stroke produced by striking the lower part of the *Shaayee* by joining the middle-finger, ring-finger and the little finger together and lifting the hand after striking in such a way that the little finger comes up last. This stroke is employed sometimes to add a bit of colour to the performance and also sometimes after completion of tuning the Tabla. The sound of the "**Thaap**" is like the sound of "**TIN**" produced by striking the "*Luv*" with the fore-finger i.e. : the sound of "*Saa*" of that particular scale.

15) **Chilla**: This is a form of practice-session (or *Riyaaz*) which is characteristic of the *Hindustani* Music Tradition. In this, the musician decides on a period – usually 40 days, during which he will be engaged

in *Riyaaz*. During this time, the elders of the community take over the responsibility of supporting his family. If *Chilla* is assiduously followed, the artiste emerges superior in his "*Taiyaari*" or speed and clarity.

16) *Chh'nd*: Any short, repetitive piece of music or rhythm that gives a sense of fulfillment or happiness to one's mind is "*Chh'nd*". Basic folk rhythms fall in this category and consequently must have led to the development of classical *Taals* in Pakhawaj or Tabla. *Chh'nds* have been used in the recitation of *Rig Ved* and *Saam Ved* chants.

Although *Laya* and *Chh'nd* are two separate concepts, there can be no *Chh'nd* without the limits of *Laya*. (*Laya-badh*)

17) *Dohra*: Generally, the first variation of a *Kaida* is termed as the *Dohra* wherein, the first half of a *Kaida* is played twice followed by the full *Kaida* upto *Khaali* and similarly same followed in *Khaali* part.

18) *Dudhaara*: This is a variation of a composition in which each phrase of the composition is played twice. Similarly, in *Tidhaara*, each phrase is played thrice and so on.

19) *Farmaishi*: Farmaishi is an Urdu word which means "Request". It can also imply a challenge. A Farmaishi Composition has some important characteristics attached - eg. It can be an *Anaghaat* or *Ateet* or *Visham Bol*, or it can be a *Chakradaar* which, when played the first time, the 1st DHA of the *Tihaai* falls on the sum, when played the 2nd time, the 2nd DHA falls on the sum and when played the 3rd time, the last DHA of the *Tihaai* falls on sum.

20) *F'rsh B'ndi*: *F'rsh* in Persian means floor. Applying this term, *F'rsh B'ndi* means demarcating the parameters of the *Taal* and *Theka* and then composing and presenting the *Peshkaar* as per parameters laid down. Hence the parameters viz : *Theka bols*, divisions, *Khaali-Bhari*, etc are always given due weightage while playing a composition.

21) *Ganda Bandhan:* This term implies the ritualistic acceptance of a disciple by a Guru.

This function is conducted in the presence of a host of invited guests, who are mostly reputed musicians and also sometimes people who have gained eminence in other fields. The Guru ties a sacred thread on the hand of the Shishya amidst chanting of prayers. The Guru then gives the Shishya some jaggery and a fistful of roasted gram to eat. The Shishya does likewise and then an announcement is made by the Guru that he has accepted the person as his Shishya and that he would fulfil that responsibility as best as he can. The Shishya in turn promises that he would put in his best efforts to practise the art taught to him by his Guru and try to make a name not only for himself but also for his Guru and the Gharana to which he belongs. This is followed by a musical soiree in which both the Guru and the Shishya perform and so also do some of the invited artists.

22) *G'th:* This is a beautiful composition in that it is endowed with aesthetic appeal. The *G'th* is a composition which has come about on similar lines as the *Paran* in Pakhawaj. It is a lyrical composition and just like poetry, has both rhyme and rhythm. Most of the G'ths are in the *Poorab* and *Farrukhabad* traditions. There are G'ths based on Natural phenomena such as Thunder and Lightning, movement or behaviour of animals, birds etc., sound of other Instruments such as Wind Instruments (*Sushir Vadya*) or *Nagara* etc. These effects are woven into compositions interspersed with Tabla or Pakhawaj bols.

23) *Guldastaa*: Literally means a bouquet of flowers. It is generally said with reference to the presentation of a Tabla player who is able to perform in all the traditions or *Gharanas* – i.e. : he who presents compositions of different *Gharanas* as they should be played in their respective styles.

24) *Gharana*: Literally, this means family or clan. In musical parlance, it means school or sometimes style of performance. It is established by generations of sons or disciples being trained in one particular tradition. The *Gharanas* are named not after its originator but by the place from where the stalwarts originated and conducted the propagation of their art. Hence we have names of *Gharanas* such as **Delhi, Lucknow, Farrukhabad, Meerut (Ajrada), Punjab** and **Benares** in Tabla and **Gwalior, Agra, Jaipur-Atraoli**, etc in vocal music.

25) *Jaati*: In Hindi, *Jaati* means class or section, as applicable to Society. In the same sense this is applicable to *Taal Shastra*. Hence we have

Jaatis according to the conglomerate of *Matras*. There is *Tishra Jaati* for groups of 3 *matras*, *Chatushra Jaati* for groups of 4 *matras*, *Khanda Jaati* for groups of 5 *matras*, *Mishra Jaati* for groups of 7 *matras* and *Sankeerna Jaati* for groups of 9 *matras*.

Originally there were only 2 **Jaatis** i.e. – *Tishra* and *Chatushra* and these were basic forms of *Taals* according to the *Laghu / Guru* concepts. Thus, we had **CHAA CHA PUT'** as *Tishra* with one *Guru* and one *Laghu* and **CHA CHAA CHA PUT'** as *Chatushra* with a combination of *Laghu – Guru – Laghu*.

26) *Kaida*: This is a well-defined and structured composition replete with syllables and phrases of Tabla language, generally ending with a resonating phrase and one which shows **Khaali-Bhari**, also lending itself to making permutations leading to *Paltas*.

Kaida comes from the Persian word "*Kaid*" meaning prison. In these compositions, some typical phrases are imprisoned i.e. : they cannot break free into any other variation and hence one sees and hears the same phrases being repeated in different combinations while expanding a **Kaida**. **Kaida** in Hindi or Urdu means 'Rule'. Thus we see that a Kaida is expanded along set patterns and rules.

27) *Kaal*: This is one of the ten vital characteristics (*Dasha-Praan*) of a *Taal*. In a broad sense it means time, but in today's musical parlance it means a gesture of the hand denoting *Khaali* i.e. : a wave of the hand as against a *Taali* or clap.

28) *Kism*: This literally means an example. Variations of a *Theka* are termed as **Kism** where, without changing the *Taal*-structure, merely the *bols* are changed or inter-changed and presented in a disciplined manner.

29) *Khand*: Pre-determined groups of *matras* in a *Taal* are called *Khand*. A *Taal* is not just a collection of *matras* but one in which the matras are grouped together. This grouping is what gives a *Taal* its character. There are many examples of *Taals* with the same number of *matras* but different groupings eg : *Jhumra* and *Aadachautaal*, *Jhaptaal* and *Surfaak Taal*. **Khanda** is also the name of a *Jaati* in which the *bols* are in groups of five syllables.

30) **Khaali-Bhari**: Any part of the *Taal* which is shown by a *Taali* is termed as **Bhari**. That is one which has stressed *bols* such as **DHA, DHIN**, etc. **Khaali** means that part of the *Taal* shown by a wave of the hand and this has unstressed *bols* such as **TA, TIN**, etc. This concept is very closely followed in Tabla playing. Generally a *Khaali* is expressed in the middle of a long *Guru*.

31) **Khulaa (Baaz)**: Resonating sounds are a hallmark of this style of playing – as against *B'nd Baaz* which involves playing with a compact hand close to the Tabla-top. In **Khulaa-Baaz** the *bols* are played with an open hand, fingers loosely spaced and the hand always at a distance above the Tabla, giving enough scope for the sound to resonate before striking again.

32) **Laggi**: This is the smallest possible composition in Tabla, that can be treated like a *Kaida* i.e. : one which can be expanded. It is made up of small, attractive *bols* which are in consonance with the *Chalans* of the *Thekas* viz : *Keharwa, Dadra, Chaachar*. The variations are done as in a *Kaida* though one need not follow the strict regulations as in a *Kaida*. The *L'di* pattern is used to make *Paltas* or variations.

33) **L'di**: Literally *L'di* means a round thin rope, which is generally used to lace or tie a garment. The comparison to a Tabla composition comes from the fact that, the *L'di* composition is smooth and rounded and one in which the end *bol* merges into the Sum *bol* in such a fashion that after sometime it becomes diffcult to latch on to the Sum (i.e. : for the listener).

Another version stems from the derivation of *L'd* meaning fight. According to this the *bols* of the Tabla and Dugga are so positioned as if to indicate that they are fighting each other. Also, there are compositions which are constantly fighting or going against the expected stresses of a *Theka*. These are *L'di G'ths*. Normally a *G'th* is played once or twice but a *L'di-G'th* can be played any number of times.

In the **Benares** *Gharana*, variations or *Paltas* of *Laggi* are called *L'di*.

34) **L'dhant**: The friendly repartees between a *Sitar / Sarod* player and the Tabla player or where the Tabla player plays or attempts to play the

84

same (or similar) strokes as the instrumentalist are termed as *L'dhant*. This generally involves mathematical expression or *Layakari* and is a good thing if artistically done and not extended. It needs the alertness and quick reaction of a Tabla player to make for a successful *Ladhant*.

35) *Laya*: The uniform speed or rate of time-division by means of sounds or strokes is called *Laya*. It is the cumulative effect of the time-gap between two successive strokes over a period (assuming that the strokes are uniformly spaced).

36) *Loam-Viloam*: This is a composition which reads the same both ways i.e. : left to right or right to left. In English language this is termed as a 'Palindrome'.

37) *Laut-Palat*: Some small collection of *bols* which are turned back to front or reversed and played is called *Laut-Palat*.

38) *Matra*: This is a device used to measure a *Taal*. It is referred to in English as "Beat". *Taal* is used to measure the time-span in Music. A *Laghu* is generally taken as one *Matra* and a *Guru* as two *matras*.

39) *Mukhda*: In musical parlance, a *Mukhda* is a phrase which leads to the Sum of the composition. Similarly, in Tabla, a *Mukhda* is a short composition which is played to enhance the Sum. A *Mukhda* could be as small as a matra to as much as 8 *matras*.

40) *Mohra*: This a small composition which ends in a *Tihaai*, coming to Sum. It is also compared to a golden coin which in olden times was known as a *Mohur*, or even to a "seal" which was also known as a *Mohur* or *muhar,* as given to official documents by kings or *Nawabs*.

41) *Nikaas*: This is a term used for the process of producing Tabla *bols* by striking the Tabla / *Dugga* by fingers / palms at various points. Generally every *Gharana* has its own pattern of *Nikaas*. Normally by noting the way a Tabla player plays the instrument and listening to the sounds produced, one can guess as to which *Gharana* he represents or is influenced by.

42) *Nauhakka*: This is a form of *Tihaai*. In fact, it is a *Tihaai* of a *Tihaai*. But playing a *Tihaai* 3 times itself does not make a *Nauhakka*. For

this, the same *bol* has to be played 9 times with 8 equal gaps between them. Also, it has to start on Sum and end on Sum.

43) ***P't***: This is generally used when we talk of multiples eg : ***Dup't*** i.e. – twice, ***Choup't*** or four times, etc. Of course this is with reference to a particular *Laya*.

44) ***Paran***: The word has come from the *Sanskrit* word "*Parn*" meaning leaf, as in a tree. These are mainly compositions of Pakhawaj – nowadays also played on Tabla. These are long compositions having weighty, forceful *bols*, played in the open-handed style or *Khulaa-Baaz*, are uniform in structure and end with a *Tihaai*. The comparison to a leaf is because, just as in a leaf, veins branch out from the central big vein on either side uniformly, similarly, *bols* are distributed evenly in a *Paran*.

There are four types of *Paran* :-

Saath Paran: *Parans* which are played during accompaniment (generally in *Dhrupad* / *Dhamaar*).

G'th Paran: *Parans* without a *Tihaai*. This can be played with the principles of *Khaali-Bhari*.

Bol Paran: *Parans* which are based or built around a poem, *Shloka* or a lyrical composition.

Taal Paran: These are generally of *Chakradhaar* type.

45) ***Palla***: Some compositions are split into 2, 3 or 4 parts. Each of these are themselves complete, though smaller bits. But they are distinct in that each of them is in a *Laya* of its own. Each is then called a *Palla*. Thus we have a *Dupalli*- a composition of 2 distinct *Layas* / parts ; *Tripalli*— a composition of 3 distinct *Layas* / parts ; *Choupalli*— a composition of 4 distinct *Layas* or parts.

46) ***Pain-ch***: There are some compositions whose expansion or elaboration becomes quite tricky because of placement of *bols*. It requires great skill on the part of the Tabla player to present such compositions and

86

make their variations without affecting the inherent beauty of the composition. Hence the name *Pain-ch* in Hindi or *Urdu* means a tricky or difficult situation confronting someone.

47) ***Peshkaar***: This is a composition that is based on the *bols* and the divisions of the *Theka* – or rather, is an off-spring of the *Theka*. It has the elements of *Khaali-Bhari* and is played in a slow tempo in a resonant manner. Also, there is no restriction in introducing new patterns or *Layas* while playing the *Peshkaar*.

Generally, *Peshkaar* is compared to the *Aalaap* that is presented in Vocal or Instrumental Music.

48) ***Rela***: This is a composition which is made up of *bols* or phrases that lend themselves to faster playing and form a sort of a chain. It takes the form of a *Taal*, in that it is played keeping the divisions of the *Taal* and the *Khaali-Bhari*. It can be played like a *Kaida* in single, double or fourth speeds.

49) ***Raon***: This is like a *Rela*, but it is generally played as a sequel to a *Chalan*. A *Chalan* is played and then keeping the prominent *bols* of the *Chalan*, the rest of the spaces are filled with smaller, faster *bols* such as TIRI KIT', GID' NAG', TIT' TIT', DHIN'GIN', DHIN'DHIN'. The *Chalan* when played thus, i.e. : with the smaller, faster *bols,* sounds like a *Rela*. The only difference is that the speed of the *Chalan* remains the same as in the *Vilambit*. This form is generally found in the **Ajrada** and **Farrukhabad** *Gharanas*.

50) ***Sum***: This is the starting point of a *Taal / Theka*. It is the point around which a *Taal* is played. It is the aim of every composition to achieve this point in as attractive a manner as possible.

51) ***Tukda***: *Tukda* is a composition of forceful *bols* which is generally 2 or 3 cycles long in the *drut* phase of a *Taal*. It can be with or without a *Tihaai*. Hence it is distinct from the ***Paran, G'th*** or ***Chakradhaar*** which are generally long drawn out. Originally, a ***Tukda*** was a piece of *bols* lifted out of a ***Paran***.

52) **Theka**: A **Theka** is a pre-determined and widely accepted composition made up of a collection of sounds (*Varnaas* or *bols)* produced by striking the Tabla / Pakhawaj at different points, representing the different divisions of the *Taal* that is to be presented.

One can say that the **Theka** is the first "*Bandish*" or Composition of a *Taal*.

53) **Taal**: It is a cycle of beats that lends musical or Dance-compositions a sort of pre-determined and preset ambit which can be demonstrated by means of sound producing actions (*Sashabda Kriyaa*) and Silent actions such as **Khaali** or counting of matras on fingers (*Nih-Shabda Kriyaa*).

54) **Taali-Khaali**: These are "*Kriyaas*" or actions which demonstrate a *Taal*. These are given at specific points such as beginning of each "*Khand*" or section of *matras*. There can be two successive *Taalis* but there cannot be two successive *Khaalis*.

55) **Taalim**: Ordinarily "**Taalim**" means *Riyaaz* or practice. But it is also used as a term that conveys the Extensive Tutelage under a *Guru* or *Ustad* and a *Riyaaz* that is done under his supervision. When one listens to a Tabla player, one generally hears this term being mentioned – that he has had **Taalim** under so and so (*Guru*).

56) **Tihaai**: A composition of *bols* which is repeated thrice with equal spaces in between the 3 repetitions is known as **Tihaai**. — and coming to Sum, there are two types of **Tihaais** viz : "*Be d'm*" and "*D'm daar*".

"*Bedum*" **Tihaais** are those that have very small or no gaps between the three parts of the **Tihaai**. *Dum* in Hindi or *Urdu* means rest or gap. As against this, "*Dumdaar*" **Tihaais** are those that have gaps or rests of atleast half a *matra*.

57) **Uthaan**: The composition that is presented at the very outset of a Tabla Solo item, in the **Benares** *Gharana* is called **Uthaan**. This is also true of *Kathak* Dance. This is just like a **Tukda**, but much bigger than that in shape and size. Just as in other *Gharanas* one starts out with a *Mohra* before playing the **Peshkaar**, in **Benares** *Gharana* an **Uthaan** is played.

88

This must have come into the tradition because it creates an impact on the audience and the artist can make a good impression at the very outset. Generally at the beginning of a concert, the audience is restless and consequently lot of disturbances are going on. Probably, playing the **Uthaan** must have been done to capture their attention immediately.

58) **Udaan**: This is a composition (**Tukda**) that starts from any given *matra* and comes to Sum suddenly.

58) **Upaj**: A spontaneous, unplanned execution of a *bol*, suitable to the occasion is termed as **Upaj**.

Changing or re-phrasing some parts of a *bol* that has been played and making a new *bol* and presenting it immediately thereafter is called **Upaj Ang** creation. This is more evident during accompaniment. This is possible only if the artist has a keen sense of rhythm and a deep understanding of the *Taal*.

60) **Varnas**: These are the same as Akshars or Syllables. Combinations of these form Bols.

61) **Zarab**: This is a small, fast compostion which is played to heighten the effectiveness of the Sum.

Biographies Of Eminent Tabla Players

Over the past few centuries, many a stalwart Tabla player has left a lasting impression on future generations of young and aspiring Tabla players. Some have made a name as excellent performers while some others as prolific composers. The lives of such great men are bound to inspire anybody who wishes to emulate them.

Given hereunder are short Life sketches of eminent Tabla players of the past, without whose contribution, the art of Tabla playing would not have reached the level of excellence that we witness today.

Ustad Miyan Bakshu-ji-Khalifa – Lucknow Gharana.

One of the famous three brothers of **Lucknow Gharana** i.e. : Makku Khan, Modu Khan and Bakshu Khan, he was famous as a *Meetha* Tabla-player i.e: one whose Tabla playing was very sweet (melodious) to listen to and was also known as a good composer. He had a good collection of both Tabla and Pakhawaj compositions. He is credited with being the one who popularized the *Poorab* **tradition** of Tabla playing as distinct from the Delhi style. He had no sons and hence he taught all he knew to his only daughter, whom he married off to Ustad Haji Vilayat Ali Khan who founded the **Farrukhabad Gharana**.

Ustad Muhammad Khan Saheb – Lucknow Gharana.

We know of the three brothers from Lucknow, Ustads Makku Khan, Modu Khan and Bakshu Khan who were well-known as being one better than the other. Very little is known of their children. But it is a well-known fact that Ustad Mammu Khan was a descendent of this family and was also a *Khalifa* of the Gharana. His son is Ustad Muhammad Khan. He enriched the repertoire of the **Lucknow Gharana** with many of his own compositions in addition to those of his illustrious fore-fathers. The Ustad had two sons. The elder of the two, Bade Munne Khan, was taught and trained by him very assiduously. He even made him perform at concerts where he himself was performing. The younger son, Aabid Hussein Khan, was very much younger than Bade Munne Khan and although he did receive some training from his aging father, he received a lot of guidance from his elder brother.

Ustad Bade Munne Khan Saheb — Lucknow Gharana.

The eldest son of Ustad Muhammed Khan Saheb and the elder brother of Ustad Aabid Hussein Khan Saheb, he started making his compositions after the death of his father. His compositions bear the influence of Ustad Haji Vilayat Ali of **Farrukhabad Gharana**.

Ustad Bade Munne Khan seems to have shifted his inclination towards **Farrukhabad Gharana** Hence his compositions are very attractive because of the influence of both **Gharanas**. Although Ustad Aabid Hussein Khan, his younger brother, learnt from him for 10 to 12 years, the presentation of Aabid Hussein Khan reveals that his playing did not have the impress of **Farrukhabad Gharana**.

Ustad Miyan Aabid Hussein Khan – Lucknow Gharana.

Born in 1867 in Lucknow. He learnt Tabla from his father Ustad Muhammed Khan Saheb – from the age of 7 years. After the death of his father, he learnt for a further 10 to 12 years from his elder brother Ustad Bade Munne Khan. A very *Riyaazi* (diligent) Tabla player, he was very knowledgeable and impressive and was famous for his clarity in playing. Music lovers of those days felt that Ustad Aabid Hussein Khan was an artist from whom one could get to hear authentic **Lucknow Gharana Tabla**. He taught Tabla at Lucknow's Marris College of Music and produced a number of outstanding students, famous among them being his nephew Ustad Waajid Hussein Khan, Ustad Jehangir Khan of Indore and Pandit Biru Mishra of Benaras Gharana. He died in June 1936.

Khalifa Waajid Hussein Khan – Lucknow Gharana.

Born in the year 1896, he was the longest surviving Khalifa of Lucknow Gharana. He expired recently. Son and disciple of the famous Tabla Nawaz and composer, Ustad Bade Munne Khan, Waajid Hussein Khan carved a niche for himself for his erudition and forceful presentation. He was also the nephew of the famous Tabla Nawaz Ustad Aabid Hussein Khan of the same Gharana.

Even at an advanced age, Ustad Waajid Hussein Khan impressed listeners with his skill and dexterity and forceful playing with both Tabla and Dugga being equally prominent.

Renowned for his presentation of *Relas, G'ths, G'th parans, Tihaais* and *Chakradaars*, he was not so much inclined towards *Kaidas*. Most of the compositions played were straight forward and rarely in other *Jaatis.*

Ustad Miyan Haji Vilayat Ali Khan – Farrukhabad Gharana.

Haji Saheb as he is also known is credited to be the founder of the **Farrukhabad Gharana**. There is no record of his birth and death dates, but it is known that he was a contemporary of Ustad Kader Baksh, the father of noted singers Ustads Haddu and Hassu Khan. It is not known who was his first teacher. But by the time he was married to the daughter of Ustad Bakshu Khan of Lucknow, he was already a well-known Tabla player in his own right. At the time of his marriage, he received in dowry 1000 *G'ths* and *G'th-parans* from Ustad Bakshu Khan. Haji Saheb continued his further training under his father-in-law. It is for this reason that he considered his wife as his Guru. A great composer, Haji Saheb is supposed to have made "*Haj*" pilgrimage seven times and hence the honorific.

Haji Saheb established his school in a small town, Farrukhabad, in U.P. The students here used to practice on wooden Tablas and Duggas under the supervision of both Haji Saheb and his wife. He had one son, Ustad Hussein Ali Khan, who later turned out to be the Ustad of Ustad Munir Khan. Some of the prominent disciples of Haji Saheb are *Choodiyanwale* Imam Baksh, Salari Khan, Mubarak Ali Khan, Channu Khan, Karam Ittal Khan and his brother Ilaahi Baksh. Because of the predominant influence of both **Lucknow** and **Delhi** styles of playing, this Gharana presents very aesthetic and pleasant sounding compositions.

Ustad Miyan Choodiyanwale Imam Baksh Khan Saheb – Farrukhabad Gharana.

This is a case which exemplifies how a *Shishya* can make a *Guru* well-known. Imam Baksh Khan Saheb was a well-known *Pakhawaji*, belonging to the **Batola Gharana** having accompanied the likes of Haddu-Hassu Khan. However, he was enamoured of Ustad Haji Vilayat Ali Khan Saheb's Tabla playing and wanted to learn under him. The Ustad refused his request as he was already a well-known *Pakhawaji*. Imam Baksh Khan Saheb somehow managed to enter Haji Saheb's school incognito, as a servant, whose job it was to refill the *Hukkahs* or smoke-pipes of students who were doing their *Riyaaz*. This he did for a period of 12 years and in the process, learnt a lot of Tabla. When the Ustad realized this, instead of getting angry, he welcomed Ustad Imam Baksh and had the *Ganda-Bandhan* ceremony performed by his wife, whom he held in great respect as an *"Ustad-ni"* being, the daughter of his Ustad, i.e. : Ustad Bakshu Khan Saheb. Now, in the absence of a *Ganda* or sacred 5-coloured thread, the *Ustad-ni* used one of her bangles or *"Choodi"* and put it on the hand of Ustad Imam Baksh Khan who later came to be known as *Choodiyanwale* Imam Baksh.

Ustad Salari Khan Saheb – Farrukhabad Gharana.

Salari Khan Saheb was initially a student of Ustad Bakshu Pakhawaji. Later on he started learning from Ustad Haji Vilayat Ali. A contemporary of Ustad Choodiyan Imam Baksh, Salari Khan Saheb was also one of Haji Vilayat Ali Khan Saheb's senior disciples. He had a great reputation as a good Tabla player and an excellent composer. Some of his compositions, which are *Jods* (parallel compositions) for his Ustad's creations are well-known.

Ustad Miyan Boli Baksh Khan Saheb – Delhi Gharana.

Son of the famous Tabla *Nawaz* of **Delhi Gharana**, Ustad Bade Kaale Khan, Miyan Boli Baksh trained under his father and also obtained training in *Poorab* style of playing from various Ustads of *Poorab* **Gharana**. During his concerts (solo), he would play *Peshkaar*, *Kaidas* and *Relas* in the Delhi Tradition and later on play *G'th-Todas, Chakradaars* and other *Bandishes* in the *Poorab* style. He was greatly influenced by the playing of Ustad Haji Vilayat Ali Khan Saheb. According to his son, Ustad Nathu Khan, there was no Tabla player to match Ustad Boli Baksh in many many generations.

Ustad Faiyaz Khan Moradabadi.

More famous as Ustad Ahmedjan Thirakawa's maternal uncle. He taught both Thirakawa Khan Saheb and Shamsuddin Khan Saheb which explains why their style of playing is similar and distinct from that of Ustad Amir Hussein Khan. All the three of them have subsequently learnt under Ustad Munir Khan Saheb.

Faiyaz Khan Moradabadi was the son of Ustad Karam Ittal Khan. Ustad Karam Ittal Khan and his brother Ustad Ilaahi Baksh were the disciples of the great Haji Vilayat Ali Khan of Farrukhabad. In fact, Karam Ittal Khan who studied with Haji Vilayat Ali for over thirty long years, also resided with the Ustad and was considered a premier student of Haji Vilayat Ali.

Ustad Munir Khan Saheb – Lucknow Gharana.

Born in 1863 in the village of *Laliyana* in Merut District, he took his early lessons in Tabla from his father Ustad Kaale Khan Saheb, who was himself a noted Tabla player. At the age of 15, he became a *Ganda-Bandha Shagird* of Ustad Hussein Ali Khan, the son of Haji Vilayat Ali Khan Saheb, of the Farrukhabad Tradition. Having learnt for about 15 years, he became a *Ganda-Bandha Shagird* of Ustad Boli Baksh of **Delhi Gharana**. This made him a *Guru-Bandhu* of the great Ustad Nathu Khan of **Delhi**

Gharana. He further learnt from 24 other Ustads prominent among them being Ustad Nazar Ali Khan Saheb and Ustad Naṣir Khan Saheb Pakhawaji, and made his repertoire richer.

Besides being an excellent soloist, Munir Khan Saheb was also a well-known accompanist of vocalists and instrumentalists. He was a composer par-excellence and a very prolific Ustad who produced a string of noted Tabla players. Prominent among his innumerable disciples are Ustads Ahmedjan Thirakawa, Shamsuddin Khan, Amir Hussein Khan, Ghulam Hussein Khan, Habibuddin Khan and Subbarao-mama Ankolekar.

Ustad Munir Khan Saheb, due to his own aesthetic abilities, was able to combine the best of the different styles of Tabla he had imbibed from so many Ustads. Thus he founded a new style which came to be known as the *"Laliyana"* or **Bombay Gharana** – one, his birth place and the other his *Karmabhoomi* (the place where he acheived most of his success as a performer and as an Ustad or Teacher).

Ustad Ahmedjan Thirakawa – Farrukhabad Gharana.

Born in Lucknow around 1882, it is said that the hands of young Ahmedjan used to quiver or tremble or dance so fast that he was nicknamed *"Thirku"* from the Hindi word *Thirakna*-to dance. This sorbiquet stuck with him for the rest of his life. He took his lessons as a young boy from his paternal uncle, the well-known Ustad Sher Khan of **Lucknow Gharana**, and then from his maternal uncle Ustad Faiyaz Khan of Moradabad. Later on he, along with Ustad Shamsuddin Khan, who was his *Gurubhai*, came down to Bombay in search of better opportunities. In Bombay he came in contact with Ustad Munir Khan, who at that time, was a name to reckon with. Thirakawa Khansaheb, along with Shamsuddin Khansaheb did their *"Ganda-bandhan"* with Ustad Munir Khan Saheb and were his *Shagirds* till the Ustad passed away.

It is said that Ustad Thirakawa Khan Saheb used to practice Tabla for 16 to 18 hours a day, for years together. This, along with the immense knowledge that he had acquired, made him into a Tabla player of the highest order. He is the one who popularized **Solo Tabla Playing** among the audiences, who initially, used to shy away from Tabla Solo Concerts thinking that they would not be able to understand and appreciate it.

Thirakawa Khan Saheb was also a highly gifted accompanist, much sought after by musicians of the day. His association with the Late Baal Gandharava, a stalwart singer - actor and dramatist of the Marathi stage, is legendary.

Although he was not inclined to teach a lot, he did have many notable Shagirds. Thirakawa Khan Saheb has left an indelible impression on the peoples' mind mainly because of his individual brilliance. He used to teach at the Marris College of Music in Lucknow and later at the National Centre for Performing Arts in Bombay.

Among his noteworthy disciples are Late Pandit Jagannaath-buwa Purohit, Pandit Laalji Gokhale, Pandit Nikhil Ghosh and Pandit Bhai Gaitonde.

Ustad Shamsuddin Khan:-Farrukhabad Gharana.

Shamsuddin Khan was born in the year 1890, in Aligarh a small village in Uttar Pradesh, India. His childhood was spent in Moradabad. Acutely interested in music and particularly rhythm, young Shamsuddin started learning the art of Tabla playing under the watchful guidance of Ustad Faiyaz Khan of Moradabad. Another youngster, Ahmedjan, who happened to be the maternal nephew of the Ustad was also a co-student. Faiyaz Khan Moradabadi was the son of Ustad Karam Ittal Khan. Ustad Karam Ittal Khan and his brother Ustad Ilahi Baksh were the disciples of the great Haji Vilayat Ali Khan of Farrukhabad. In fact, Karam Ittal Khan who studied with Haji Vilayat Ali for over thirty long years, also resided with the Ustad and was considered a premier student of Haji Vilayat Ali.

Both Shamsuddin Khan and Ahmedjan, who later on came to be known as "Thirkawa", later migrated to Bombay, where they came under the tutelage of another legendary maestro, Ustad Munir Khan. Shamsuddin Khan also learnt from Ustad Tega Jaffer Khan of the Delhi Gharana.

Shamsuddin Khan Saheb had also learnt Vocal music and was a very good vocalist of the Kirana Gharana. Shamsuddin Khan Saheb mostly accompanied Ustad Abdul Karim Khan, a doyen of the Kirana Gharana until the latter passed away. After the death of Ustad Abdul Karim Khan, Shamsuddin Khan started accompanying the Ustad's daughters Roshanara Begum and Hirabai Barodekar. Shamsuddin Khan Saheb was also known for his magnificent Tabla Solos. He once performed a Tabla solo in Teen Taal, all night, without repeating a single composition. At a time when most of the soloists preferred to play only Teen Taal, Shamsuddin Khan Saheb was known to have played solos in various Taals such as Jhaptaal, Aada Choutaal, Surfaak Taal and Vardan Taal of 19 matras. Most of the old 78 rpm records of Roshanara Begum, Hirabai and Krishna Rao have the Tabla accompaniment of Ustad Shamsuddin Khan.

Around 1930, Shamsuddin Khan visited Mangalore for a concert and there he met a young and impressionable lad, Taranath Rao Hattiangadi. This young boy was so taken up by the Ustad's effortless and classy performance, that he immediately took some lessons from him. After Taranathji came to Bombay in pursuit of a Degree from the J. J. School of Arts, he had a Ganda Bandhan ceremony with Ustad Shamsuddin Khan and started learning from the great master. It is rather unfortunate that very few solo recordings of Shamsuddin Khan Saheb exist today. Shamsuddin Khan Saheb passed away on the ship whilst on his return after performing Haj— a death which is considered auspicious among Muslims. Shamsuddin Khan Saheb did not teach many students. His foremost students have been Late Pandit Taranathji and Pandit Ravi Bellare, who now lives in Los Angeles, U.S.A.

Ustad Shamsuddin Khan Saheb's style of playing Tabla was unique. It is said that at any of Hirabai's concert, there was a section of the audience which would come to hear Khan Saheb. Some even believed that given an opportunity, Khan Saheb could replicate every nuance of the Kirana Gayaki on his Tabla. Khan Saheb's tuning of the Tabla closely resembled the tuning of the Taanpura. It was precise. The Dugga was tuned to very low tone, giving it a deep sound with a lot of feeling. The deep variable tone of the Dugga synchronized with the highly resonant tone of the Tabla producing a highly balanced and soothing effect, giving rise to a kind of nostalgic or yearning effect, that only a few artists could create. His style of playing was melodious and always in tune with the singer. When he played, it seemed as if his hands were dancing on the Tabla. His playing was spontaneous and never mechanical. When one saw Shamsuddin Khan Saheb playing, it seemed that the Tabla and he were one identity. Today, those age old compositions and style of playing can only be heard from Pandit Ravi Bellare.

Ustad Amir Hussein Khan – Farrukhabad Gharana.

Ustad Amir Hussein Khan's father was a *Sarangi* player who was a court-musician with the *Nizam* of Hyderabad. Initially, he learnt music from his father and later on started training in Tabla from his illustrious maternal uncle, Ustad Munir Khan, who was based in Bombay. Ustad Munir Khan Saheb used to teach the young Amir Hussein Khan whenever he would visit Hyderabad either for a concert or to meet his sister. However, Amir Hussein Khan decided to come to Bombay to be with his Ustad. This was in the year 1914. From then on his training went on uninterrupted and he also began moving out with his Ustad to places like Baroda, Delhi, Meerut, Raigad where Ustad Munir Khan was a court-musician for sometime with the Maharaja. He was given opportunities by the Ustad to play Solo Tabla recitals as well as accompany different artists. By the age of 24 years, Amir Hussein Khan was such an accomplished Tabla player that Ustad Munir Khan Saheb sent for him and made him perform in the presence of the *Maharaja* of Raigad. Highly impressed by his performance, the *Maharaja* honoured him by presenting him with handsome gifts in cash and kind.

Ustad Amir Hussein Khan Saheb was not only an accomplished Tabla player, but an excellent composer, an erudite scholar, teacher and above all a very humane and good soul.

He has left behind a great legacy in the form of innumerable Shishyas who today are carrying on the tradition of passing on the knowledge to the younger generation. Prominent among Khan Saheb's students are Pandit Pandharinath Nageshkar, Pandit Nikhil Ghosh, Pandit Arvind Mulgaonkar, Ustad Babasaheb Mirajkar and many others.

Ustad Karamatullah Khan – Farrukhabad Gharana.

Born in the year 1918, he was the son of Ustad Masit Khan. Began taking lessons in Tabla from his father at the age of 6 years. His Tabla appears to have an influence of the **Benaras Gharana** insofar as his handling of the *Baayaan,* although he kept the *Shaayee* away from himself, enabling him to get better sonority or *Aas*. He was well-known for the clarity and precision of his **Bol-production** and was in great demand both as a Soloist and Accompanist.

Among his famous disciples are the great Guru, Pandit Gyan Prakash Ghosh and son Ustad Sabir Khan.

Pandit Ram Sahai – Benaras Gharana.

Prominent among the Tabla players of the **Benaras Gharana**, Pandit Ram Sahai was born in the year 1830 in Benaras. Very *Taiyar* due to assiduous *Riyaaz*, he was noticed by Ustad Modu Khan, the *Khalifa* of the **Lucknow Gharana**, who made him a *Shagird*. He was profusely praised by noted musicians of the *Nawab* Wajid Ali Shah's *Durbar* when they heard his Tabla playing and was honoured by the *Rasikas* of Benaras. He enriched his already rich repertoire by adding many of his own compositions. Notable among his disciples are Pandit Bhairav Sahay, who was his nephew (brother's son) and Pandit Janaki Sahai Pratap. He died quite young, at the age of 46.

Pandit Kanthe Maharaj – Benaras Gharana.

A great Tabla player, Pandit Kanthe Maharaj was born around 1880 in Benaras. He started learning Tabla under Pandit Baldev Sahay-ji, son of Pandit Bhairav Sahay. After about 3 years of studentship, Pandit Baldev Sahay left for Nepal at the invitation of the King and settled there. Unable to bear the absence of his mentor and consequently the lessons in Tabla, young Kanthe Maharaj also left for Nepal and stayed there for four years, during which time Pandit Baldev Sahay extracted rigorous practice from his student. Pandit Kanthe Maharaj was fond of playing the **G'ths, Parans** and **Chh'nds** of the **Benaras Gharana** and excelled himself in doing so. He achieved name and fame with his performances all over India and continued playing even at an advanced age. Among his disciples is the great Pandit Kishen Maharaj who happens to be his nephew. Pandit Kanthe Maharaj expired in the year 1961 at the age of 89. Such was his faith in the fact that the way to Salvation was through Tabla that even on his death bed he called' for Kishen Maharaj-ji and taught him a **G'th-Paran.** This fact Pandit Kishen Maharaj relates with great reverence.

Pandit Kishen Maharaj – Benaras Gharana.

Born on *Gokul-Ashtami* day (birthday of Lord Krishna) in September 1923, Pandit Kishen Maharaj started learning Tabla at a very young age from his uncle, Pandit Kanthe Maharaj. Drawn towards **Layakaari** and complicated **Taals**, he concentrated more on odd **Taals** of 9, 11, 13, 15, 19, 21—beats and mastered them. Consequently, playing in even-*matra Taals* of 12, 14, 16 – beats was no big deal for him. He started making a name for himself very early because of his skills on the Tabla and also with the way he presented his concerts on stage. A very handsome and fair-complexioned personality added to his stature on the stage. Apart from Solo-playing, Pandit Kishen Maharaj excelled in accompaniment to instrumental and **Kathak** Dance. Artists all over India clamoured to have him accompany them.

Pandit Anokhelal Mishra – Benaras Gharana.

Born in a poor family in 1914, Anokhelal lost his parents at a very early age and was brought-up by his grandmother. From the age of 5 or 6 years, he started learning Tabla from Pandit Bhairav Prasad – for 15 years. Training under a **Guru** of Pandit Bhairav Prasad's erudition and immense **Riyaaz**, made Anokhelal-ji into a great Tabla player who made a name all over India. He is known even today for his fast *Teen-Taal Theka* played with one finger – something that is unsurpassed even to this day. Apart from his skills as an accompanist, his Solo-recitals were also proof of his excellent **Taiyaari** and tonal sweetness. It is said that true **Benaras Gharana Tabla** was heard from Anokhelal-ji. He expired in March 1958, suffering from gangrene of the left foot. Prominent among his disciples are late Pandit Mahapurush Mishra and his son Pandit Ramji Mishra.

Pandit Samta Prasad Mishra – (Gudai Maharaj).

A descendent of *"Partappu"* (Pratap) Maharaj he was born in July 1921 at *Kabir Chaurah*, in Benaras. Initial training was under his father, Pandit

Bacha Mishra, but after he lost his father at the age of seven, young Gudai learnt with Pandit Bikkuji Mishra. After mastering the instrument with assiduous *Riyaaz*, Samta Prasad made a name for himself as a brilliant Soloist and a much sought-after accompanist especially of *Kathak* Dance and Instrumental Music. His clarity of playing and tonal excellence is unrivalled even today. His favourite *Taals* were *Teen-Taal, Rupak* and *Dhamaar*. He expired in Pune.

Laya Bhaskar Khaprumama Parvatkar.

Khaprumama alias Laxmanrao Parvatkar, was born in a village *Parvati* in Goa in a family known for its Sarangi-playing. He started learning Sarangi from his uncle Raghuvir Parvatkar, *Dhrupad Dhamaar* from Antubuwa Dhawalikar and Tabla from his uncle Harischandra Parvatkar. Soon, he started accompanying noted vocalists both on Sarangi and Tabla and achieved quite a bit of fame. Being interested in *Layakaari* from a young age, he was always seen counting *Matras* and *Aavartans*, unmindful of the amusement he was causing to passers-by. He played the *"Ghumat"*, a popular percussion instrument of Goa expertly. Later on in life, he astounded people with his uncanny ability to keep track of 4 to 5 Taals using his hands, legs and voice :- e.g. : He would show *Teen-Taal* with one leg, *Japtaal* with the other leg, *Roopak* with one hand, *Choutaal* or *Ektaal* with the other hand and recite *Pancham-Savaari*. He was also credited with the ability of reciting a particular composition in 3 *Aavartans* and play the same *bol* 5 times in the same span i.e. in 3 *Aavartans*. Also he was able to play a *Paran* on the Tabla and at the same time recite it in reverse i.e. end to *Sum*. He composed many odd *Taals*, well-known among them being "*Yog*"-Taal or 15½ beats and "*Parabrahma*"-Taal of 15¾ beats. In this *Taal (Parabrahma)* he composed the "*Maha Sudarshan*" *Paran* which had 125 *Dha's*. The title of "*Laya-Bhaskar*" was bestowed on him by vocalist Ustad Alladiya Khan (Jaipur / Atrauli Gharana).

Ustad Miyan Nanhe Khan Saheb — Delhi Gharana.

He was born in the year 1872 to Ustad "Langde" Husseinbaksh, a prominent Tabla Nawaz   (performer of excellence) of the Delhi Gharana. His early years were spent learning Tabla from his illustrious father. But, due to his father's early death, he began learning Tabla from his eldest brother, Ustad Ghasit Khan.

Ustad Nanhe Khan spent a considerable part of his life in Bombay and was also considered as a *Khalifa* of one of the branches of the Delhi Gharana. Among his disciples, mention must be made of Ustad Jugna Khan. Ustad Nanhe Khan Saheb passed away in the year 1940, at the age of 68.

Ustad Qadir Baksh Khan Saheb – Punjab Gharana.

Son of noted *Pakhawaji*, Ustad Fakir Baksh, Qadir Baksh was born in Lahore in the year 1902. His training started early and by the age of 9 to 10 years, he could play like a professional. He was adept at playing both Tabla and Pakhawaj. He was as good if not better, in accompaniment as he was in Solo and thus received invitation from far and wide for his services. Among his illustrious disciples are Ustad Allarakha Khan in Bombay and Ustad Shaukat Hussein of Pakistan.

Ustad Allarakha Khan Saheb – Punjab Gharana.

Born in a farming family in *Rattangadh* village of *Gurudaspur* District of Punjab in the year 1919, Allarakha had an instinctive feel for music right from childhood, which can only be attributed to his achievements in the same field in an earlier birth. He joined a roving drama company as a child artist and at the tender age of 15 or so he started learning Tabla from Ustad Laal Mohammed Khan a disciple of Ustad Qadir Baksh Khan, at *Pathankot*. Having learnt from him for a few years, he returned to *Gurudaspur* and set up a small school to teach music.

Once, on a visit to Lahore, he happened to hear the master, Ustad Qadir Baksh Khan's Tabla and was so overwhelmed by the experience that he immediately became his *Ganda-Bandha Shagird*. He spent a few years with the Ustad and later started giving programmes independently, all over India. In 1937, Shri Bukhaari, who was Station Director of Bombay Station of All India Radio, offered Allarakha Khan Saheb a job of Tabla accompanist – a job, which Khan Saheb held until 1942. He then trained his immense talent in another direction altogether i.e. the budding Film Industry of Bombay and providing Music-Direction under the name of A.R. Qureshi.

In his playing, one finds more of his own genius coupled with fantastic *Taiyari* and a phenomenal control over *Layakaari* – more than the original **Punjab Gharana** Tabla. Khan Saheb's accompaniment of Instrumental Musicians and *Kathak* Dancers, particularly Pandit Ravi Shankar, Ustad Ali Akbar Khan and Birju Maharaj-ji, has remained unparalleled even today. If one takes an overview of the Tabla scene today, one finds scores of young Tabla players trying to emulate Khan Saheb and his son Ustad Zakir Hussein. It would not be out of place or inappropriate to say that, Khan Saheb has set up an independent Gharana of his own.

Pandit Nannu Sahai (S*ur*) alias Durga Sahai.

He was the son of Pandit Baldev Sahai. Born in 1892, he was blind since birth. But due to this fact, his power of concentration and memory were tremendous and thus he had with him a big treasure of knowledge of **Benaras Gharana** *Bol*s. He was nicknamed *Surdas* or "*Sur*", because of his blindness. Being a person of big built, his Tabla playing was forceful. He was awarded a Gold-Medal for his outstanding Tabla performance at the *Bhawanipore Sangeet Sammelan* in Calcutta. He was the recipient of an honourarium of Rs.100/- per month from *Maharaja* Shashikant Acharya Chaudhuri, of Mymensing. He expired on 4th March 1926, at the age of 34.

Ustad Khalifa Nathu Khan Saheb – Delhi Gharana.

Son of Ustad Bolibaksh Khan Saheb and grandson of Ustad Kaale Khan Saheb, Nathu Khan Saheb was born in the year 1875. Most of his training was under his father. It is said that he used to practice 16 to 18 hours a day and due to this, had attained total mastery over the difficult *Kaidas* of **Delhi Gharana** – especially those with DIT'TIT' using two fingers. All the same, his immense *Taiyaari* notwithstanding, Nathu Khan used to play each *Kaida* in the appropriate speed at which the nuances of the composition could be appreciated. He expired at the age of 65 in the year 1940.

Zorawar Singh

He was a Tabla player in the *Durbar* of Jiyajirao Scindia of *Gwalior* and a close associate of *Kudow Singh Maharaj*. He was well-known for his clarity of *Bols* and tone and excelled in accompaniment of vocalists. He passed away at the end of the 19th century.

Pandit Hari Sunder alias Bacha Mishra – Benaras Gharana.

He was born in 1876 to Pandit Jagannath Maharaj. His elder brother was Shiv Sunder. His son is the famous Pandit Samta Prasad. Bacha Mishra-ji took training from his father and was a contemporary of Ustad Nathu Khan of Delhi and Ustad Azim Khan of Barreili. He earned a good name for himself with his assiduous *Riyaaz*.

Pandit Biru Mishra – Benaras Gharana.

An excellent Tabla player and a good composer, Pandit Biru Mishra, born in 1896, was the son of Pandit Bhagwan Prasad-ji, under whom he took his initial training. He later studied under Pandit Vishwanath-ji of the same Gharana. Subsequently, he also trained under Ustad Aabid Hussein Khan of Lucknow Gharana and Ustad Chammu Khan of Barreili.

Pandit Bhairav Prasad. – Benaras Gharana

He was born in the year 1840 in Patna. His father died quite early and so his mother took the young Bhairav Prasad to her father's house in Benares. Her father, Pandit Bihari Mishra was a Sarangi player. It was here that Bhairav Prasad grew up. His uncle looked after the boy like his own son. Bhairav Prasad started learning Tabla from the famous Bhagat Maharaj. With his assiduous *Riyaaz* and sincerity, he won his Guru's heart, who opened his vast treasury of knowledge to his young student. His style of playing was very aggressive and he used a wide-topped Tabla. Because of the above reasons and also that he possessed a good physique, his Tabla playing was considered to be very Masculine. Pandit Bhairav Prasad was very kowledgeable and taught quite a few leading lights of Tabla. Pandit Baldev Sahay, Pandit Jagannath-ji, (grandfather of Pandit Samta Prasad-ji), Baiju-ji, Gokul-ji, Vishwananth-ji, and Pandit Bhairav Sahay-ji were his contemporaries. Pandit Bhairav Prasad-ji was also a connoisuer of vocal music and had quite a good knowledge of *Dhrupad, Dhamar, Hori* and other compositions. He was a very generous and religious person. He expired at the age of 100 years with a volume of Bhagwat-Gita in his hands. Among his students are Moulvi Ram Mishra, Mahavir Bhat, Mahadev-ji Mishra, Nageshwar Prasad-ji and Pandit Anokhelal-ji.

Pandit Bhairav Sahay – Benaras Gharana.

Son of Pandit Gouri Sahay, he started learning from his uncle, the noted reformist of **Benaras Gharana**, Pandit Ram Sahay-ji, at a very early age – of 5 years. Within 6 years he had already achieved a good mastery over the instrument. His daily routine was to perform puja of the "*Aas – Bhairav*" idol at '*Nichi Baag'* precincts and do his *Riyaaz* for the rest of the time. By the time he was 20 years of age he was a master – who astounded knowledgeable people. He was incomparable both in Solo and accompaniment. Hearing tales of his greatness, the king of Nepal invited him to participate in a Music Conference. Here, he accompanied the noted *Sarodiya*, Ustad Niamatullah Khan who was so impressed with his accompaniment that he complimented Bhairav Sahay-ji saying that "He is not a *Tabaliya*, but a "Farishta" (Angel). God has given eyes to his fingers so that they can see at the *Gat-Todas* of the musicians at the same time". The King of Nepal gifted Bhairav Sahay-ji with a Sword and Rifle.

Ustad Masit Khan Saheb – Farrukhabad Gharana.

Son of Ustad Nanhe Khan who was attached to the *Durbar* of Nawab Wajid Ali Shah of Lucknow, he was born in the year 1892. He studied under his father and attained fame as an excellent Tabla player, and was absorbed by the *Rampur Durbar* as a court musician. He retired from the service in due course and settled down in Calcutta. His son Ustad Karamatullah Khan and grandson Sabir Khan along with disciple Pandit Gyan Prakash Ghosh have done a lot for the popularity of Tabla today in Calcutta.

Ustad Habib-ud-din Khan – Ajrada Gharana.

Born in Merut in 1899, he studied Tabla from his father Ustad Shammu Khan from the age of 12 years. After assiduous *Riyaaz* for over 15 years, he became a disciple of the famous Ustad Nathu Khan of Delhi Gharana. After spending a few years under Nathu Khan Saheb, he became a *Ganda-Bandh Shagird* of Ustad Munir Khan, who was known for his rich repertoire spanning all the Gharanas.

Well-known for his sweetness of tone, clarity at high speeds and vast knowledge, Habib-ud-din Khan Saheb was equally at ease in Solo-playing and Accompaniment. He was a much sought after artist and taught many students such as Ramzan Khan of Delhi and Sudhir Kumar Saxena of Baroda. He expired on 20th July 1972, at the age of 73 due to a severe paralytic stroke.

Ustad Gami Khan Saheb – Delhi Gharana.

He was the son of Ustad Chote Kale Khan Saheb, the famous **Delhi Gharana** tabla player. He took to Tabla at a very young age of 5 years and studied for about 10 years with his father, who died when Gami Khan Saheb was yet a boy of only 15 years. Thereafter, he did *Riyaaz* without rest or respite, and fine-tuned the knowledge gained by him from his father and within a short span of time achieved great fame. He was later made the *Khalifa* of **Delhi Gharana** and trained many good Tabla players prominent among them being his son Ustad Inam Ali Khan Saheb, Ustad Fakir Mohammed Khan ("*Peeru*") of Punjab, Tufail, Narayanrao Indorkar and others. He expired in the year 1958.

Pandit Baldev Sahai – Benaras Gharana.

Son of the highly regarded Tabla exponent of **Benaras Gharana** Pandit Bhairav Sahai-ji, Baldev Sahai-ji was born in the year 1872 and started his stewardship with his father at the age of 5 years. His training continued for 20 years, along with hard *Riyaaz* and thus, shortly, Baldev Sahai-ji turned out to be an artist of great merit and was given the title of "*Vaadya Rasraaj*". He had a good command over *Laya* and was able to play in odd-*matra Taals* with the same ease as *Teen-Taal* – a rarity in those days. Equally well-known for his Solo-recitals as well as Accompaniment, Baldev Sahai-ji excelled in his accompaniment of Instrumental Music and *Kathak* Dance. Pandit Nannu or Durga Sahai, more popularly known as *"Sur"* owing to his blindness, was his son and one who continued his glorious tradition, making a name for himself and his father.

The King of Nepal invited him to Nepal in 1924, where he settled down. Prominent among his disciples are Pandit Kanthe Maharaj, Pandit Bikku Mishra and Pandit Bholanath Sreshtha of Nepal.

Ustad Jehangir Khan – Indore

Son of Bahadur Khan, Ustad Jehangir Khan was born in 1869 at Benaras. He started his lessons at the age of 11 years under Ustad Mubarak Ali Khan of Patna. After 9 years, he became a disciple of Ustad Chhanu Khan Saheb, of the **Farrukhabad Gharana** (disciple of Haji Saheb). Later on, after a brief stint with Ustad Feroze Khan Saheb of **Delhi Gharana**, he became a *Ganda Bandha Shagird* of Ustad Aabid Hussein Khan of the **Lucknow Gharana**. He is known to have accompanied leading musicians of his time viz :- Ustad Alladiya Khan, Ustad Rajab Ali Khan, Ustad Faiyaz Khan, among others.

An Ustad who had a profound knowledge of **Lucknow, Delhi** and **Farrukhabad Gharanas**, Jehangir Khan Saheb was recorded by *Sangeet Natak* Academy in 1959. Also, the same year he was given a National Award by the President of India and also by the *Khairagadh* University with the title of "**Doctor of Music**". He had come to settle down in Indore at the invitation of Tukoji Rao Holkar, the Maharaja of Indore.

Pandit Chaturlal – Purab/Farrukhabad Gharana.

The elder brother of famous Sarangi wizard Pandit Ram Narayan, Chaturlal-ji was a pioneer in so far as popularizing Tabla in Western countries is concerned. He was the first Tabla player who toured the West along with Pandit Ravi Shankar and Ustad Ali Akbar Khan way back in the 1950's. Pandit Chaturlal was born in the year 1925 in Udaipur and expired at the young age of 40 in the year 1965.

Chaturlal took his initial lessons from Pandit Nathu Prasad in Udaipur. At about 15 to 16 years of age, he performed *Ganda-Bandhan* with Ustad Hafiz Miyan, also of Udaipur. Chaturlal-ji was well-known for the sweetness of his Tabla playing with great control over both Tabla and *Baayaan*. He brought a new dimension to the art of accompaniment, especially of Instrumental music. His early concerts and association with Pandit Ravi Shankar and Ustad Ali Akbar Khan are legendary and even today, young Tabla players keep trying to duplicate the tonal qualities of Chaturlal-ji's Tabla, as also his ready response to the Instrumentalists' posers. He was also one of the first Hindustani percussionists who interacted with *Carnatic* Musicians and introduced many facets of that branch into our Tabla playing especially *Khanda-Jaati* and *Sankeerna* patterns. *Tishra* and *Mishra* were being played in Hindustani Music even earlier.

Had it not been for his early death, he would have contributed much more than is being credited to him today.

Pandit Pandharinath Nageshkar – Purab/Farrukhabad Gharana.

Born on 16th March 1913 at Nageshi in Goa. Started learning Tabla from Valle-mama alias Yeshwant Vitthal Naik, who was attached to "*Balwant Sangeet Natak Mandali*" – at the age of 13 years. After about 2 years, he began learning from the great Subrai-mama, a *Shagird* of Ustad Munir Khan Saheb. After the death of Subrai-mama, he started learning from *Laya Bhaskar* Khaprumama Parvatkar and later from Ustad Anwar Hussein Khan and Ustad Jatin Bux Khan. Ultimately, being completely captivated by the Tabla of Ustad Amir Hussein Khan, Nageshkar-ji became a *Ganda-Bandha Shagird* of the Ustad, from whom he continued to learn till Khan Saheb's death.

Nageshkar-ji was an able accompanist of Vocal Music and was much sought after. But, it was as a teacher that he is well-known, having produced many outstanding students such as Shripad Nageshkar (his younger brother), Vasantrao Achrekar, Suresh Talwalkar, Vibhav Nageshkar (his son) and many more.

Pandit Nikhil Ghosh – Purab/Farrukhabad Gharana.

Nikhil Ghosh-ji started learning Tabla from the eminent Pandit Gyan Prakash Ghosh, a *Shagird* of Ustad Masit Khan of the **Farrukhabad Gharana**. Later, at the suggestion of his elder brother, the pioneer Flautist, Pandit Pannalal Ghosh, he became a student of Usatd Amir Hussein Khan. After Khan Saheb's demise, he became a *Shagird* of Ustad Ahmed Jan Thirakawa. Pandit Nikhil Ghosh was a person who was well-versed in other branches of music such as *Sitar* and Vocal. He has written books on music which have been translated in different languages. He started the monumental project of compiling an encyclopedia of music which is now nearing its completion. An able administrator and organiser, Pandit-ji's Music-School *"Arun Sangeetalaya"*, started on a small scale has now become the famous musical institution *"Sangeet Mahabharati"*. His legacy is being carried on by his talented sons Nayan Ghosh who is an admirable Tabla and Sitar player and Dhruva Ghosh, a talented Sarangi player.

Ustad Sheikh Dawood Khan – Purab/Farrukhabad Gharana.

Born in *Solapur*, he spent a considerable part of his life – until his death, in Hyderabad. His initiation in Tabla was under Ustad Mohammed Khan, (a disciple of Ustad Munir Khan) and later from Ustad Mehboob Khan Mirajkar. He later became a *Shagird* of Ustad Jehangir Khan of Indore. He was quite well-known all over India but more popular down South where he was referred to as *"Dakhan ke Thirakawa"* or the Thirakawa of the South. A very *Taiyar* Tabla player, he had good control over *Daayaan* and *Baayaan*.

Ustad Nizamuddin Khan – Lucknow/Farrukhabad Gharana.

Son of Ustad Azim Khan (Jawarewale), he mainly obtained *"Taalim"* or training from his father and later from Ustad Ahmed Jan Thirakawa. He was well-known for his accompaniment of Instrumental Music and in particular for his *"Laggis"* while accompanying *Thumri, Dadras*, etc.

Ustad Afaq Khan – Lucknow Gharana.

Son of the *Khalifa* of the **Lucknow Gharana**, Ustad Wajid Hussein Khan, he learnt from his father and attained great fame for his sonorous style of playing.

Pandit Narayan Rao Indorkar.

Learnt most of his Tabla from Ustad Gami Khan of **Delhi Gharana** and later from Ustad Jehangir Khan of Indore. Very knowledgeable and good for Vocal accompaniment. He was in great demand by Vocalists all over the country. He also carried on the important task of imparting knowledge of Tabla to students.

Ustad Inam Ali Khan – Khalifa (Delhi).

Son of the famous **Delhi Gharana** Tabla *Nawaz*, Ustad Gami Khan, it was but natural that he should be the *Khalifa* of the Gharana after his father. The most important feature of **Delhi Gharana** i.e. : stroke production with only two fingers on the *Daayaan* i.e. Tabla, was very much in evidence in his playing. Extremely knowledgeable, Khan Saheb could hold discussions for hours on topics such as *Taal, Kaida, Peshkaar, Rela,* etc. He passed away lately in Delhi, having lived most of his productive life in Bombay.

Pandit Taranath Rao – Farrukhabad Gharana.

Pandit Taranath-ji as he was known to a legion of his students, well-wishers and admirers, was born on 6th March 1915 in Mangalore into a musical family. His father H. Rama Rao was a well-known exponent of the *"Yakshgana"* a ballet-form from the South of India. He was dancer, singer and a *Maddalam* player and a dramatist known for his portrayal of female characters. As a child, Taranath-ji studied *Mridangam, Pakhawaj* and Tabla with his illustrious father. In 1932, he migrated to Bombay to study Arts and Painting in the J.J.School Of Arts. His attraction towards Tabla made him a disciple of Subrai-mama Ankolekar, who was one of the distinguished disciples of Ustad Munir Khan of the Lucknow Gharana. During the 11 to 12 years that he spent under Subrai-mama's tutelage, Taranath-ji distinguished himself as a Soloist and accompanist of great merit. After the passing away of his mentor, Taranath-ji became a *Ganda-*

Bandha Shagird of Tabla maestro Ustad Shamsuddin Khan, whose knowledge and sweetness of playing was legendary. Simultaneously he was also assisting the master of *Laya, Laya Bhaskar* Khaprumama Parvatkar, who passed on valuable compositions and a deep insight into the intricacies of *Layakari*. Taranath-ji also had the priviledge of being in the company of Ustad Faiyaz Mohammed of Kanpur. With his inborn talent and relentless pursuit of the art form for over 50 years, Taranath-ji earned the peak of perfection in his scholarship and wizardry and earned many encomiums from a galaxy of prominent personalities. The title of "*Vadan Kushal*" was bestowed by the *Maharaja* of Mysore at a ceremony hosted by him to honour Pandit-ji. *Jagadguru Shankaracharya* of *Sringeri Peetam* bestowed the honorific "*Vadan Kaustubh*". He was also similarly honoured by the *Maharajas* of Kolhapur, Baroda and Sawantwadi. Top musical institutions vied with one another to avail of Taranath-ji's erudition and expertise – prominent among them being, *Bhatkande* University, both at Lucknow and Bombay, *Maharaja Sayaji-Rao Gaekwad* University of Baroda and *Kala Academy*, Goa.

Taranath-ji was invited by Al India Radio to give an hour's talk on the "Comparison between *Hindustani* and *Carnatic Sangeet Paddhati*". Musical giants such as Ustad Allaudin Khan of Maihar, Ustad Ali Akbar Khan, Pandit Ravi Shankar, Pandit Pannalal Ghosh, Pandit Omkarnath Thakur, Dagar Brothers (Moinuddin Khan and Aminuddin Khan), Ustad Faiyaz Khan, Ustad Vilayat Hussein Khan – just to name a few, solicited not only his accompaniment skills but also his erudite scholarship. Pandit Ravi Shankar took him to the United States to teach Tabla and Pakhawaj at his "*Kinnara*" school of music. Pandit Taranath-ji was equally good in Pakhawaj playing, having learnt under Shankarrao Alkutkar and Baburao Gokhale.

Pandit Taranath-ji devoted the last twenty-five years of his life exclusively to teaching Tabla and Pakhawaj to young and aspiring Tabla players. Pandits Ravi and Shashi Bellare, his twin nephews (sister's sons) were his first students who gained wide recognition. Then followed a host of disciples who started as tots with their *Guru-ji* and burst forth in their teens to achieve excellence at an age when many others start with rudiments. Prominent among his disciples besides Pandits Ravi and Shashi who are themselves recognized as Masters today, are Pandit Sadanand Naimpalli, Pandit Omkar Gulvady, Pandit Mohan Balwally, Pandit Maruti Khurdikar, Dr. Kedar Muthe, Shri Anand Badamikar and Shri Balkrishna Iyer. Some of his prominent foreign disciples are Bengt Berger, Jef Feldman, Greg Johnson, Adam Rudolph, Peter Fagiola Roland Drogemueller and many others. It was a sight for the Gods when Pandit Taranath-ji would be sitting amongst his students, teaching them and also simultaneously playing the *Lehra* on the *Harmonium*, encouraging them to give it a better try with epithets such as "*Shabash*", "*Jeete Raho*" and "*Wah-Wah*".

The last 12 years or so of Pandit-ji's life were spent teaching Tabla, Pakhawaj and other ethnic drums at the **"Cal Arts"** in Los Angeles, U.S.A. Over those 12 years, Taranath-ji trained innumerable American students, who, today remember him not only for the instructions given by him in Music, but also his warmth, generosity, sense of humor and above all the affection with which he and his wife taught them and fed them and made them part of their family.

One faculty of Pandit Taranath-ji was his ability to recite any composition in any *Jati* while at the same time, providing a very melodious *Lehra* of the *Taal* in which that composition was set. About his artistic abilities in various other spheres such as carpentry, painting, serving, cooking and even such mundane activities such as packing of suitcases, it would need a volume to describe them.

Pandit Taranath-ji, if one were to describe him in a nutshell, could be termed a **Musical** *Maharishi* who, not only taught his wards Tabla and other percussion Arts but also to live life artistically.

Pandit Ravi Bellare

(Composer, Multi-Instrumentalist, Dancer, Visual-Artist, Scholar and Educator).

The artistry of Pandit Ravi Bellare provides a vital link to the ancient traditions of classical music, dance and visual arts of India. From the earliest days of his childhood in Mangalore, South India, Ravi Bellare exhibited a precocious genius for absorbing information. His childhood was singularly graced by intimate contact with legendary and *gharanedar* Ustads and Pandits of music of that time, many of whom were still performing as court musicians and dancers.

Being the nephew (sister's son) of the great scholar and performer Pandit Taranath-ji, Ravi-ji grew up in an atmosphere of the highest quality of music and Arts at his uncle's house. Early in his life, he came into contact with people of the caliber of Ustad Allaudin Khan, Pandit Ravi Shankar, Ustad Ali Akbar Khan, famous *Pakhawaji* and **Jaipur Gharana** *Kathak Guru* – Pandit Sunder Prasad-ji, Ustad Vilayat Hussein Khan of **Agra Gharana** and many many more, who had a profound influence on the musicality and erudition of Pandit Ravi Bellare. He too, like his *Guru* and uncle acquired proficiency in Arts especially painting and passed out from Sir J.J.School of Arts with flying colours. It was Pandit Taranath-ji who put Pandit Ravi Bellare under the guidance of the great Tabla stylist of **Farrukhabad Gharana**, Ustad Shamsuddin Khan, whom, the cognoscenti speak of in the same breath as Ustad Ahmed Jan Thirakawa. With this background, it was no wonder that Ravi Bellare was to achieve international acclaim as a Tabla player of eminence.

Later on in life, Pandit Ravi Bellare, not one to rest on his laurels, went on to study Dance both *Kathak* and *Bharata-Natyam*. He acquired proficiency not only in Dancing, but also the *"Natwangam"* or handling of the *"Taalam"* (cymbals) to the Dance *Bols* or *"Thirmanam"*. He travelled all over the world as a *Kathak* and *Bharat-Natyam* Dancer, dabbling in Folk styles in between. His eclectic talents led him to a long term association with the great Ram Gopal, as choreographer, musician and arranger. He later joined Pandit Ravi Shankar's *Kinnara* School of Music as its Principal in Bombay, before the school moved to Los Angeles in 1967. Pandit Ravi Bellare was also invited by the University of Berlin as an associate Professor to conduct important research work in their libraries of Ancient Indian texts.

In addition to the practical application of Visual and Musical Arts, Ravi

113

Bellare has also produced visual arts in the medium of oil, acrylic, bass-relief, silk-screen, wood-carving and sculpture. His work depicts the poetics of India's classical music as reflected in the "*Naayikas*" or emotional expressions inherent in *Raga* and *Tala* systems. Ravi Bellare has also collected a vast compendium of knowledge from ancient and modern scholarship in the field of history and theory of Rhythm and *Tala*, *Raga* and the dance forms of North and South India. With this Background, Pandit Ravi Bellare is able to speak and write with great authority on the arts of India in their ancient forms as well as development of modern idioms.

Pandit Shashi Bellare

Twin brother of Pandit Ravi Bellare, Shashi was an extrovert by nature and may be this was the reason he was very much liked by musicians who craved for his highly stylized accompaniment. Indeed, there was a time around the late 50's and 60's when Shashi Bellare was as much in demand as say, Ustad Zakir Hussein is today.

Shashi Bellare used to represent his school Robert Money High School in Cricket. It is said that he was very good at what he did and could well have gone on to represent India at the highest level in Cricket. But music being in the family and with well known personalities visiting their household, it was little wonder that young Shashi was soon enamoured of Sangeet Mehfils rather than the Cricket Greens. Staying with his maternal uncle the redoubtable Pandit Taranathji, Shashi had the opportunity to meet and listen to a host of musical giants like Ustad Allauddin Khan of Maihar, Ustad Vilayat Hussein of Agra Gharana, Pandit Ravi Shankar, Ustad Ali Akbar Khan, Pandit Kishen Maharaj etal.

Although Shashi Bellare learnt Tabla from Pandit Taranathji and Ravi Bellare, he was impressed by the personality of Pandit Kishen Maharaj-ji and began to follow his style of playing. He has accompanied a long list of top musicians like Pandit Ravi Shankar, Ustad Ali Akbar Khan, Pandit Ram Narayan and others, both in their live concerts and record albums. He is at present settled in Pune. Shashiji had once accompanied Pandit Ravi Shankar in a concert where they together played non-stop for eleven hours.

Shashiji has a happy knack of being able to stop his playing abruptly along with the main artist and rejoin him when the artist resumes his playing, all the while keeping the Taal constant.

Pandit Arvind Mulgaonkar

A senior student of Ustad Amir Hussein Khan, Mulgaonkarji was a brilliant soloist and accompanist in his younger days. At the prodding of his Ustad Mulgaonkarji undertook the onerous task of authoring what turned out to be one of the best treatises on every aspect of Tabla. Ofcourse, this involved deep studeis of various Traditions and their characteristic compositions– which Mulgaonkarji carried out meticulously. He is a winner of innumerable awards, prominent among them being the 1992 Maharashtra state Govt. award for excellence in instrumental music and the 1995 award of Senior Fellowship from Human Resources Development Ministry of the Govt. of India.

Biographies Of Pakhawajis.

Ustad Nasir Khan

Born in 1825, he spent most of his life in Hyderabad. He was under the patronage of *Rajahs* and *Nawabs* for sometime. He was famous as a performer and composer and a contemporary of the famous *Pakhawaji*, Kudow Singh Maharaj. It is believed that Nasir Khan Saheb used to practice for 18 to 20 hours a day. Both these great *Pakhawajis* had a memorable *Jugabandi* (contest) and acknowledged each other's greatness. He expired in 1917 of old age.

Pandit NanaSaheb Paanse

Born as *Narayan Thaarpe* in a village near Waai in Maharashtra, Nanasaheb adopted the surname Paanse as he had gained popularity as an accompanist of a Devotional singer (*Kirtankaar*) whose name was Paanse.

His initial training was under the famous *Pakhawaji* of that period Chounde Maharaj. Later on he happened to go to *Kashi* along with his father. There he happened to hear the *Pakhawaj-Vaadan* (performance) of a *Rajput Brahmin* called Jodh Singh and was so taken up by it that he insisted that he would stay back and learn under the master. His father gave in to young Nana's insistence, albeit reluctantly. Here, NanaSaheb stayed for a period of 12 years and underwent intensive training and severe *Riyaaz*, before returning home.

Using his mathematical skills, he set about rectifying the mistakes in certain compositions that had been carried on for generations. He also enriched his repertoire with many of his own compositions. He attracted a large following of students with his ability to impart quality knowledge.

Besides being an ace *Pakhawaji*, he was also an able Tabla player and dancer. Among his prominent disciples are his son Balwantrao Panse, Wamanrao Chandwadkar and Sakharampant Agle. He was under the patronage of the Royal family of Indore.

Pandit KudowSingh Maharaj

Born in 1815, in the village *Banda* of UP, he had his training under noted *Pakhawaji BhawaniSingh Maharaj*. It is well nigh impossible that there is any *Pakhawaji* or Tabla player of today who does not play Kudow Singh-ji's compositions. He was a hot-headed individual who was proud of his knowledge and prowess of the Pakhawaj playing. He would undertake tours to different places to meet and challenge the *Dhrupadiyas* or *Pakhawajis* there and defeat them. He was employed as a *Pakhawaji* by *Jiyaji Rao Scindia*. He challenged and defeated a noted *Pakhawaji Jyot Singh*, employed by *Nawab* Wajid Ali Shah of Lucknow, thereby winning 1000 Royal Silver coins, and a title "*Kunwar Daas*". During the War of Independence of 1857, he went to stay with some Freedom fighters at *Datia* and was there till his last days and death in 1880. His Pakhawaj playing was very profound with great clarity. His method of *Riyaaz* is legendary. He would sit with his students and practice for 18 hours a day even under candle-light. There are many stories connected to his supernatural personality. It is said that he had the *Vardaan* (Blessing) of Goddess *MahaKaali*. There is a story of Kudow Singh-ji incurring the wrath of the *Maharaja* under whom he was serving and getting a death sentence – to be trampled under the foot of an elephant. When the time came for execution of the death penalty, Kudow Singh-ji was asked to name his last wish. He naturally asked that he be allowed to play the Pakhawaj. As the elephant entered, Kudow Singh Maharaj, with a characteristic flourish, played the *Rela* and went into an ecstacy playing his very famous "*G'ja-Paran*". A miracle was witnessed by the large collection of people. The elephant stopped in its advance and began dancing. The *Maharaja* was amazed at what he witnessed and granted a Royal pardon to Kudow Singh-ji.

Gurudev Patwardhan

Born in a *Vaidik* (priestly) Family in 1869 at *Miraj*, he started learning Tabla from Rambhau Gurav of Miraj at a relatively late stage. Once, when Patwardhan-ji asked for some further lessons, his tutor insulted him by saying that the knowledge of Tabla was not suited to *Sanskrit Pandits*. After this episode, Patwardhan-ji left for Hyderabad where he learnt both Tabla and Pakhawaj from Wamanrao Chandwadkar, a student of Nana Saheb Paanse, for almost 28 years after which he went to stay with Pandit Vishnu Digambar Paluskar, at the latter's request, at Lahore. Here, he taught both Tabla and Pakhawaj and also accompanied Pandit-ji in his concerts. In 1903, he wrote a book entitled "***Mridang Tabla Vaadan Paddhati***". He died in 1916 at Miraj. Among his disciples was Pandit Baburao Gokhale.

Pandit Govindrao Devrao Barhanpurkar

He belonged to the *Paanse* **Gharana**. Born in 1875 to Devrao Barhanpurkar, a musicologist, he was encouraged to take to music. He learnt Pakhawaj for about 15 years from Pandit Sakharampant Agle, a disciple of NanaSaheb Paanse and Tabla from Pandit Wamanrao Chandwadkar, another disciple of Paanse. He learnt *Dhrupad Dhamaar* Compositions from Harihar Rao Kopargaonkar. He toured Burma and Ceylon with Pandit Vishnu Digambar Paluskar. With encouragement from Paluskar-ji, he wrote three volumes of *"Mridang Taal Vaadan Subodh"* and also *"Bharatiya Taalmanjiri"*. He was given the title *"Mridangacharya"* by Shri Vallabh bhai Patel at a Music Conference held in Ahmedabad in 1929. He was honoured by the *Sangeet Natak* Academy in March 1955 and by Dr.Rajendra Prasad on the occasion of the Golden Jubilee Celebration of *Gandharva Maha-Vidyalaya,* (a school for Music, started by Pandit Vishnu Digambar Paluskar). He expired on 20th June 1957.

Parvat Singh Pakhawaji

Born in *Gwalior* around 1876, he was the great grandson of Zorawar Singh and son of Sukhdev-Singh, who was appointed court-musician by Jankoji Rao of *Gwalior*. Later on, Parvat Singh was also appointed as court musician by Madhavrao Scindia. Parvat Singh-ji started learning Pakhawaj from his father at the young age of 5 years and acquired proficiency quite early. At the age of 25, he came to Bombay where he met reputed artists, whom he also accompanied during their concerts, notably artists like, Pandit Vishnu Digambar Paluskar, Ustad Alladiya Khan, Ustad Nazir Khan, Pandit Bhaskarbuva Bakhale, *Sitarist* Barkatullah Khan and many others. He spent around 15 years in Bombay but had to return to *Gwalior* at the demise of his father. The *Maharaja* of *Gwalior* State at that time, Madhavrao Scindia appointed Parvat Singh-ji as the court-musician in 1917. In *Gwalior* he came into contact with artists such as Pandit KrishnaRao Shankar Pandit and Ustad Hafiz Ali Khan. He was conferred the title of *"Vidya Kala Visharad"* by the *Maharaja* of *Darbhanga* in 1926. He expired on 18th July 1951.

Pandit Balwant Rao Panse Pakhawaji

Son of the legendary Pakhawaji Nana Saheb Paanse, he achieved mastery over the Pakhawaj at a very young age under the able tutelage of his illustrious father. His performances drew spontaneous appreciation everywhere mainly due to the clarity and sonorous tone of his playing. Unfortunately, he died young and because of this tragedy, Nanasaheb also passed away soon thereafter.

Pandit Ganesh Ramchandra (Baburao) Gokhale

He was born in 1896 at *Kurundwad Sansthan*. He was the nephew of Pandit Vishnu Digambar Paluskar (sister's son) and learnt Vocal music under Pandit-ji. He was later attracted to Tabla and Pakhawaj. He went to Lahore to learn from Pandit Vishnu Digambar-ji, but ended up learning Tabla and Pakhawaj from Gurudev Patwardhan. He started performing from 1908 onwards, attracting a large following with his clear and sonorous Pakhawaj playing. He migrated to Bombay in 1926, where he started the "*Maharashtra Sangeet Vidyalaya*" to propagate music. The noted Tabla and Pakhawaj maestro, Pandit Taranath-ji was one of his illustrious disciples.

Pandit Makhanji Pakhawaaji

Born in 1876 at *Mathura,* he took training from Shri Madan Mohan-ji and Gangaram-ji, students of the legendary *Pakhawaji* Kudow Singh-ji Maharaj. Later on he also learnt from Shri Bhawani Shankar-ji of Punjab. His touch on the Pakhawaj was very soft, though effective. He performed extensively all over India with eminent *Dhrupadiyas* craving his accompaniment. He spent 25 years in service of the eminent music lover Sir *Goculdas Pasta* as a Pakhawaj player. He spent the last years of his life in *Madhav Baug* in Bombay, playing his Pakhawaj and training students. Two of his outstanding students are Pandit Shankar Rao Shinde Appegaonkar and Pandit Ramdas-ji. Makhanji passed away in Mathura on 21st February 1951 at the age of 75 years.

Pandit Sakharam Pant Agle

Born 1858 in the *Vaijapur* village of Aurangabad, he started learning Pakhawaj at the early age of 12 from the Pakhawaj Maestro Nana Saheb Paanse, at

Indore. Owing to his unparalleled devotion to *Guru* and equally arduous *Riyaaz*, he achieved such mastery over the instrument that he was appointed as the court *"Pakhawaji"* in the Indore *Durbar*. He became popular all over India and even Nepal due to his outstanding performances. He was highly respected by noted musicians of his time. Among his innumerable disciples are Pandit Govindrao Burhanpurkar and his son Ambadas Pant Agle.

Mridangacharya Narayanrao Koli

The credit for reviving and popularizing the Pakhawaj in Bombay in recent times goes to Narayan Rao Koli. His name became synonymous with Pakhawaj playing.

Narayanrao was born on 7th May 1920 at Bombay. A student of St. Xaviers High School and later St. Xaviers College, he was a Graduate in the Arts faculty and went on to get the L.L.B. degree and started practicing Law in the High Court of Bombay.

Narayan Rao learnt the basics of music before settling down to Pakhawaj. He learnt *Harmonium* from the late Dr.Dabhade, *Khayal Gayaki* from Ustad Aman Ali Khan of **Bhendi Bazar Gharana** and *Dhrupad-Dhamaar* from Pandit Shankar Buwa Puranik. He even learnt *Kathak* Dance from Pandit Jailal. He ultimately decided that Pakhawaj would be his *be all and end all* and started learning from Pandit Shankar Rao Alkutkar, a senior disciple of Nanasaheb Paanse.

He was a master of *"Padhant"* (Recitation), whereas his handling of the Pakhawaj was immaculate, holding the listeners spellbound with the clarity and intonations of the various compositions he played.

He expired on 5th January 1968 at the young age of 48 years.

Pandit Arjun Shejwal

A senior and pet student of Narayan Rao Koli, Shejwal-ji had a sweet temperament and also stroke production ability. He had imbibed a lot from his *Guru* and carved a niche for himself as a leading Pakhawaj Soloist and Accompanist. Arjunji, because of his affable nature was in great demand as an accompanist and very popular amongst audiences all over the world. he has played a great hand in popularising Pakhawaj in foreign countries and has a number of disciples all over the world.

PART - II

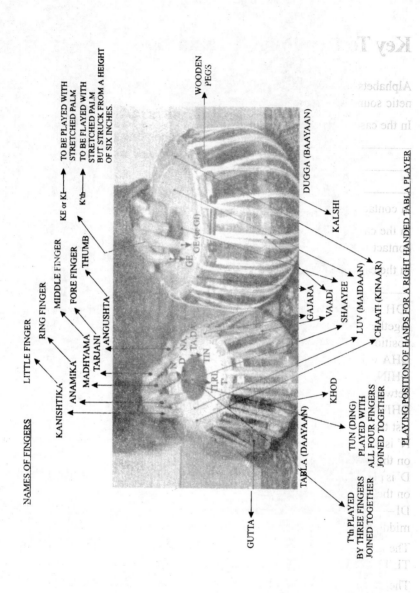

NAMES OF FINGERS

LITTLE FINGER
RING FINGER
MIDDLE FINGER
FORE FINGER
THUMB

KANISHTIKA
ANAMIKA
MADHYAMA
TARJANI
ANGUSHTA

KE or KI → TO BE PLAYED WITH STRETCHED PALM
K'th → TO BE PLAYED WITH STRETCHED PALM BUT STRUCK FROM A HEIGHT OF SIX INCHES.

GE
GE (or GH)

WOODEN PEGS

DUGGA (BAAYAAN)

KALSHI

GAJARA
VAADI
SHAAYEE
LUV (MAIDAAN)
CHAATI (KINAAR)

TABLA (DAAYAAN)

KHOD

TUN (DING)
PLAYED WITH ALL FOUR FINGERS JOINED TOGETHER

GUTTA

Tth PLAYED BY THREE FINGERS JOINED TOGETHER

PLAYING POSITION OF HANDS FOR A RIGHT HANDED TABLA PLAYER

122

Key To Reading Of Tabla Bols

Alphabets such as T',K',G,' N',D',G' are to be pronounced as per the phonetic sound they represent.

In the case of TA, the A should sound as in TABLA

————do———DHA , ——————————do——————————

————do———TIN, the I should sound as in THIN and BIN

————do———T'th , the sound of th is produced with the tongue flatly in contact with the palate and trying to pronounce T'.

In the case of K'th , the sound of th is produced with the tongue flatly in contact with the palate and trying to pronounce T' .

In the case of TUN , the U should sound as in INPUT.

————do———TI , KI , GI and DI the I should sound as in TIN

DH is the initial sound produced by striking the Tabla and Dugga together. The latter portion of the syllable is obtained from the striking position of the hand on the Tabla where the stroke is played. eg: you get DHA when the stroke on the Tabla is on the Chaanti (border).

DHIN,——————do———————————LUV, i.e. the portion between the Chaanti and the Shaayee.

DHIT——————do———————————T'th, struck by the last three fingers in the center of the Shaayee.

N' is played on the Tabla by middle finger and ring finger joined together on the lower part of Shaayee.

D' is played on the Tabla by ring finger or middle finger (not joined together) on the lower part of Shaayee.

DI——————————do———————————TI, struck by the middle finger in the center of the Shaayee and GE on the Dugga.

The alphabets played on the Tabla or Daayaan are:-NA, TIN, TUN, T'th, TI, T', D', N.'

The alphabets played on the Dugga or Baayaan are:-GI (GE or G'), KI (KE or K'), K'th.

Strokes played on the Dugga by the tips of the fore-finger and the middle finger are both GE's. Striking the Maidaan, i.e. the surface of the Baayaan below the Shaayee, also gives the sound of GE. This is used more often in the Benares Gharana, or when there is a need to stress on a particular beat eg. 'Sum'. This is unlike K'th , where the palm has to remain on the Baayaan for sometime after striking to prevent the skin from vibrating.

Strokes such as DHA , DHIN , DHIT , DI are combinations of Tabla strokes of NA , TIN , T'th , TI with GE on the Baayaan.

K'DASN is played with K'th , immediately followed by NA (DA).

G'DASN is played with G' , immediately followed by NA (DA).

K'D'GESN is played by the fore-finger of the right hand on the Chaanti immediately followed by the fore-finger of the left hand on the Tabla at the same place on the Chaanti and again immediately followed by the fore-finger of the right hand at the same place on the Chaanti (the sound should be a fast NA-NA-NA).

G'D'GESN – Similar as above , but the strokes are played with an open palm on the Maidaan of the Baayaan giving scope for unrestricted vibrations of the skin of the Baayaan (the sound should be a rapid GE-GE-GE).

DIRI – The DI is played by the right half of the palm on the Shyaaee of the Tabla along with GE on the Baayaan and the RI by the left half of the palm on the Shyaaee of the Tabla without GE.

Note:- Diagram on page 122 shows a right handed Tabla player.
Pictures on page 138 show the position for playing DIRI on Tabla. (figures 30 and 31)

Bol : **"NA"** or **"TA"** or**"DA"** *(Fig. 1)*

played on the Chaanti (Kinaar). In the above picture,the little and ring fingers are kept loosely on the Tabla.The middle finger (madhyama) is held above the pudi-level while the fore finger (tarjani) is used to strike the Chaanti and lift immediately thereafter to the level of the middle finger.

Bol : **"TIN"** *(Fig. 2)*

In the same position as in (1), this Bol is struck by the Tarjani (fore finger) on the "Luv"of the pudi (skin between Chaanti and Shaayee). The impact should be very light and instantaneously it should be lifted to the original position.

125

Bol : "TUN" *(Fig. 3)*

In this case, all the four fingers i.e. excluding the thumb are joined together and then used to strike the lower part of the Shaayee with the tips and the hand is once again raised to allow the Shaayee to resonate. This sound is the second note on the musical scale, when the Tabla is tuned to the first note or "Shadj"

Bol : "T 'th" *(Fig. 4)*

The bol is struck in the center of the Shaayee by joining the Kanishtika Anamika and Madhyama (little finger, ring finger and middle finger) and with a certain degree of force to get a non-resonating sound.

Bol : **"TI"** *(Fig. 5)*

The Bol is struck by the Madhyama (middle finger) in the center of the Shaayee and is a non- resonating sound.

Bol : **T'** *(Fig. 6)*

This bol is struck in the center of the Shaayee using the Tarjani (fore finger) and is a non-resonating bol. Most of the time TI and T' occur in sequence. T' is also sometimes referred to as "RI"

127

Bol : **D'** *(Fig. 7)*

This bol is struck by the Madhyama (middle finger) or sometimes by the Anamika (ring finger) on the lower part of the Shaayee and is a non resonating bol.Commonly used is phrase such as GID'NAG,KID'NAK' etc.

Bol : **N'** *(Fig. 8)*

This bol is played on the lower part of the Shaayee by the Madhyama (middle finger) and Anamika (ring finger) joined together-lightly so that slight resonance is obtained.

Bol : **"GE"** or **"GI"** *(Fig. 9)*

This bol is struck with the middle finger (madhayma) of the left hand on the Dugga.The hand is placed just behind the Shaayee and the stroke is played on the other side of the Shaayee.

Bol : **"GE"** or **"GI"** *(Fig. 10)*

Evereything is the same as the earlier stroke except that this is struck with the forefinger (tarjani).

129

Bol : **"K'th"** *(Fig. 11)*

    This is shown in 2 stages. The above fig. shows the hand raised about 6 inches above the Dugga.

    The above fig. shows the final position of the hand as in "KI". *(Fig. 12)*

    The stroke is played with some degreee of force and the hand is not lifted immediately to kill the vibrations.

Bol : "GE" *(Fig. 13)*

This stroke is played with an open hand and is shown in two stages. The above fig. shows the hand raised above the Dugga, just about to strike.

The above fig. shows the hand has struck the dugga pudi below the Shaayee. In this case, the hand has to be raised instantaneously to allow the Dugga to vibrate to the maximum extent possible. *(Fig. 14)*

Bol : **"KI"** or **"KE"** *(Fig. 15)*

The hand is placed as described for "GE". But the stroke is played with palm flat and covering the Shaayee; to cut off all vibrations.

Bol : **"DHA"** *(Fig. 16)*

This is a bol combining 2 strokes. NA on the Tabla and GE on the Dugga. The two are played at the same time.

Bol : **"DHIN"** *(Fig. 17)*

This is a combination of TIN on the Tabla and GE on the Dugga,played together.

Bol : **"DING"** *(Fig. 18)*

This is a combination of TUN on the Tabla and GE on the Dugga played together.

Bol : **"DHIT"** *(Fig. 19)*
    This is a combination bol of T'th on the Tabla and GE on the Dugga played together.

Bol : **"DI"** *(Fig. 20)*
    This is a combination bol of TI on the Tabla and GE on the Dugga played together.

Bol : **T'DASN'** *(Fig. 21)*
This bol is played in 3 stages on the Tabla. T'th as shown as above.

DA as shown above. *(Fig. 22)*

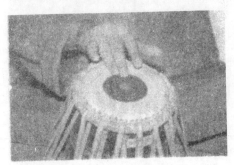

N ' as shown above. *(Fig. 23)*

Bol : **"K'D GESN"** or **"T'R TESN"** *(Fig. 24)*
This bol is played in 3 stages.
NA or DA with the Right hand.

NA or DA with the Left hand. *(Fig. 25)*

NA or DA with Right hand. *(Fig. 26)*

Bol : **"G 'D 'GESN"** *(Fig. 27)*
   This bol is played in 3 stages.
   GE (open handed) with Left Hand.

GE (open handed) with Right Hand. *(Fig. 28)*

GE (open handed) with Left Hand *(Fig. 29)*

Bol : **"DIRI"** *(Fig. 30)*

This is played in 2 stages.

DI-Right half of the Right Palm on Tabla along with GE on the Ḍugga as shown above.

RI-Left half of the Right Palm on Tabla without GE as shown above. *(Fig. 31)*

Bol:- "**TI & T**" *(Fig. 32)*

This is as played in Purab Gharana. The RI is played with the Fore - finger (tarjani) as shown in *fig. 6*

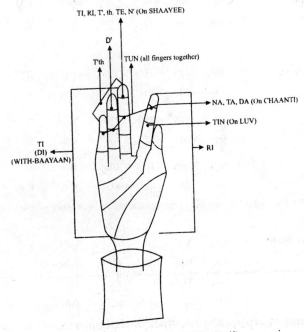

TI, RI, T', th. TE, N' (On SHAAYEE)

D'

T'th

TUN (all fingers together)

NA, TA, DA (On CHAANTI)

TIN (On LUV)

TI
(DI)
(WITH-BAAYAAN)

RI

POSITION OF PALM TO PLAY DIRI DIRI *(Fig. 33)*

Exercise 1:

				NA			
			NA	TI			
		NA	TI	T'			
	NA	NA	TI	T'			
NA	TI	NA	TI	T'			
NA	TI	T'	NA	TIN	NA		
NA	TI	T'	NA	NA	TIN	NA	
NA	NA	TI	T'	NA	NA	TIN	NA

Exercise 2:

NA	NA	TI	T'	GI	GI	TI	T'
NA	NA	TI	T'	KI	KI	TI	T'

Exercise 3:

(1)

NA	TIN	TUN	T'th	TI	T'	D'	N'
GI	GI	KI	KI	K'th	S	S	S

(2)

NA	TIN	TUN	T'th	TI	T'	D'	N'
GI	GI	KI	KI	K'th	S	K'th	S

(3)

NA	TIN	TUN	T'th	TI	T'	D'	N'
GI	GI	KI	KI	K'th	K'th	K'th	K'th

NOTE :- The symbol "S" indicates a rest equal to the duration of one syllable.

Exercise 4:

NA	S	TI	T'	TUN	S	NA	S
NA	NA	TI	T'	TUN	S	NA	S
NA	TI	T'	NA	TI	T'	NA	NA
TI	T'	TUN	S	TUN	S	NA	S

TUN may be replaced by TIN struck on the border the of Luv and the Shaayee in exercise 4.

140

Exercise 5:

(1)

NA	NA	TI	T'	GI	GI	TI	T'
K'th	S	TI	T'	GI	GI	TI	T'
NA	NA	TI	T'	GI	GI	TI	T'
TUN	S	TI	T'	GI	GI	TI	T'
NA	NA	TI	T'	GI	GI	TI	T'
DHA	S	TI	T'	GI	GI	TI	T'
DHA	S	TI	T'	GI	GI	TI	T'
DHA	S	TI	T'	DHA	S	TI	T'

(2)

TI	T'	GI	GI	TI	T'	NA	NA
TI	T'	GI	GI	TI	T'	K'th	S
TI	T'	GI	GI	TI	T'	NA	NA
TI	T'	GI	GI	TI	T'	TUN	S
TI	T'	GI	GI	TI	T'	NA	NA
TI	T'	GI	GI	TI	T'	DHA	S
TI	T'	GI	GI	TI	T'	DHA	S
TI	T'	DHA	S	TI	T'	DHA	S

(3)

GI	GI	TI	T'	NA	NA	TI	T'
GI	GI	TI	T'	K'th	S	TI	T'
GI	GI	TI	T'	NA	NA	TI	T'
GI	GI	TI	T'	TUN	S	TI	T'
GI	GI	TI	T'	NA	NA	TI	T'
GI	GI	TI	T'	DHA	S	TI	T'
GI	GI	TI	T'	DHA	S	TI	T'
DHA	S	TI	T'	DHA	S	TI	T'

141

(4)	TI	T'	NA	NA	TI	T'	GI	GI
	TI	T'	K'th	S	TI	T'	GI	GI
	TI	T'	NA	NA	TI	T'	GI	GI
	TI	T'	TUN	S	TI	T'	GI	GI
	TI	T'	NA	NA	TI	T'	GI	GI
	TI	T'	DHA	S	TI	T'	GI	GI
	TI	T'	DHA	S	TI	T'	GI	GI
	TI	T'	DHA	S	TI	T'	DHA	S

Combined Strokes of Tabla and Dugga

NA + GI = DHA ;   TI + GI = DI;   TIN + GI = DHIN;

TUN + GI = DING;   T'th + GI = DHIT.

Exercise 6:

DHA	GI	TI	T'	GI	GI	TI	T'
K'th	S	TI	T'	GI	GI	TI	T'
K'th	S	T'th	S	K'th	S	TI	T'
K'th	S	T'th	S	K'th	S	TI	T'

If the same exercise is played in double speed, there will be two Syllables (bols) per Matra (beat). Thus, we have

(1)	DHA GI	TI T'	GI GI	TI T'	K'th S	TI T'	GI GI	TI T'
	K'th S	T'th S	K'th S	TI T'	K'th S	T'th S	K'th S	TI T'
(2)	DHA GI	TI T'	GI GI	TI T'	K'th S	TI T'	GI GI	TI T'
	K'th T'th	K'th S	TI T'	K'th T'th	K'th S	TI T'	GI GI	TI T'
(3)	DHA GI	TI T'	GI GI	TI T'	K'th S	S S	K'th T'th	K'th S
	TI T'	K'th T'th	K'th S	TI T'	GI GI	TI T'	DHA S	K'th T'th
	K'th S	TI T'	K'thT'th	K'th S	TI T'	GI GI	TI T'	DHA S
	K'th T'th	K'th S	TI T'	K'th T'th	K'th S	TI T'	GI GI	TI T'
	DHA							
(4)	(K'th T'th	K'th T'th	K'th T'th	K'th T'th	K'th T'th	K'th T'th	K'th S	
	TIT'	GI GI	TIT'	DHA S) X 3				

142

Exercise 7 : (For Baayaan Fingering)

1)	DHA GI	TI T'	GI GI	TI T'	K'th S	TI T'	GI GI	TI T
	TA KI	TIT'	KIKI	TIT'	K'th S	TIT'	GIGI	TI T'
2)	DHA S	GI GI	TI T'	KI T'	DHA GE	TI T'	GI GI	TI T'
	TA S	KI KI	TI T'	KI T'	DHA GE	TI T'	GI GI	TI T'

Exercise 8:

GE	GE	TI	T'	GE	GE	NA	NA
TI	T'	GE	GE	TI	T'	NA	NA
KE	KE	TI	T'	KE	KE	NA	NA
TI	T'	GE	GE	TI	T'	NA	NA

DUGUN (Double Speed)

GEGE	TIT'	GEGE	NANA	TIT'	GEGE	TIT'	NANA
KEKE	TIT'	KEKE	NANA	TIT'	GEGE	TIT'	NANA

Taal Dadra

A cycle of 6 Matras (beats). Taali (clap) on 1, Khaali (wave of hand) on 4(0)

Theka

1	2	3	4	5	6
DHA	DHIN	NA	DHA	TIN	NA
x 1			0		

Dugun:

1	2	3	4	5	6
DHA DHIN	NA DHA	TIN NA	DHA DHIN	NA DHA	TIN NA
x			0		

Chaugun:

1	2	3
DHA DHIN NA DHA	TIN NA DHA DHIN	NA DHA TIN NA
x		

4	5	6
DHA DHIN NA DHA	TIN NA DHA DHIN	NA DHA TIN NA
0		

Tihaai:

1	2	3
DHA DHIN NA DHA	TIN NA DHA S	S DHA DHIN NA

4	5	6
DHA TIN NA DHA	S S DHADHIN	NA DHA TIN NA

DHA (Come back to Theka)
x

Peshkaar

1) (DHA TI   DHA DHA   TIN NA   TA TI   DHA DHA   DHIN NA) *x 4 times*

2) DHA TI   DHA TI   DHA TI   DHA TI   DHA DHA   TIN NA
    TA TI   TA TI   TA TI   DHA TI   DHA DHA   DHIN NA } *x twice*

3) DHA TI   DHA DHIN   NA DHA   TI DHA   DHIN NA   DHA TI
    DHA TI   DHA DHA   TIN NA   TA TI   DHA DHA   DHIN NA
    TA TI   TA TIN   NA TA   TI TA   TIN NA   TA TI
    DHA TI   DHA DHA   TIN NA   TA TI   DHA DHA   DHIN NA

4) (DHA DHA   TIN NA   TA TI   DHA DHA   DHIN NA   DHA TI)   *x 4 times*

5) (TIN NA   TA TI   DHA DHA   DHIN NA   DHA TI   DHA DHA)   *x 3 times*

144

Tihaai:

TIN NA	TA TI	DHA S	TA TI	DHA S	TA TI
DHA x					

Kaida

1)

GI NA	TI T'	GI NA	DHA GE	DHI NA	GI NA
DHA TIRI	KIT' DHA	GI NA	DHA GE	TIN NA	KI NA
KI NA	TI T'	KI NA	TA KE	TIN NA	KI NA
DHA TIRI	KIT' DHA	GI NA	DHA GE	DHIN NA	GI NA

2)

(GI NA	TI T'	GI NA	DHA GE	DHI NA	GI NA) x 3 times
DHA TIRI	KIT' DHA	GI NA	DHA GE	TIN NA	KI NA
(KI NA	TI T'	KI NA	TA KE	TIN NA	KI NA) x 2 times
GI NA	TI T'	GI NA	DHA GE	DHI NA	GI NA
DHA TIRI	KIT' DHA	GI NA	DHA GE	DHIN NA	GI NA

3)

GI NA	TI T'	GI NA	(DHA GE	DHI NA	GI NA) x 3 times

Followed by 1st two lines of Theme i.e. (1) and then Khali

4)

[(GI NA	TI T'	GI NA) x 2	DHA GE	DHI NA	GI NA] x 2 times
DHA TIRI	KIT' DHA	GI NA	DHA GE	TIN NA	KI NA
[(KI NA	TI T'	KI NA) x 2	TA KE	TIN NA	KI NA)] x 2 times
DHA TIRI	KIT' DHA	GI NA	DHA GE	DHIN NA	GI NA

5)

GI NA	TI T'	GI NA	TI T'	GI NA	TI T'
GI NA	DHA GE	DHI NA	DHA GE	DHIN NA	GI NA

Followed by 1st two lines of Theme i.e. (1) and then Khali

Tihaai:

[DHA TIRI	KIT' DHA	GI NA	DHA GE	TIN NA	KI NA
DHA S x	S S		S S] x 3 Times (No gaps the 3rd time)		

Rela

1)	DHA S	TI T	GI D'	NA G'	TIN NA	KI NA
	TA S	TI T'	GI D'	NA G'	DHIN NA	GI NA

} x 4 times

2)	DHA S	TI T'	GI D'	NA G'	TIN NA	KI NA
	DHA S	S S	GI D'	NA G'	TIN NA	KI NA
	DHA S	TI T'	GI D'	NA G'	TIN NA	KI NA
	TA S	TI T'	GI D'	NA G'	DHIN NA	GI NA

In Khaali, play the 1st two lines in Khaali i.e.without using

'GE' on the Baayaan and then play the next two lines as they are.

3)	DHA S	TI T'	GI D'	(NA G'	DHIN NA	GI NA) x3 times
	DHA S	TI T'	GI D'	NA G'	TIN NA	KI NA
	TA S	TI T'	GI D'	NA G'	DHIN NA	GI NA

In Khaali , play the 1st line in Khaali i.e.without using

'GE' on the Baayaan and then play the next two lines as they are

4)	DHA S	TI T'	GI D'	NA G'	(DHIN NA	GI NA) x4 times
	DHA S	TI T'	GI D'	NA G'	TIN NA	KI NA
	TA S	TI T'	GI D'	NA G'	DHIN NA	GI NA

In Khaali , play the 1st line only in Khaali i.e.without using

'GE' on the Baayaan and then play the next two lines as they are

5)	DHIN N'	DHIN NA	GINA	DHIN N'	DHIN NA	GINA
	DHA S	TI T'	GI D'	NA G'	TIN NA	KI NA
	TIN N'	TIN NA	KI NA	TIN N'	TIN NA	KI NA
	DHA S	TI T'	GI D'	NA G'	DHIN NA	GI NA

Tihaai:

[DHA S	TI T'	GI D'	NA G'	TIN NA	KI NA
DHA S	S S	S S] x 3 times (No gaps the third time)			

Tukdas

1) DHIT DHIT   DIT' TIT'   DHAGE TIT'   K'D'DHA TIT'   (K'thTI T'DHA

   SK'th ST'th   DHAS SS) x3 Times

2) K'thS TIT'   K'thT'th K'thT'th   (K'thTI T'DHA   SK'th ST'th   DHAS K'thT'th

   DHA S—) x3 Times

*NOTE:- The hyphen after DHA S denotes an incomplete matra. The second part of Tihaai should
start immediately in this matra.*

3) DHAS TIRI   KIT' T'K'   TAS TIRI   KIT' T'K'   TIRI KIT'   T'K'T'K'

   TIRI KIT'   (DHA TI   DHA S   DHA TI   DHA S   DHA TI

   DHA S) x3 Times

4) DIT' TIT'   DHAGE TIT'   K'D'DHA TIT'   K'thS TIT'   G'DI GI N'   TAKE TIRIKIT'

   TUNNA K'thT'th   DHAS SS   (K'D' GE   SN G'D   GE SN   K'thS SS

   DHAS SS   SS SS) x 3 Times (No gaps the third time)

Varieties Of Dadra Theka

1)	DHA	TIN	TIN	TA	DHIN	DHIN
2)	DHIT	DHA	TIN	T'th	DHA	DHIN
3)	DHA TI	DHA GE	TIN NA	TA TI	DHA GE	DHIN NA
4)	DHA S	TIN NA	KI NA	TA S	DHIN NA	GINA

147

Taal Teentaal

(A Cycle of 16 Matras with Taali on 1, 5 & 13; Khaali on 9)

Theka

1	2	3	4
DHA	DHIN	DHIN	DHA
x			
1			

5	6	7	8
DHA	DHIN	DHIN	DHA
2			

9	10	11	12
DHA	TIN	TIN	TA
0			

13	14	15	16
TA	DHIN	DHIN	DHA
3			

Dugun:

DHA DHIN	DHIN DHA	DHA DHIN	DHIN DHA
x			
1			

DHA TIN	TIN TA	TA DHIN	DHIN DHA
2			

DHA DHIN	DHIN DHA	DHA DHIN	DHIN DHA
0			

DHA TIN	TIN TA	TA DHIN	DHIN DHA
3			

Chougun:

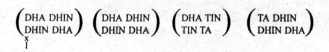

$$\begin{pmatrix} \text{DHA DHIN} \\ \text{DHIN DHA} \end{pmatrix} \begin{pmatrix} \text{DHA DHIN} \\ \text{DHIN DHA} \end{pmatrix} \begin{pmatrix} \text{DHA TIN} \\ \text{TIN TA} \end{pmatrix} \begin{pmatrix} \text{TA DHIN} \\ \text{DHIN DHA} \end{pmatrix}$$

x
1

148

$\underline{}$—do——	——do——	—do——	—do——
2			
——do——	——do——	—do——	—do——
0			
—do——	——do——	—do——	—do——
3			

Tihaai:

$$\left(\begin{matrix} \text{DHA DHIN} \\ \text{DHIN DHA} \\ \underset{1}{x} \end{matrix}\right) \left(\begin{matrix} \text{DHA DHIN} \\ \text{DHIN DHA} \end{matrix}\right) \left(\begin{matrix} \text{DHA TIN} \\ \text{TIN TA} \end{matrix}\right) \left(\begin{matrix} \text{TA DHIN} \\ \text{DHIN DHA} \end{matrix}\right)$$

$$\left(\begin{matrix} \text{DHA S} \\ \text{DHA DHA} \\ 2 \end{matrix}\right) \left(\begin{matrix} \text{DHA S} \\ \text{DHA DHIN} \end{matrix}\right) \left(\begin{matrix} \text{DHIN DHA} \\ \text{DHA DHIN} \end{matrix}\right) \left(\begin{matrix} \text{DHIN DHA} \\ \text{DHA TIN} \end{matrix}\right)$$

$$\left(\begin{matrix} \text{TIN TA} \\ \text{TA DHIN} \\ 0 \end{matrix}\right) \left(\begin{matrix} \text{DHIN DHA} \\ \text{DHA S} \end{matrix}\right) \left(\begin{matrix} \text{DHA DHA} \\ \text{DHA S} \end{matrix}\right) \left(\begin{matrix} \text{DHA DHIN} \\ \text{DHIN DHA} \end{matrix}\right)$$

$$\left(\begin{matrix} \text{DHA DHIN} \\ \text{DHIN DHA} \\ 3 \end{matrix}\right) \left(\begin{matrix} \text{DHA TIN} \\ \text{TIN TA} \end{matrix}\right) \left(\begin{matrix} \text{TA DHIN} \\ \text{DHIN DHA} \end{matrix}\right) \left(\begin{matrix} \text{DHA S} \\ \text{DHA DHA} \end{matrix}\right)$$

$$\underset{x}{\text{DHA}}$$

Kaida
(DELHI GHARANA)

1)
DHA	DHA	TI	T'	DHA	DHA	TIN	NA	
TA	TA	TI	T'	DHA	DHA	DHIN	NA	} x 2 times

Dugun:

(DHA DHA TI T' DHA DHA TIN NA TA TA TI T' DHA DHA DHIN NA) x 4 times

2)
DHA DHA	TI T'	DHA DHA	TI T'	DHA DHA	TI T'	DHA DHA	TIN NA
TA TA	TI T'	TA TA	TI T'	DHA DHA	TI T'	DHA DHA	DHIN NA

3)
DHA DHA	TI T'	TI T'	DHA DHA	TI T'	TI T'	DHA DHA	TIN NA
TA TA	TI T'	TI T'	TA TA	TI T'	TI T'	DHA DHA	DHIN NA

4) DHA DHA   TI T'   TI T'   TI T'   DHA DHA   TI T'   DHA DHA   **TIN NA**

   TA TA   TI T'   TI T'   TI T'   DHA DHA   TI T'   DHA DHA   DHIN NA

5) DHA TI   T' DHA   DHA DHA   TI T'   DHA TI   T' DHA   DHA DHA   TIN NA

   TA TI   T' TA   TA TA   TI T'   DHA TI   T' DHA   DHA DHA   DHIN NA

6) DHA TI   T' DHA   DHA DHA   TI T'   DHA DHA   DHA DHA   DHA DHA   TI T'

   DHA TI   S DHA   TI T'   DHA TI   S DHA   TI T'   DHA DHA   TI T'....Khaali

7) DHA DHA   DHA DHA   TI T'   DHA DHA   DHA DHA   TI T'   DHA DHA   TI T'

   DHA TI   S DHA   TI T'   DHA TI   S DHA   TI T'   DHA DHA   TI T'....Khaali

Tihaai:

(DHA TI   S DHA   TI T'   DHA TI   S DHA   TI T'   DHA TI

S DHA   TI T'   **DHA DHA**   DHA S) *x 3 Times*

Kaida

DHA DHA   TIRI KIT'   DHA DHA   TIN NA   TA TA   TIRI KIT'

DHA DHA   DHIN NA

This Kaida is similar in all respects to the first Delhi Gharana Kaida except that TIRIKIT' takes the place of TI T'. Hence, it may be given the same treatment for making variations.

Peshkaar

1) DHE K'D   DHIN DHA   S DHA   DHIN DHA   DHIN DHIN   DHA DHIN

   DHA DHA   TINTA

   TE K'D   TIN TA   S TA   TIN TA   DHIN DHIN   DHA DHIN

   DHA DHA   DHINDHA

2) DHE K'D   DHIN DHA   S DHA   DHIN DHA   DHE K'D   DHIN DHA

   S DHA   DHIN DHA

   DHE K'D   DHIN DHA   S DHA   DHIN DHA   DHIN DHIN   DHA DHIN

   DHA DHA   TINTA

   TE K'D   TIN TA   S TA   TIN TA   TE K'D   TIN TA

   S TA   TIN TA

DHE K'D	DHIN DHA	S DHA	DHIN DHA	DHIN DHIN	DHA DHIN
DHA DHA	DHIN DHA				

3)

DHE K'D	DHIN DHA	S DHA	DHE K'D	DHIN DHA	S DHA
S DHA	DHIN DHA	DHE K'D	DHIN DHA	S DHA	DHIN DHA
DHIN DHIN	DHA DHIN	DHA DHA	TINTA —Khaali		

4)

DHE K'D	DHIN DHA	DHE K'D	DHIN DHA	DHE K'D	DHIN DHA
S DHA	DHIN DHA	DHE K'D	DHIN DHA	S DHA	DHIN DHA
DHIN DHIN	DHA DHIN	DHA DHA	TINTA —Khaali		

5)

DHE K'D	DHIN DHA	S DHA	DHIN DHA	DHIN DHIN	DHA DHIN
DHA DHA	DHIN DHA	KID'NAK'	TIRIKIT'	T'K T'K	TIRIKIT'
DHIN DHIN	DHA DHIN	DHA DHA	TINTA —Khaali		

6)

DHE K'D	DHIN DHA	S DHA	DHIN DHA	DHIN DHIN	DHA DHIN
DHA DHA	DHIN DHA	KID'NAK'TIRIKIT'	T'K' T'K' TIRIKIT'	DHIN DHA	
SK'D'DHA	DHIN DHIN	DHA DHIN	DHA DHA	TIN TA —Khaali	

7)

(KID'NAK'TIRIKIT'	T'K' T'K'TIRIKIT	DHIN DHA	K'D' DHA) *x 3 times*
DHIN DHIN	DHA DHIN	DHA DHA	TIN TA —Khaali

Tihaai:

[(KID'NAK'TIRIKIT'   T'K' T'K'TIRIKIT'   DHIN DHA) *x 2 times*

DHIN DHIN   DHA DHIN   DHA DHA   TIN TA   DHA S] *x 3 times*

Rela

1)	GID' NAG'	TIT' TIT'	GID' NAG'	NAG' TI T'
	KID' NAK'	TIT' TIT'	GID' NAG'	NAG' TI T'
2)	GID' NAG'	TIT' TI T'	GID' NAG'	TIT' TI T'
	GID' NAG'	TIT' TI T'	GID' NAG'	NAG' TI T'
	Khaali———			
3)	GID' NAG'	TIT' TIT'	TIT' TIT'	GID' NAG'
	TIT' TIT'	TIT' TIT'	GID' NAG	NAG' TIT'
	Khaali———			

151

4)	GID' NAG'	NAG' TIT'	GID' NAG'	TIT' TIT'
	KID' NAK'	NAK' TIT'	GID' NAG'	TIT' TIT'
5)	GID' NAG'	NAG' TIT'	GID' NAG'	NAG' TIT'
	GID' NAG' Khaali———	NAG' TIT'	GID' NAG'	TIT' TIT'
6)	TIT' TIT'	GID' NAG'	NAG' TIT'	GID' NAG'
	TIT' TIT'	KID' NAK'	NAG' TIT'	GID' NAG'
7)	TIT' TIT'	GID' NAG'	TIT' TIT'	GID' NAG'
	TIT' TIT' Khaali———	GID' NAG'	NAG' TIT'	GID' NAG'

Tihaai:

[GID' NAG'	TIT' TIT'	GID' NAG'	TIT' TIT'
GID' NAG'	TIT' TIT'	GID' NAG'	NAG' TIT'
GID' NAG'	DHA DHA	DHA S] x *3 times*	

Rela (Composition of Ustad Nathu Khan Saheb of Delhi Gharana)

GID' NAG'	TIT' GID'	NAG' TIT'	GID' NAG
TAGE TIT'	GID' NAG	TIT' GID'	NAG' TIT'
KID' NAK'	TIT' KID'	NAK' TIT'	KID' NAK'
TAGE TIT'	GID' NAG'	TIT' GID'	NAG' TIT'

Rela (In Angushtaan Style i.e. Closer to the Chaanti & hence the Thumb)

GI N'	DHIN N'	GI N'	DHA GE	TIRI KIT'	DHIN N'	GI N'	TI T'
KI N'	TIN N'	KI N'	TA KE	TIRI KIT'	DHIN N'	GI N'	TI T'

In the above composition TI T' is played in the reverse fashion

DRUT TEENTAAL

In Drut TeenTaal, i.e. in the Fourth speed, only four main matras i.e. 1st (Sum), 5th (Taali), 9th (Khaali) & 13th (Taali) are shown by the hands. On the Tabla though, the full Theka is played.

Mukhdas

1) DHA DHIN DHIN DHA DHA DHIN DHIN DHA
   $\overset{x}{\underset{1}{}}$ $\underset{2}{}$

   DHA TIN TIN TA SS TIRIKIT' T'KT'K TIRIKIT'
   $\underset{0}{}$ $\underset{3}{}$

2) DHA DHIN DHIN DHA DHA DHIN DHIN DHA
   DHA TIN TIN TA KID'NAK' TIRIKIT' T'KT'K' TIRIKIT'

3) DHA DHIN DHIN DHA DHA DHIN DHIN DHA
   DHA TIN TIN KID'NAK' TIRIKIT' T'K'T'K' TIRIKIT' DHADHA

4) DHA DHIN DHIN DHA DHA DHIN DHIN DHA
   DHA TIN TIRIKIT' T'K'T'K' TIRIKIT' DHATIRI KIT'DHA TIRIKIT'

5) DHA DHIN DHIN DHA DHA DHIN DHIN DHA
   DHA KID'NAK' TIRIKIT' T'K'T'K' TIRIKIT' DHATIRI KIT'DHA TIRIKIT'

6) DHA DHIN DHIN DHA DHA DHIN DHIN DHA
   KID'NAK' TIRIKIT' T'K'T'K' TIRIKIT' DHAT'K' TIRIKIT' DHAT'K' TIRIKIT'

7) DHA DHIN DHIN DHA DHA DHIN DHIN KID'NAK'
   TIRIKIT' T'K'T'K' TIRIKIT' DHAT'K' T'K'TIRI KIT'DHA T'K'T'K' TIRIKIT'

8) DHA DHIN DHIN DHA DHA DHIN KID'NAK' TIRIKIT'
   T'K'T'K' TIRIKIT' DHAKIT' T'K'T'K' TIRIKIT' DHAKIT' T'K'T'K' TIRIKIT'

9) DHA DHIN DHIN DHA DHA KID'NAK' TIRIKIT' T'K'T'K'
   TIRIKIT' DHATIRI KIT'T'K' T'KTIRI KIT'DHA TIRIKIT' T'K'T'K' TIRIKIT'

10) DHA DHIN DHIN DHA KID'NAK' TIRIKIT' T'K'T'K' TIRIKIT'
    DHA T'K' TIRIKIT' T'K'T'K' TIRIKIT' DHA T'K' TIRIKIT' T'K'T'K' TIRIKIT'

11) DHA DHIN DHIN KID'NAK' TIRIKIT' T'K'T'K' TIRIKIT' DHAKID'
    NAK'TIRI KIT'T'K' T'K'TIRI KIT'DHA KID'NAK' TIRIKIT T'K'T'K' TIRIKIT'

12) DHA DHIN KID'NAK' TIRIKIT' T'K'T'K' TIRIKIT' DHA S KID'NAK'
    TIRIKIT' T'K'T'K' TIRIKIT' DHA S KID'NAK' TIRIKIT' T'K'T'K' TIRIKIT'

13) DHA KID'NAK' TIRIKIT' T'K'T'K' TIRIKIT' DHADHA DHA S TIRIKIT'
    T'K'T'K' TIRIKIT' DHADHA DHA S TIRIKIT' T'K'T'K' TIRIKIT' DHADHA

14) KID'NAK' TIRIKIT' T'K'T'K' TIRIKIT' DHADHA DHAKID' NAK'TIRI KIT'T'K'
T'K'TIRI KIT'DHA DHADHA KID'NAK' TIRIKIT' T'K'T'K' TIRIKIT' DHADHA
DHA
x

NOTE: No. 6 onwards, can also be classified as Mohras & Nos. 11 to 14 can be classified as Tihaais.

Mohras

1) TIRIKIT' T'KT'K TIRIKIT' TAKITIRI KIT'T'K TIRIKIT' T'KT'K TIRIKIT'
   x
   1   2

   DHA S   S GE   S T'   DHA S   GE S   T' DHA   S GE   S T'
   0   3

   DHA
   x

2) TIRIKIT' T'KT'K TIRIKIT' TAKITIRI KIT'T'K TIRIKIT' T'KT'K TIRIKIT'

   DHA S   S T'K   TIRIKIT' DHA S   T'K TIRI KIT' DHA S T'K   TIRIKIT

   DHA
   x

3) TIRIKIT' T'KT'K TIRIKIT' TAKITIRI KIT'T'K TIRIKIT' T'KT'K TIRIKIT'

   TAKITIRI KIT'TAKI TIRIKIT' TAKITIRI KIT'TAKI TIRIKIT' T'KT'K TIRIKIT'

   DHA S   S TAKI   TIRIKIT' TAKITIRI KIT'TAKI TIRIKIT' T'KT'K TIRIKIT'

   DHA S   S TAKI   TIRIKIT' TAKITIRI KIT'TAKI TIRIKIT' T'KT'K TIRIKIT'

   DHA
   x

4) DHA TI   T' TI   T' DHA   TI T'   TI T'   TI T'   DHA DHA   TI T'

   DHA DHA DHA TI   T' TI   T' DHA   DHA DHA TI T'   TI T'   DHA DHA

   DHA
   x

154

Tukdas

1)

DHA S	DHIN NA	TUN NA	K'th T'th	KIT' DHA	S DHA	TUN NA	K'th T'th
DHA S	S DHA	TUN NA	K'th T'th	DHA S	K'th T'th	DHA S	K'th T'th
DHA S	S DHA	TUN NA	K'th T'th	DHA S	K'th T'th	DHA S	K'th T'th
DHA S	S DHA	TUN NA	K'th T'th	DHA S	K'th T'th	DHA S	K'th T'th

DHA
x

2)

DHA S	DHA S	TUN S	TUN S	NA NA	TI T'	KI T'	K'th TIRI
KIT' T'K	TA S	DHA TIRI	KIT' T'K	TA S	K'th T'th	DHA S	K'th T'th
DHA S	S S	DHA TIRI	KIT' T'K	TA S	K'th T'th	DHA S	K'th T'th
DHA S	S S	DHA TIRI	KIT' T'K	TA S	K'th T'th	DHA S	K'th T'th

DHA
x

3)

DHIT S	DHIT S	DHA S	TIRI KIT'	DHIT S	TA S	GI GI	TI T'
K'th S	TI T'	G' DIN	GI N'	DHA S	TIRI KIT'	DHIT S	TA S
GI GI	TI T'	K'th S	TI T'	G' DIN	GI N'	DHA S	TIRI KIT'
DHIT S	TA S	GI GI	TI T'	K'th S	TI T'	G' DIN	GI N'

DHA
x

155

4) DHIT S   DHIT S   TIRI KIT' DHIT S   DHA GE   TI T'   TA KE   TI T'

K'D DHIT   S TUN   GE N'   NA G'   TI T'   K'th TA   G' DIN   GI N'

DHA S   DHA S   TIRI KIT' DHIT S   TAGE   S N'   DHA S   TIRIKIT'

DHIT S   TAGE   S N'   DHA S   TIRI KIT' DHIT S   TAGE   S N'

DHA
x

5) DHA TI   S DHA   TI S   DHA TI   DHA TIRI KIT' T'K   TA TIRI   KIT' T'K

TIRI KIT'   T'K T'K   TIRI KIT'   DHA TI   DHA S   DHA TI   DHA S   DHA TI

DHA S   S T'K   TIRI KIT'   DHA TI   DHA S   DHA TI   DHA S   DHA TI

DHA S   S T'K   TIRI KIT'   DHA TI   DHA S   DHA TI   DHA S   DHA TI

DHA
x

6) GIN TIRI   KIT' T'K   TA GE   TI T'   K'th TA   S GE   NA S   DHAS

TUN S   NA S   GE NA   TUN NA   DHA TUN   NA DHA   TUN NA   DHA TUN

NA S   K' th TA   GE NA   TUN NA   DHA TUN   NA DHA   TUN NA   DHA TUN

NA S   K' th TA   GE NA   TUN NA   DHA TUN   NA DHA   TUN NA   DHA TUN

NA
x

156

Chakradaars

1) [DHA TI   SDHA   TI S   DHA TI   DHA TIRI   KIT' T'K   TA TIRI   KIT' T'K
(TIRIKIT'   T'K T'K   TIRIKIT'   DHA TI   DHA S   DHA TI   DHA S   DHA TI
DHA S   S S) *x 3 Times*] *x 3 Times*

2) [DHA TIRI   KIT' T'K   TA S   K'th S   S S   DHA S   TUN S   TA S
KI T'   DHA S   TUN S   TA S   DHA TIRI   KIT' T'K   TA S   DHA TIRI
KIT' T'K   TA S   DHA TIRI   KIT' T'K   TA S   S S] *x 3 Times*

3) [DHA TI   T' DHA   TI T'   DHA DHA   TI T'   KIT' DHA   TI T'   DHA TI
T' DHA   S N'   TIRI KIT'   T'K TA   TIT' K'T'   G'DIN G'N'   DHA S   TIT'K'T'
G'DI G'N'   DHA S   TIT' K'T'   G'DIN G'N'   DHA S   S S] *x 3 Times*

Pranaam G'th

DHIT S	DHIT S	DI T'	TI T'	DHA GE	TI T'	KIT' DHA	TI T'
DHA S	S S	T'DAS N	S S	G'DAS N	S S	K'th S	S S
Shree S	S S	*Guru De*	S *V'*	*D'th* S	S *T'*	*Pr'naa*	S *M'*
DHA S	S S	*Pr'naa*	S *M'*	DHA S	S S	*Pr'naa*	S *M'*
DHA							

[Note:- All words & letters in Italics are from Sanskrit language which mean "Salutations to the Guru" Pranaam means Salutation and should be shown by joining hands in the gesture of praying.]

157

An Introduction To Layakaari

NOTE:- Give Taali (Claps) at the rate of One Clap per second.

Ek gun (Single speed)   ——1——   ,   ——2——   ,   ——3——   ,   ——4——
i.e. One count per Matra $\overset{x}{I}$

Du gun (Double speed)   1——2   ,   2——2   ,   3——2   ,   4——2
i.e Two counts / Matra

Ti gun (Triple speed) *   1—2—3   ,   2—2—3   ,   3—2—3   ,   4—2—3
i.e 3 counts / Matra

Chougun (4th speed)   1—2—3—4 , 2—2—3—4 , 3—2—3—4 , 4—2—3—4
i.e. 4 counts / Matra

Paanch gun(5th speed)# 1—2—3—4—5 , 2—2—3—4—5 , 3—2—3—4—5 , 4—2—3—4—5
i.e. 5 counts / Matra

Cheh gun (6th speed)
i.e. 6 counts / Matra   1-2-3-4-5-6   ,   2-2-3-4-5-6   ,   3-2-3-4-5-6   ,   4-2-3-4-5-6
Double of Tigun

Saat gun (7th speed)$
i.e.7 counts / Matra   1-2-3-4-5-6-7   ,   2-2-3-4-5-6-7   ,   3-2-3-4-5-6-7   ,   4-2-3-4-5-6-7

Aath gun (8th speed)   1-2-3-4-5-6-7-8 , 2-2-3-4-5-6-7-8 , 3-2-3-4-5-6-7-8 , 4-2-3-4-5-6-7-8
i.e.8 counts / Matra   —double of Chougun

*NOTE:-   * These speeds are also referred to as "Dedhi", or 1 1/2 times the original speed.*

   # ———————do——————— "Sawai" or 1 1/4 times the original speed.

   $ ———————do——————— "Paune Dugun" or 1 3/4 times the original speed.

Again, in terms of "G'ti", Tigun is "Tishra G'ti"; Chougun or Dugun is "Chatushra"; Paanch gun is "Khanda G'ti" & "Saath gun is "Mishra G'ti" If there was a count of NINE per clap, that would be Naugun which is "Sankeerna G'ti".

Aad Kaidas (Kaida in Dedhi)

1) DHA TIRI KIT'   DI KI T'   GI NA DHA   TI GI NA

   DHA TIRI KIT'   DI KI T'   GI N' TIN   NA KI NA

| TA TIRI KIT' | TI KI T' | KI NA TA | TI KI NA |
| DHA TIRI KIT' | DI KI T' | GI N'DHIN | NA GI NA |

(In the above Kaida, the phrases DI KI T' & TI KI T' are played as DI TI T' & TI TI T' where DI & first TI of TI TI T' are played with the Fore-finger in the center of the Shaayee)

Paltas or Variations can be made as usual and so also the Tihaai. But, throughout the "Prastaar"the character of the Kaida i.e. Dedhi must be maintained.

2)	DHA GE NA	DHA TIRI KIT'	DI KI T'	DHA GE NA
	DHA TIRI KIT'	DI KI T'	GI N' DHIN	NA GI NA
	GI NA K'	DHIN N' DHIN	NA S S	DHA GE NA
	DHA TIRI KIT'	DI KI T'	GI N' TIN	NA KI NA
	Khaali——			

3)	DHA S DHA	S DHA S	GI NA DHA	S GI NA
	DHA TIRI KIT'	DI KI T'	GI N' DHIN	NA GI NA
	DHA TIRI KIT'	DI KI T'	GI NA DHA	TI GI NA
	DHA TIRI KIT'	DI KI T'	GI N' TIN	NA KI NA
	Khaali——			

Ajrada Peshkaar — 1 (Dedhi Ang)

1) DHA S TI   S DHA SD'   DHA S TIN   S NA SD' ⎫
   TA S TI   S DHA SD'   DHA S DHIN   S NA SD' ⎬ x 4 times

2) DHA S TI   S DHA SD'   DHA S S   TAKE TIRI KIT' ⎫
   DHA S TI   S DHA SD'   DHA S TIN   S NA SD ⎬ x 2 times
                                            Khaali——

3) DHA S TI   S DHA SD'   DHA S S   TIRI KIT' T'K T'K TIRI KIT' ⎫
   DHA S TI   S DHA SD'   DHA S TIN   S NA SD ⎬ x 2 times
                                      Khaali——

4) (DHA S TI   S DHA SD'   DHA S S   TIRI KIT' T'K T'K TIRI KIT') x 3 times
   DHA S TI   S DHA SD'   DHA S TIN   S NA SD
                                      Khaali——

5) DHA S TI   S DHA SD'   (DHA S S   TIRI KIT' T'K T'K TIRI KIT') *x 3 times*

    DHA S TI   S DHA SD'   DHA S S   TIRI KIT' T'K T'K TIRI KIT'

    DHA S TI   S DHA SD'   DHA S TIN   S NA SD   Khaali———

6) DHASTI   SDHASD'   DHASGINA   DHAGETIN NAKINA

    DHASTI   SDHASD'   DHASTIN   SNASD'   } *x 2 times*
    Khaali———

7) DHA S TI   S DHA SD'   (DHASGINA   DHAGE TIN NA KI NA) *x 3 times*
    followed by 6th Palta and then Khaali

8) GINA DHAGE TIN NA   KI NA GINA DHAGE   TINNA KINA GIN

    DHAGE TINNA KINA

    DHASTI   SDHASD'   DHASTIN   SNASD'   Khaali——

9) (GINA DHAGE TINNA) *x 2* (GIN' TINNA—) *x 3*

    DHASTI   SDHASD'   DHASTIN   SNASD'   Khaali——

10) DHA TIRIKIT' T'K T'K DHA   TIRIKIT DHA TI DHA GE   DHIN NA GI NA DHA TI

    DHA GE TIN NA KI NA

    DHASTI   SDHASD'   DHASTIN   SNASD'   Khaali——

Tihaai:

    [DHA TIRIKIT' T'K T'K DHA   TIRIKIT (DHA TI DHA GE   DHIN NA GI NA DHA TI

    DHA GE TIN NA KI NA   DHA ——) *x3* With a gap of 1 Matra] *x 3 times*

Ajrada Peshkaar—2 (Dedhi Ang)

1) (DHA TI DHA   DHA TIN NA   TA TI DHA   DHA DHIN NA)   *x 8 Times* ——(Chalan)

2) DHA TIRI KIT' T'K T'th KIT'   DHA DHA TI   DHA TI DHA   DHA TIN NA}
                                                  Khaali——— } *x 4 Times*

Further Paltas (Variations) can be made as usual.

Rela In Dedhi Ang:

    (DHA S DHIN   DHIN NA S   DHA S TIN   TIN NA S) *x 8 Times* ——Chalan

Raon:

DHA TIRI GID' N'G DHIN TIRI GID' N'G DHA TIRI GID' N'G
DHA TIRI GID' N'G TIN TIRI KID' N'K TA TIRI KID' N'K } x 4 Times

Variations to be made as usual.

Rela In Chatushra Jaati:

DHAS TIT'	GID' N'G'	DIT' TIT'	GID' N'G'
DHAS TIT'	GID' N'G'	TINS NAS	KID' N'K'
TAS TIT'	KID' N'K'	TIT' TIT'	KID' N'K'
DHAS TIT'	GID' N'G'	DHINS NAS	GID' N'G'

Variations to be made as usual.

Some More Tukdas In Drut Teen Taal

Theka:

DHA DHIN DHIN DHA	DHA DHIN DHIN DHA	DHA TIN TIN TA	TA DHIN DHIN DHA
x	2	0	3
1			

1)

DIT' TIT'	DHAGE TIT'	K'DDHA TIT'	DHAGE TIT'
DHATIRI KIT'DI	T'T'th K'thT'th	K'thT'th K'thT'th	K'thSTIT'
(DHA TUN SNA	NA K'th S T'th	DHAS TIRIKIT') x 3 (No TIRIKIT', the 3rd time)	

2)

TUN TUN	DIT' TIT'	DHAGE TIT'	K'thTA SN'
DHAS GES	TUNS GES	N'S DHAS	SS K'thS
(GEGE TUNS	GEGE TIRIKIT'	DHAS K'thS) x 3 Times	(No K'thS the 3rd time)

3)

DHIT DHIT	DHIT DHIT	DIT' TIT'	DIT' TIT'
DHAGE TIT'	K'DDHA TIT'	DHAGE TIT'	K'DDHA TIT'
DHATIRI KIT'T'K	TAS TAS	TAS K'DDHIN	NAS DHAS
DHAS K'D TIN	NAS TAS	TAS K'DDHIN	NAS DHAS
DHA			
x			

161

4)

GINA TIT'	NATI T'TA	STUN STA	K'thS SS
TUNS SS	SS NAS	SS SS	GES SS
NATIRI KIT' T'K	TAS K'th T'th	K'thS DHATIRI	KIT'T'K T'th KIT'
DHAS DHATIRI	KIT'T'K T'th KIT'	DHAS DHATIRI	KIT'T'K T'th KIT'
DHA			

x

5)

DHAGE TIT'	TAKE TIT'	DHAS K'thTI	T'K'th TIT'
K'thS T'D'	SN' NAS	NAS DHATIRI	KIT'T'K T'th KIT'
DHAS T'D'	SN' NAS	NAS DHATIRI	KIT'T'K T'th KIT'
DHAS T'D'	SN' NAS	NAS DHATIRI	KIT'T'K T'th KIT'
DHA			

x

G'ths of 'n' Dha's

1) 6 DHA's:

DHA DHIN NA	DHA KIT' T'K	TA KIT' T'K	DHATIRI KIT' T'K DHA
DHA KIT' T'K	DHATIRI KIT' T'K DHA	DHA KIT' T'K	DHATIRI KIT' T'K DHA

DHA....... (The above G'th is in Dedhi)

x

2) 9 DHA's:

DHATIRI KIT'T'K	TATIRI KIT'T'K	TIRIKIT' T'KT'K	TIRIKIT' TAKITIRI
KIT'T'K TIRIKIT'	T'KT'K TIRIKIT'	TAS K'thT'th	DHATIRI KIT'T'K
DHAS DHAS	DHAS TAS	K'thT'th DHATIRI	KIT'T'K DHAS
DHAS DHAS	TAS K'thT'th	DHATIRI KIT'T'K	DHAS DHAS
DHA			

x

3) 12 DHA's:

DHAGE TIT'	TAKE TIT'	KIT'DHA TIT'	DHAGE TIT'
K'thS DIT'	TIT' KD'DHA	TIT'DHAS·	DHAS DHAS
(DHAS DIT'	TIT' KD'DHA	TIT'DHAS	DHAS DHAS) x 2 Times
DHA			

x

162

4) 15 DHA's:

DIT'TIT'	DHAGE TIT'	KIT'DHA TIT'	DIRIDIRI K'thS
DIRIDIRI K'thS	DHAS DHAS	DHAS DHAS	DHAS DIRIDIRI
K'thS DIRIDIRI	K'thS DHAS	DHAS DHAS	DHAS DHAS
DIRIDIRI K'thS	DIRIDIRI K'thS	DHAS DHAS	DHAS DHAS
DHA			
x			

5) 3, 6, 9 DHA's:

DHIT DHIT	DIT'TIT'	DHAGE TIT'	KIT'DHA TIT'
DIRIDIRI KIT'T'K	TAKITIRI KIT'T'K	T'th K'DASN	DHAS DHAS
DHAS SS	DHIT DHIT	DIT'TIT'	DHAGE TIT'
KIT'DHA TIT'	DIRIDIRI KIT'T'K	TAKITIRI KIT'T'K	T'th K'DASN
DHASDHAS	DHAS SS	DHAS DHAS	DHAS SS
DHIT DHIT	DIT'TIT'	DHAGE TIT'	KIT'DHA TIT'
DIRIDIRI KIT'T'K	TAKITIRI KIT'T'K	T'th K'DASN	DHAS DHAS
DHAS SS	DHASDHAS	DHAS SS	DHASDHAS
DHA			
x			

NOTE:- In some of the compositions given above, the phrase DIRIDIRI KIT'T'K has been used. Until the phrase is properly practiced and set, one may play DHATIRI KIT'T'K in its place.

DIRI is a sequence of two strokes.

1) DI—This comprises of TI on the Tabla, either in the center of the Shaayee with the Middle finger only for the B'nd Baaz OR with the full Right Half of the Palm on the Shaayee, together with GE on the Baayaan. (For Right Hand on Tabla)

2) RI—This comprises of T' with the Forefinger in the center of the Shaayee on the Tabla in case of the B'nd Baaz OR with the Left Half of the Palm on the Shaayee. There is no stroke on the Baayaan. (For Right Hand on Tabla)

NOTE:- Refer Diagram on Page No. 138 " Position of Palm to play DIRI" also refered figs. 30 & 31

Dupalli: This is a G'th with two different Layas eg. Dedhi and Dugun or Paune Dugun and Dugun.

*(DHING' DIN	N' GIN'	DHING' DIN	N' GIN'	T'th KIT'	DHAS TIRIKIT'
DHING' DIN	N' GIN')*	#[G'DA SN	G'DA SN	TAKI TIRI	KIT' T'K
DHATIRI KIT'T'K		TATIRI KIT'T'K	TATIRI KIT'T'K	T'thS K'DASN]#
DHA *(NOTE:- DHING' DIN is to be played as DHIN N' DHIN.)*

x

In the above composition, bols marked with * are in Tishra Jaati and bols marked with # are in Chatushra Jaati.

This composition can be expanded into a "Farmaishi" Chakradaar by repeating the last Four Matras & DHA three times & then the whole thing three times.

In case of a Farmaishi Chakradaar, when the composition is played the first time, the 1st DHA of the Tihaai falls on the Sum. When played the second time, the 2nd DHA comes to Sum & the last DHA of the Tihaai falls on Sum when played the third time. "Farmaish is a Urdu word which means "Request".

Tripalli: This is a G'th with three different Layas e.g. Dedhi, Dugun, Tigun

DHA G' S	T'th KI T'	DHA GE TI	T' KI T' ⎫ Dedhi or Tishra
DHA TIRI KIT'	DI KI T'	K'th TA GE	DI G' N' ⎭
(TI RI KI T'	DHATIRI KIT'DI	KIT' K'th TA	G' DI G' N) Dugun or Chatushra
(DHAG' S T'thKIT'	DHAGE TIT'KIT'	DHATIRIKIT' DIKIT'	K'thTAG' DI G' N') Tigun
			or double of Dedhi
DHA

x

Some Kaidas in Teen Taal

The "Prastaar" or development of the following Kaidas is on similar lines as shown earlier, ending with an appropriate Tihaai

1) DHA TI	T' DHA	TI T'	DHA DHA	TI T'	DHA GE	TIN NA	KI NA
TA TI	T' TA	TI T'	DHA DHA	TI T'	DHA GE	DHIN NA	GI NA

2) DHA TI   DHA GE   NA DHA TIRIKIT' DHA TI   DHA GE   TIN NA   KI NA
TA TI   TA KE   NA DHA TIRIKIT' DHA TI   DHA GE   DHIN NA GI NA

3) DHA TIRI KIT' DHA DHIN NA DHA DHA DHIN NA DHA TI   DHA DHA DHIN NA
DHA TI   S DHA   TIRI KIT' DHADHA TIRI KIT' DHA TI   DHA DHA TIN NA
TA TIRI   KIT' TA   TIN NA   TA TA   TIN NA   TA TI   TATA   TIN NA
DHA TI   S DHA   TIRI KIT' DHA DHA TIRI KIT' DHA TI   DHA DHA DHI NNA

4) DHIN NA S DHA   TIRI KIT' DHIN NA KID' NAK' TIRI KIT' T'K T'K TIRI KIT'
TINNA   S TA   TIRI KIT' DHIN NA   KID' NAK' TIRI KIT' T'K T'K TIRI KIT'

5) DHA S   TIRI KIT' DHIN NA GINA   DHA GE TIRI KIT' DHIN NA GI NA
DHA GE   NA DHA   TIRI KIT' DHIN N'   DHA GE TIRI KIT' TIN NA   KI NA
Khaali——

6) DHA TIRI   KIT'DHA   TI T'   GI NA   TI T'   GI N'   DHIN NA   GINA
TI T'   TIT'   DHA TIRI   KIT'DHA   TI T'   GI N'   TIN NA   KI NA
Khaali——

7) GI NA   TI T'   GI NA   DHA GE   DHIN NA   GI NA   TI T'   GI NA
DHA TIRI   KIT'DHA GI NA   TI T'   GI NA   DHA GE TIN NA   KI NA
Khaali——

8) DHA TIRI   KIT' T'K TIRI KIT' DHA TI   GI NA   DHA GE   TIN NA   KI NA
TA TIRI   KIT' T'K TIRI KIT' DHA TI   GI NA   DHA GE   DHIN NA GI NA

9) DHA S   GI GI   TI T'   GIN'   DHIN NA   GI NA   DHA GE TI T'
GI GI   TI T'   DHA S   GI GI   TI T'   GI N'   TIN NA   KINA
Khali——

10) DHINN'GIDA   SN'DHAS   GID'NAG'   DHINN'GIN'
DHASGID'   NAG'DHAS   GID'NAG'   TINN'KIN'
TINN'KIDAS   SN'TAS   KID'NAK'   TINN'KIN'
DHASGID'   NAG'DHAS   GID'NAG'   DHINN'GIN'

This is a Kaida of Lucknow Gharana; to be played in Khula Baaz

Rela: (With DIRI DIRI)

1) DHA TIRI KIT' T'K DIRI DIRI KIT' T'K DHA TIRI KIT' T'K TIN NA   KIT' T'K
TA TIRI   KIT' T'K TIRI TIRI KIT' T'K DHA TIRI KIT' T'K DHIN NA KIT' T'K

2) DHA TIRI KIT' GIRI   DIRI DIRI   KIT' T'K   DHA TIRI   KIT' T'K   TIN NA   KIT' T'K
   TA TIRI   KIT' KIRI   TIRI TIRI   KIT' T'K   DHA TIRI   KIT' T'K   DHIN NA   KIT' T'K

3) In Mishra Jaati:-
   TIRI KIT' T'K   DIRIDIRI KIT'T'K   TIRI KIT' T'K   TINNA KIT'T'K
   TIRI KIT' T'K   TIRITIRI KIT'T'K   TIRI KIT' T'K   DHINNA KIT'T'K

Rela In Angushtan

1) DHIN N' DHIN N'   NAGE DHIN N'   NAGE DHIN N'   DHIN N' NA GE
   TIN N' TIN N'   NAKE TIN N'   NAGE DHIN N'   DHIN N' NA GE

2) DHIN N' GI N'   T'K T'K   DHIN N' GI N'   DHA DA GI N'
   TIN N' KI N'   T'K T'K   DHIN N' GI N'   DHA DA GI N'

Peshkaar In Delhi Gharana

1) DHAS SK'D   DHA TIRI   KIT' DHA   TI DHA
   TIRI KIT'   DHA TI   DHA DHA   DHIN NA
   KIT' DHA   TIRI KIT'   DHA TIRI   KIT' DHA
   TI DHA   DHA TI   DHA DHA   TIN NA......Khali

————Paltas (Variations) to be made as in a Kaida

2) DHA TI   DHA DHA   DHIN NA   DHA TI
   DHA SK'D   DHA TI   DHA DHA   TI DHA
   SK'D DHA   DHIN NA   T'K GIN'   DHA TI
   DHA SK'D   DHA TI   DHA DHA   TIN NA......Khali

————Paltas(Variations) to be made as in a Kaida

Assorted G'th's

1) DHAGE TIT'   KIT' DHAGE   TIT' KIT'   DHAS SS ⎫
   GID' NAG'   NAGE TIT'   GID' NAG'   T'thS SS ⎬ .....Baraabar (1:1)
                                                   ⎭
   (T'K TIRIKIT' DHA G'DASN SS   DHA TIRI KIT'   T'K G'DASN SS)......Dedhi

   (DHA TIRI KIT'DHA TIRI KIT' DHA S   GID' NAG' DHA TIRI   KIT' DHA TIRI KIT')
                                                             ....Dugun

   DHA   (A composition of Kudow Singh Pakhawaji)
   x

166

2) (DIRIDIRI KIT'T'K   T'thS KIT'DHA) x 3   SST'thKIT'   DHAS T'thKIT'

   DHAS SS   TIS T'S   K'thS TAS   SS GES   DIS GES   SSN'S   DHASSS

   (TIT'K'thTA   G'DI GIN'   DHAS TAS   K'thSDIRIDIRI   KIT'T'KT'thKIT'

   DHAS SS) x 3
   x

3) **DUPALLI FARMAISHI CHAKRAHDAR G'th (Ustad Sher Khan)**

   [DHASN'   DHATIT'   DHATIRIKIT'   DIKIT'   K'thTA GE   GETIT'   GISN'

   DASN'   K'thSTIT'   GIGI TIT'   DHAGETIT'   GIGITIT'

   (DIRIDIRIKIT'T'K   TAKITIRI KIT'T'K   T'thK'DASN   T'thK' DASN

   DHAS SS) x 3] x 3

Note : In the above G'th the first line and first matra of second line are in Dedhi.

4) **DUPALLI:**

   DHA TIRI KIT'   DHA S S   K'th S TI   T' KI T'   K'thTAK'th   TAK'thTA⎤

   K'th TI T'   TA GE N'   N'G'N'   G'N'G'   TA GE TI   T' KI T' ⎬Dedhi

   DHA TIRI KIT'   DI KI T'   K'th TA GE   DI G' N'...........................⎦

   (GINS T'RA   SN' DHAS   TIS K'thS   SST'S   DHAS SS   TIRI KIT') x 3 Dugun

   (No TIRIKIT' 3rd time)

5) K'thS DIRIDIRI   KIT' T'K T'thKIT'   DHAS DHATUN   STA K'thS

   SS TIT'   K'thTAG'DIN   G'N' NA G'   TIT' K'thT'th

   GINS T'RA   SN' DHAS   SS DIRIDIRI   KIT'T'K T'thKIT'

   DHAS DIRIDIRI   KIT'T'K T'thKIT'   DHAS DIRIDIRI   KIT'T'K T'thKIT'

   DHA
   x

6) K'thS DIRIDIRI   KIT'T'K T'thKIT'   DHAS SS   SS SS   SS DHAS

   TUNS TAS   K'thS SS   SS SS   SS TIT'   K'th T'th G'DIN   GIN' NAGE

   TIT'K'th T'th   GINS T'RA   SN'DHAS   (SS DIRIDIRI   KIT'T'K T'KIT'

   DHA SSS) x 3 with gap of SSSS

7) K'thS DIRIDIRI   KIT'T'K T'thKIT'   DHAS SS   SS SS   SS DHAS

   TUNSTAS   K'thS TIT'   K'th T'th G'DIN   GIN'NAGE   TIT' K'th T'th   GINS T'RA

   SN' DHAS   TUNS TAS   K'thS DHAS   TAS (K'thS   DIRIDIRI KIT'T'K

   T'th KIT' DHAS) x 4 bed'm (without gaps)

167

8) N'G DHITS TIRI   KIT'T'K TAS   TUNS TAS   K'th TA TUN TA   KIDN'K TIRIKIT'
T'K T'th KDASN   (KID'N'K TIRIKIT'   T'KDIRI DIRIKIT'   DHAS KDASN   DHAS—) x 3

9) TIRIKIT' DHITS   DIT' TIT' ĠESTIRI KIT'T'K   DIN'GIN'DHAS   TIRIKIT' T'KDIRI
DIRIKIT' DHAS   (GEGE TUNS   TAS KDASN   DHAS K'th T'th   DHAS—) x 3

[The above G'th is a composition of "Laya Bhaskar" Khaprumama Parvatkar]

NOTE:- In both the above compositions, the hyphen after DHA S indicates an incomplete Matra and the second part of the Tihaai should start there.

10) DIRIDIRI KITT'K   DHASSS   T'th S KIT   DHASSS   KIT' DHITS   SS TAS
GINS T'RA   SN' DHAS   GINS T'RA   SN' DHAS   TIS T'S   K'thS TAS
(DIRIDIRI KITT'K   TAS K'thS   SS TIS   SS T'S   SS TAS   G'DIN GIN' DHASSS) X 3

11) DIRIDIRI KITT'K   TASSS   K'th TA GEGE   TUNSSS   N'G'DHITS   SS K'th TA
GINS T'RA   SN'DHAS   TUNS TAS   K'thS TIS   T'S (DIRIDIRI
KIT'T'K T'thKIT'   DHAS—) X3

12) **EK DHARA** (All phrases played only once each)
DIRIDIRI KITT'K   TASSS   K'th TA GEGE   TUNSSS   N'G'DHITS   SS K'th TA
GINS T'RA   SN'DHAS   SS TUNS   SS TAS   SS K'thS   SS TIS   SS TS
SS DHAS   K'thS DIRIDIRI   KITT'K T'thKIT   DHA

13) **DU DHARA** (All phrases played twice each)
(DIRIDIRI KITT'K   TASSS) x 2   (K'th TA GEGE   TUNSSS) x 2 N'G' DHITS   SS N'G'
DHITSSS   (K'th TA GINS   T'RASN'   DHAS TUNS   TAS K'thS   TI S T S
DHA S K'th S   SS DIRIDIRI   KITT'K T'th KIT   DHAS DIRIDIRI
KITT'K T'th KIT   DHASSS) x 2

14) **TI DHARA** (All phrases played thrice each)
(DIRIDIRI KITT'K   TAS—) x 3   —SSS   SSSS   (K'th TA GEGE   TUNS –) x 3
—SSS   SSSS   (N'G' DHITS SS —) x 2   N'G'DHITS
[K'th TA GINS   T'RASN'   DHAS TUNS   TAS K'thS   DHAS TAS

K'thS DIRIDIRI   KITT'K T'th KIT   DHAS K'thS   DIRIDIRI KITT'K

T'th KIT DHAS   K'thS DIRIDIRI   KITT'K T'th KIT   DHASSS SSSS] *x 3*

15) BENARES G'th

TIRIKIT T'K'TA   GINA TIT'   DHAS K'D DHA   SN' K'thS   TUNS TUNS

NANA TIT'   GINA TIT'   GIN' TINNA   TIRIKIT' T'K' TIRI   KIT'T'K TIRIKIT'

GINS T'RA   SN'K'thS   (K'thT'th K'D DHA   TIT' DHAGE   TIRIKIT' T'K'DIRI

DIRIDIRI GID'N'G'   DHASSS   SS TAS   DHASSS) *x 3*

16) N'V' GRAH' KR' MIK

DIRIDIRIKITT'K   T'th KITDHA   K'thSSS   DHASSS   DIRIDIRI KITT'K

DHASSS   DIRIDIRI KITT'K   DHAS KIT   DHASSS   DIRIDIRI KITT'K

T'th KIT DHA   K'th SSS   (DIRIDIRI KITT'K   TA S KIT'   DHA SSS   TA SSS

DIRIDIRI KITT'K   TA S KIT'   DHA SSS) *x 3*

17) **KAMAALI G'th:** Kamaal means something that is extraordinary. In this case the phrase *K'D GE S N and G'D GE S N are played by both hands on the Tabla and Baayaan respectively and K'th is given by a clap of the hands in the position of a Namaskaar. This is a Chakradaar.

[DIT' TIT'	DHAGE TIT	K'D DHA TIT	K'th S TIT
G'DIN GIN'	TAGE TIRIKIT	TUNNA K'th T'th	DHA SSS
* K'D GE S	SS N G'D	GE SSS N	K'th SSS
(SS DIRIDIRI	KIT'T'K T'th KIT	DHA SSS) *x 3 gap of* SSSS] *x 3*	

18) DIRIDIRI KITT'K TA SSS   TASTIRI KITT'K   T'th SSS

TIT GIGI   N'K' DHIN N'   DHAGE TIRIKIT   TUNNA K'th T'th

GINA S GI   NA S GINA   DHAGE TIRIKIT   TUNNA K'th T'th

[(DIRIDIRI KITT'K) *x 6*   DHA SSS] *x 3*

19) DIRIDIRI KITT'K   TA SSS   TIRITIRI KITT'K   TA SSS

(DIRIDIRI KITT'K) *x 2*   TA SSS   DIRIDIRI KITT'K   TA S K'th T'th

GIN T'RA   SN'DHA S   DHIN S TA [DIRIDIRI KITT'K   TA S TIRI KITT'K

DIRIDIRI KITT'K TASDIRIDIRI   KIT'T'KTAS   DIRIDIRIKIT'T'K   TAS SS] *x 3*

20) {(DHIN N' DHIN NAGI N') x 2   T'K DHIN   N'T'K DHIN N'DHIN   NAGI N'}-Dedhi

(TIT K'th TA   KITT'K) x 2   (DIRIDIRI) x 2   GID'N'G'   TING'N G'

(DHA SSS   SS KIT'   TA SSS   SS KIT') x 2   (DIRIDIRI) x 2   GID'N'G'

TING'N'G'   (DIRIDIRI KIT'T'K   TA TIRI KIT'T'K   TA TIRI KIT'T'K

TUN NA KIT'T'K   DHA SS DI   S GE N S T'   DHA SSS) x 3

The last four lines are in Dugun Laya. TING'N'G' should be played as TIN N'N'G'

Paran

1) (DHAGE TIT') x 4   (TAKE TIT') x 4   (K'D DHATIT'   DHAGE TIT') x 2

(K'D DHA TIT') x 3   DHAGE TIT'   DHIT DHIT   (TIRI KIT'DHIT) x 2

DIT' TIT'   DIT' K'th TA S   N'DHA S   TIT'K'th TA

S N'TAS   DHIN S DHA S   KIT'T'K' DHA S   TIN S TA S   KIT'T'K' TA S

N'G'NA S   TIRIKIT' 'TAS   GE GE GE S   TIRI KIT' TA S   G'DIN GIN'

NA GE TIT'   G'DI GIN'   DHA SSS

[N'G'S N'   DHIT SSS   GE GE S N'   DHIT SSS

DHIT S T'GE   S N'DHIT S   T'GE S N'   DHIT S DHIT S   DHA SSS   SSSS] x 3

2) [(DHAGE TIT') x 4   (TAKE TIT') x 4   (K'D DHA TIT'   DHAGE TIT') x 2

(K'D DHA TIT') x 3   DHAGE TIT'   (K'th TIRI KIT'T'K   TAKE TIT') x 4

{K'th S TIT'   (K'th T'th) x 2   K'th TIRI KIT'T'K   TAKE TIT'

K'th TIRI KIT' DHIN   NA S DHATI   K'th S T'th DHA   TI K'th S T'th

DHA SSS   SSSS } x 3] x 3 Farmaishi Chakradaar

G'th by Zoravar Singh of Gwalior

DHAS SGE	T'K DING'	DHINNA SDHA	GEN' DHIN N'
DHAGE N' DHA	TIRIKIT' DHIN N'	DHAGE TIRIKIT'	TIN NA KINA
T'th KIT'T'th	KIT' TIN N'	KID'NAK'	TIN' KIN'
(DHA S K'th T'th) x 4			

Jod or Parallel G'th for above:

DHINS SDHIN	NA K' DHIN S	DHAGE TIRIKIT'	TUNNA 'K'th T'th
T'th KIT' T'th	KIT' DHAGE	TIRIKIT' DHIN NA	GID'NAG'
GE GE NA T'	GE GE T'th S	GE GE TUNNA	KID'NA K'
(T'K DHIN N') x 3	DHINA GIN'		

170

Ganesh Paran (Padhant or Recitation)

DHAGE TIT'	K'D DHA TIT'	K'th TIT'TA	GE N'DHA S
SHRI SHAN S	*K' R' SUT'*	*U' MA S N'N*	*S D' NA S*
SI S DHI PR'	*DA S Y' K'*	*SHRI S G' JA*	*S N' NA S*
K'th S TIT'	K'D DHA TIT'	K'th TIT'TA	GE N'TAGE
TIT' K'th TA	G'DIGIN	(*L'M S BO*	*S D'R'*
VI S GHNE	*S SH W'R'*)	*G'NE' S SH*	*G'N'P'TI*
J'G' S TR'	*S KSH' KA S*	*AA DI TW'M S*	*PR' NAA S M'*
DHA SSS	*PR' NAA S M'*	DHA SSS	*PR' NAA S M'* DHA x

Note : All words appearing in Italics are Sanskrit words. (All **underlined** "S" stand for gaps. Words in brackets are in Tishra Jaati.)

Bol to be played

DHAGE TIT	K'D DHA TIT'	K'th TIT TA	GEN' DHA S
DHIN S DHA S	K'D DHA TIT'	GINA K'DIN	G'DHIN NAS
DHIT S DIT'	TA S K'th T'th	T'th S K'D DHA	SN'DHA S
K'th TIT'	K'D DHA TIT'	K'th TIT TA	GEN' TAGE
TIT' K'th TA	G'DI GIN	(DHIN S TA	S K'th T'th
T'th S GI	NA TIT')	GINA S T'	GINA TIT'
DHIT DHIT S T'	S K'D DHA S	DHA K'th TUN S	*PR'NAA S M*
DHA SSS	*PR'NAA S M*	DHA SSS	*PR'NAA S M* DHA . x

....Words in brackets are in Dedhi

Paune Duguni (in Teen Taal)

Chalan:

DHATI K'DHIN NA GINA   DHA DHAGE TINNA KINA

TATI K'TINNA GINA   DHA DHAGE DHINNA GINA.

G'th (to be played in Khula Baaz)

1)   DHA S GINA S TIT'   GINA S TIT'TIT'   GINA S GID'N'G'   DHING'DHINNA SK'thT'th

K'th TIT'TAS K'thT'th   K'th TIT'TAGE TIT'   KIT'DHINS NANANANA

TIRIKIT'T'KDIRIDIRI KIT'T'K

171

2) TIRIKIT'T'K DIRIDIRIKIT'T'K   DIRIDIRI KIT'DHASGIN'   DHITS T'DHE S GIN'
DING'DHINNA SGIN' DHA S T' DHA S KIT'T'K (TIRIKIT'T'K DIRIDIRI KIT'T'K)X 3

Repeat Chalan

Rela

(TIRIKIT'T'K T'K G'DA S N   TIRIKIT'T'K TAKI TIRIKIT'T'K) *x 2*

TIRIKIT'T'K T'K K'DA S N   TIRIKIT'T'K TAKI TIRIKIT'T'K

TIRIKIT'T'K T'K G'DA S N   TIRIKIT'T'K TAKI TIRIKIT'T'K

Paltas as usual.

G'th: (to be played in Khula Baaz)

DHAGE N' DHAGE TIT'   TAGE N' TAGE TIT'·   K'D DHIT S DIT'TIT'

DHAGE N' TINNA K'th T'th   K'th TIT'TA S K'th T'th   K'th TIT'TAGE TIT'

K'D DHIT S DIT'TIT'   DHAGE N' TINNA K'th T'th   K'th TIT'TA S K'th T'th

K'th TIT'TAGE TIT'   (DHA SS SS GIN'   DHA SS GE T'K DHIN') *x 3*   DHA

Chakradaar: (from Khali in Vilambit Teentaal)

[DHAGE N' DHAGE TIT'   TAGE N' TAGE TIT'   K'D DHIN S NA S NA S

TIRIKIT'T'K TUN SSS   TIRIKIT'T'K TUN S NANA   TIRIKIT'T'KT'KTIRIKIT'T'K

TA SSS DIRIDIRI KIT'T'K   DHA SS GET'K DHIN'   <u>DHA</u> SSS TA SSS

DIRIDIRI KIT'T'K DHA SS GE   T'K DHIN'DHA SSS   TA SSS DIRIDIRI KIT'T'K

DHA SS GE T'KDHIN'   DHA SSS—] *x 3.*

The Underlined <u>DHA</u> *indicates the first Sum in this Farmaishi Chakradaar.*

G'th (by Haji Saheb)

DHIT S DHIT S	TIRIKIT' DHIT S	DIT'TIT'	GIGI TIT'
TIRIKIT'T'K TA	SS TIRIKIT'	DHE S K'DHE	S K'TIRIKIT'
DHIT S TA S	GIGI TIT'	GIGI TUN S	SS TIRIKIT'
DHIT SS DI	T'K'TA S	S TIT'K'	TA SSS
DIT'K DI	T'K'TA S	TIT'K'TI	T'K'TA S
GID'N'G'	TING'N'G'	GID'N'G'	TING'N'G'
TA SSS	SS KIT'T'K	TA SSS	DIRIDIRI KIT'T'K

TA SSS	SS KIT'T'K	TA SSS	DIRIDIRI KIT'T'K
TA SSS	SSSS	DIRIDIRI KIT'T'K	TA S DIRIDIRI
KITT'K TA S	DIRIDIRI KITT'T'K	TA SSS	SS KIT'T'K
(TA TIRIKIT' DIRI	DIRIDIRI KIT'T'K	TAKITIRI KIT'T'K) *x 2*	
TA TIRIKIT' DIRI	DIRIDIRI KIT'T'K	DHA	
		x	

Dedhi – Dugun G'th (Haji Saheb)

TISHRA JAATI

(DHA S N'	DHA TIT'	DHA TIRIKIT'	DIKIT'
K'th TAGE	DI N GIN'	N'G'N'	G'N'G'
TAGE TI	T'KIT'	DHAGE TI	T'KIT'
DHA TIRIKIT	DIKIT'	K'th TAGE	DI N GIN')

— *Once in one Aavartan of Vilambit*

CHATUSHRA JAATI

(DHA S N'DHA	TIT'DHA TIRI	KIT'DI KIT'	K'th TA GE DIN
GIN' N'G'	N'G' N'G'	TAGE TIT'	KIT'DHAGE
TIT'KIT'	DHA TIRIKIT'DI	KIT'K'th TA	GE DIN GIN')

—— *4 times in 3 Aavartans.*

DUGUN of TISHRA

(DHA SN' DHA TIT'   DHA TIRIKIT' DI KIT'   K'th TAGE DIN GIN'

N'G' N'G' N'G'   TAGE TIT'KIT'   DHAGE TIT'KIT'

DHA TIRIKIT'DIKIT'   K'th TAGE DIN GIN')—*Twice in 1 Avartan*

DUGUN of CHATUSHRA

(DHA S N'DHA TIT' DHA TIRI   KIT'DI KIT' K'th TAGE DIN

GIN'N'G' N'G' N'G'   TAGE TIT'KIT'DHAGE

TIT'KIT'DHA TIRIKIT' DI   KIT'K'th TA GE DIN GIN') —

—— *8 times in 3 Aavartans.*

CHOUGUN–Of TISHRA

(DHA S N'DHATIT' DHA TIRIKIT'DHI KIT' K'th TAGE DIN GIN' N'G' N'G' N'G'

TAGE TIT'KIT' DHAGE TIT'KIT'   DHATIRIKIT'DHI KIT' K'th TAGE DIN GIN')

—— *4 times in one Aavartan.*

NOTE :- One can see that if each stage is played only once , the total number of matras is 46. Thus if one were to play a DHA at the end of every stage with a half matra gap , this would add upto 4 x ½ = 2 matras , thereby making the total of 48 matras i.e. ; 3 Aavartans of Vilambit Teentaal.

Some Farmaishi G'ths

Anaghaat :

1)

DIT TIT'	DHAGE TIT'	K'D DHA TIT'	DHAGE TIT'	
DHAGE N'DHA	GE DIN GIN'	N'G'TIT'	K'th TA K'th TA	
K'th S TIT'	KIT'K'th S	T'DI KIT'	DHAGE TIT'	
K'D DHA S N'	DHA S K'th S	SS K'th S	SS K'th S	S x

2)

DHIT S DHIT S	TIRIKIT'DHIT S	DHAGE TIT'	TAGE TIT'	
K'D DHIT S TUN	GEN'NAG'	TIT'K'th TA	GI DIN GIN'	
TIT'K'th TA	S N'DHA S	TIT'K'th TA	GI DIN GIN'	
DHA SSS	TA SSS	DIRIDIRI K'th S	DIRIDIRI K'th S	S x

Sum:

NOTE :- This is a composition of Pandit Taranathji.

1)

(TIRIKIT'T'K T'K	TIRIKIT'TA SSS) X 3	DIRIDIRIKIT'T'K	TAKI TIRIKIT'T'K	
T'th S DIRIDIRI	KIT'T'K T'th KIT'	DHA S DIRIDIRI	K'th S DIRIDIRI	
K'th S DIRIDIRI	K'th S DIRIDIRI	K'th S DIRIDIRI	K'th S DIRIDIRI	K'th x

2) (*Chakradaar*)

[DIRIDIRI KIT'T'K	TA TIRIKIT'T'K	TUN S NA TIRI	KIT'T'K T'th KIT'
DHA S DIRIDIRI	K'th SSS	SS NA TIRI	KIT'T'K T'th KIT'
DHA S DIRIDIRI	K'th SSS	SS NA TIRI	KIT'T'K T'th KIT'
DHA S DIRIDIRI	K'th S -] x 3		

Ateet:

1)

KIT'T'K T'th S	KIT'T'K TIRIKIT'	T'K T'K TIRIKIT'	TINNA K'th S
(S DHIN DHINNA	NA DHIN DHINNA	NA DHIN DHINNA	
DHA S TINNA	K'th S—) x 3.........K'th falls after Sum.		

2)

TIRIKIT'DHIT S	SS DIRIDIRI	KIT'T'K T'th KIT	DHA SSS
DIRIDIRI KIT'T'K	TA TIRIKIT'T'K	TA TIRIKIT'T'K	T'th S K'DA S N S

SS DIRIDIRI	KIT'T'K T'thS	K'DA S N SSS	DHA S DIRIDIRI
KIT'T'K T'th S	K'DA S N SSS	DHA S DIRIDIRI	KIT'T'K T'th S
K'DA S N SSS	DHA.........*DHA falls after Sum.*		

L'pet:

1)
DHIT S DHIT S	TIRIKIT'DHIT S	SSSS	TIRIKIT'DHIT S
DHAGE TIT'	TAGE TIT'	SSSS	TAGE TIT'
K'D DHIT S DIN	GE N'N'G'	SSS DIN	GE N'N'G'
TIT'K'th TA	GE DIN GIN'	SSK'thTA	GE DIN GIN'
(TIRIKIT DHIT S	TAGE S N'	DHIT S TAGE	S N'DHIT S
TAGE S N'	DHA S -) *x 3*		

2)
DIRIDIRI KIT'DHA	GE N'DHAGE	TIT'K'th TI	T'TA S N'
TIT'K'th TI	T'TA S N'	DHA S DIRIDIRI	KIT'T'K TUN S
SS DIRIDIRI	KIT'T'K TUN S	NA TIRIKIT'T'K	DHIT S TA S
SS NA TIRI	KIT'T'K DHIT S	TA S K'th T'th	GIGI TIT'
SS TA S	K'th TA GIGI	TIT' GIN S	T'RA S N'
SS TIT'	GIN S T'RA	S N'DHA S	DHIN S TA S
(SS DIRIDIRI	KIT'T'K T'th KIT'	DHA SSS) *x 3*	

Panch Mukhi G'th (Panchayi Chakradaar) 25 DHA's (Also Farmaishi)

[DIT TIT'	DHAGE TIT'	(K'D DHA TIT'	DHAGE TIT') *x 2*
K'th TIT' DHA	SS K'th T'th	<u>DHA</u> SSS	K'th T'th <u>DHA</u> S
SS K'th T'th	<u>DHA</u> SSS	K'th T'th <u>DHA</u> S	SS K'th T'th
<u>DHAS</u>—] X 5——Be d'm			

Farmaishi Bol of 25 DHA's (Be d'm or without gap)

[DHIT S DHIT	TIRIKIT' DHIT	DHAGE TIT'	TAKI TIT'			
K'D DHIT S TUN	GEN'NAG'	TIT' K'th T'th	GI DI GIN			
DHA SSS	SS DHA S	SSSS	DHAS SS	SS DHAS	SSSS	DHAS-] *x 5*

Ustad Salari Khan Saheb's G'th

(DHIN N'NA	GE T'K) x 3	TIT' K'th	TA S N'
(DHIN N'NAGE	T'K DHIN N'	NAGE DHIN N'	NAGE T'K) x 2
TIT' K'th TA	KIT'T'K	TIT' K'th TA	KIT'T'K
DIRIDIRI	DIRIDIRI	GID'N'G'	TING'N'K'
(TA TIRIKIT'DIRI	DIRIDIRI GID'N'G'	TAKI TIRIKIT'T'K) X 2	
TA TIRIKIT'DIRI	DIRIDIRI GID'N'G'	DHA	

x

Ustad Munir Khan Saheb's G'th (" *Gaind Uchhaal*" – bouncing ball)

DHA S KIT'T'K	T'K' DHIN S	SS T'K'	T'K DHIN S
T'K'T'K'T'K'	TIRIKIT'T'K'	TIRIKIT'T'K'	T'K' DHIN S
T'K'T'K'TIN	S T'K'T'K'	TIN S TIT'	TIT'KIT'T'K
DIT'TIT'KIT'	T'K'DHIN S	T'K' DHIN S	T'K' DHIN S S

x

Ustad Amir Hussain Khan Saheb's G'th

DHIN S TA S	K'D DHA S N	DIRIDIRI KIT'T'K	T'th S KIT' DHA
DIRIDIRI KIT'T'K	T'th S DIRIDIRI	KIT'T'K T'th KIT'	DHA SSS
DHA S KIT'T'K	DHA S TIN S	NA S TIRIKIT'T'K	TUN SSS
DHIN TA S K'D	DHIN TA S K'D	DHIN TA S K'D	DHA SSS
(DHIN NA KIT'T'K	TA TIRIKIT'T'K	T'K' DHIN N'	T'K' T'K'
DHIN N'T'K'	DHA S -) X 3		

Assorted G'ths

1)
(T'th KIT' T'th KIT'	DHIN N' GID'N'G) X 2		
DHIN N'GIN'DHIN N'	GIN T'K' T'K'	DHIN N'GID N'G'	T'K G'DA S N
DHIN S NA	S DHA S	TIN S NA	S DHA S
DHIN S NA	S DHA S	DIRIDIRI KITT'K	TAKI TIRKITT'K

All in Tishra except the last 2 matras.

2)
[(GIN S TIRIKITT'K)x2 TAGE TIT'		K'th TA S GE	NA S DHA S
TUN S NA S	GE NA TUNNA	(DHA TUNNA DHA	TUNNA DHA TUN
NADHA TUNNA	DHASST'th	DHAS–)x3 *SSS SSSS*]x3 chakradaar	

176

Mohra

(1)
SS DHIT S	DIRIDIRI KIT'T'K	TA TIRIKIT'T'K	TIRIKIT'T'K T'K
TIRIKIT' TA TIRI	KIT'T'K TA S	TIRIKIT'T'K TA	S GE S NT'
(DHA SSS	TA SSS	TIRIKIT'T'K TA	S GE S NT') x 2 DHA

        x

(2)
SSS K'th	TA S DHA S	TUN S TIT'	K'th TA GIGI
TA S N'T'th	KIT' DHA S	K'D DHA TIT'	K'th S TIT'
(K'th S DIRIDIRI	KIT'T'K T'th KIT'	DHA SSS) x 3	

PR'NAAM G'th (VISHNU PARAN by Pandit Taranathji)

DIT'TIT'TIT'   TIRIKIT'T'K TA SS   *SHA* S *NTA* S *KA* S   *R'M* SS TIRIKIT

BHUJ'G'Sh'Y'N'M S DI KIT' DIT' DIT' *P'S DM'NA* S *BH* 'M S TIRIKIT'T'K DIT'TA

TIT *SURE* S *SH'* S *M* TIRIKIT DING'N' *VI* S *SHWA* SS *DHA*SR'M S G'G'N'S'DRUSH' M S

ME S *GH'V'* S *RN'M* S   TIRIKIT *SHUBHA* S *NG'M* S   DHAGE N'DIT' *L'*S

KSHMI SS *KA* S *NT'M* S   *K'M'L'N'Y'N'M* S   DHA GIN'*YO* S *GIBHIR*

DHYA S *N'G'M* S *Y'M* S   DIT' DIT' DHAGI TIT'   K'D DHA TIT' DHAGI TIT'

*V'*S *NDE* S *VI* S *SHNU* S   *BH'V'BH'Y'H'R'M* S S   *S'*S *RV'LO* S *K'EK'*

NA S *TH'M* S DHIT DHIT   (DIRIDIRI KIT'T'K T'K DA S N   SS SS *PR'NAAM*

DHA SSS -) x 3 *(Note : All words appearing in bold italics are from Sanskrit. First three matras are in Dedhi, next sixteen are in Mishra Jaati, remaining in Chatushra Jaati.)*

Bol to be played

DIT'TIT' TIT'   TIRIKIT'T'K TASS   DHIN S TA S K'th   TUN SS TIRIKIT'

DHAGE N'DHIN DHIN   DI KIT DIT'DIT'   DHA S K'D DHA S TIN

TIRIKIT'T'K DIT'TA S   TIT'K'D DHASTUNS   TIRIKIT'DIG'N'NAG'

DHIT SS DHAS TIN   GEGEN'GEGETUNS   DHAS GE NAS TUNS

TIRIKIT'DHIN NAS TINS   DHAGE N'DIT'DHA   K'DA N S TUN S TUN S

K'th TIT'NAG'DHIN'   DHAGE N'DHA S DHIT   DIRIDIRIKIT'DHASTUNS

DIT'TIT'DHAGI TIT'   K'DDHATIT'DHAGITIT'   DHINSDHINS DIT'TUN

DIT'TIT'K'thTASN'   TIRIKITT'K TA K'th TIT'K'th   TUN SSS DHITDHIT

(DIRIDIRI KITT'K T'K T'K DA S N   SS SS PRANAM   DHA SSS -) x 3

Taal Roopak

Matras :- 7   Taali on 4 , 6 , Khaali on 1

1	2	3		4	5		6	7
TIN	TIN	NA	I	DHIN	NA	I	DHIN	NA
0				1			2	

Dugun:

TIN TIN   NA DHIN   NA DHIN I NA TIN   TINNA I DHINNA   DHINNA

Chougun:

TINTIN NADHIN   NA DHINNA TIN   TINNA DHINNA I

DHINNA TIN TIN   NA DHINNA DHIN I NA TIN TINNA   DHINNA DHINNA

Tihaai:

S TIN TIN NA   DHINNA DHINNA   TIN SS TIN I

TINNA DHINNA   DHINNA TIN S I S TIN TINNA   DHINNA DHINNA

G'th (by Khaprumama Parvatkar)

TA S K'D   TA TIT'   TIN S N'   GIN'TIN   NA KIT'T'K   TIRIKIT'T'K   TA SS

TIT' KIT'   TAKI TIT'   TIRIKIT'T'K T'K   TIRIKIT' DHIN S N' TA S K'D TA TIT'

GIN'TINNA KIT'T'K   TIRIKIT'T'K T'K TIRIKIT'

(GIN'TINNA KIT'T'K   TIRIKIT'T'K T'K TIRIKIT'   TIN SS -) x 3

Note :- *In the above G'th , Matras 1 to 7 in the 1ˢᵗ line –* Dedhi
Matras 1 to 4 in the 2ⁿᵈ line – Dugun
Matras 5 onwards in the 2ⁿᵈ line –⎫ Tigun *i.e.*
Till end of Tihaai.....................⎬ double of 1ˢᵗ line

Peshkaar:

1) TE S K'D TIN TA   S TA TIN TA   KIT' TA TIN TA I DHE S K'D DHIN DHA

S DHA DHIN DHA I   DHIN DHIN DHA DHIN   DHA DHA DHIN DHA

2) (TE S K'D TIN TA) x 3 I S DHA DHIN DHA   KIT' DHA DHIN DHA I

DHIN DHIN DHA DHIN   DHA DHA DHIN DHA

178

3) (TE S K'D TE S K'D   TIN TA—) x 2 | DHE S K'D DHE S K'D

   DHIN SS DHA K'D DHA | DHIN DHIN DHA DHIN   DHA DHA DHIN DHA

4) TE S K'D TE S K'D   TE S K'D TIN TA   TE S K'D TE S K'D | DHIN DHADHE S K'D

   DHIN DHA S K'D DHA | DHIN DHIN DHA DHIN   DHA DHA DHIN DHA

5) TE S K'D TIN TA   K'D TIN TA S K'D TIN   TA S TIRIKIT'TIN TA |

   DHE S K'D DHINDHA   K'D DHIN DHA S K'D DHIN | DHA S K'D DHATI

   DHA DHA DHIN DHA

6) TE S K'D TIN TA   S TA TIN TIN   TA TIN TA TA | DHIN DHA KIT' T'K

   DHIN SS DHA S K'D DHA | DHIN DHIN DHA DHIN   DHA DHA DHIN DHA

7) KID'N'K TIRIKIT'   T'K T'K TIRIKIT'   S TA TIN TA | KIT' DHA DHIN DHA

   DHIN SS DHA S K'D DHA | DHIN DHIN DHA DHIN   DHA DHA DHIN DHA

8) KID'N'K TIRIKIT' T'K'T'K TIRIKIT'   TIN SS TA S K'D TA   S TA TIN TA |

   KID'N'K'TIRIKIT' T'K T'K TIRIKIT'   DHIN SS DHA S K'D DHA |

   DHIN DHIN DHA DHIN   DHA DHA DHIN DHA

9) KID'N'K TIRIKIT' T'K T'K TIRIKIT'   TIN SS TA S K'D TA

   KID'N'K TIRIKIT' T'K T'K TIRIKIT' | DHIN SS DHA S K'D DHA

   KID'N'K TIRIKIT' T'K T'K TIRIKIT' | DHIN DHIN DHA DHIN   DHA DHA DHIN DHA

10) KID'N'K TIRIKIT' T'K T'K TIRIKIT'   TIN TA KID'N'K TIRIKIT'

    T'K T'K TIRIKIT'TIN TA | KID'N'K TIRIKIT' T'K T'K TIRIKIT'

    DHIN SS DHA S K'D DHA | DHIN DHIN DHA DHIN   DHA DHA DHIN DHA

11) (KID'N'K TIRIKIT' T'K T'K TIRIKIT') x 3 | S DHA DHIN DHA KIT' DHA DHIN DHA |

    DHIN DHIN DHA DHIN   DHA DHA DHIN DHA

Tihaai:

   [KID'N'K TIRIKIT' T'K T'K TIRIKIT' S DHA DHIN SS DHA   S K'D DHA DHIN DHIN

   DHA DHIN DHA DHA   DHIN DHA TIN S -] x 3 Bed'm (*without gap*)

G'th

   TE S K'D TIN TA   KID'NAK' TIN'KIN'   TAKE TIRIKIT'TINNA KID'

   NAK'DING'DHINNA GIN'   DHAGE TIT'GIDA S N'   DHAGE NAK' TING NAK'

   TIT'K'th TA KIT' T'K'

   (DHA TIRIKIT'T'K TAS DHA TIRI   KIT'T'KTA S DHA TIRIKITT'K   TINSSS -) x 3

179

Thekas for Solo and accompaniment:

1) TIN SS K'D   TIN S TIN   TA S T'th S | DHIN SSS   DHA S GE S |
    DHIN SSS   DHA S DHA S

2) TIN S K'D   TIN S NA S   TIRIKIT' | DHIN SSS   TIRIKIT' |
    DHIN SSS   DHA S DHA S

Tihaais:

1) TIN S K'D   TIN S NA S   TIRIKIT' | DHATI S DHA   TIRIKIT' DHA DHA |
    TIN S DHA DHA   TIN S DHA DHA | TIN |

2) (DHATI S DHA   TIRIKIT' DHA DHA   TIN S -) *x 3*

3) (DHATI S DHA   TIRIKIT' DHADHA   TIN S DHADHA | TIN S DHADHA   TIN SSS) *x 3*

4) (NANATIT'K'thSTIRI   KIT'T'KTAGETIT'   K'thTIT'TAGEN'
    DHASDHASDHAS   TINSS SSS) x 3 - Tihaai in Dedhi

Kaida:

1) TA TIRI   KIT' TA   TIN NA | DHIN NA   TIRI KIT' | DHA DHA   DHIN NA |
    TA TIRI   KIT' TA   TIRI KIT' | DHIN NA   TIRI KIT' | DHA DHA   DHIN NA |
    (Dugun) ———
    TA TIRI KIT' TA   TIN NA DHIN NA   TIRI KIT' DHA DHA | DHIN NA TA TIRI
    KIT' TA TIRI KIT' | DHIN NA TIRI KIT'   DHA DHA DHIN NA |

2) TA TIRI KIT'TA   TINNA TA TIRI   KIT'TA TINNA | DHA TIRI KIT'DHA
    DHINNA TIRIKIT' | DHINNA TIRIKIT'   DHA DHA DHINNA

3) TA TIRI KIT'TA S   TIRIKIT' TA TIRI   KIT'TA S TINNA |
    DHA TIRI KIT' DHA   TIRIKIT' DHA DHA | DHINNA DHATI   DHADHA DHINNA

4) TA S TIRI KIT'TA   TINNA TA TIN   NA TA TINNA |
    DHA TIRI KIT' DHA   TIRIKIT' DHA DHA | DHINNA DHATI   DHADHA DHINNA

5) TA TIN NA TA   TINNA TA TIN   NA TA TINNA |
    DHA DHIN NA DHA   DHINNA DHA DHA | DHINNA DHATI   DHA DHA DHINNA

6) TA TIRI KIT'TA   TINNA TIRIKIT'   T'K T'K TIRIKIT' |
    DHA TIRI KIT'DHA   DHINNA TIRIKIT' | DHINNA TIRIKIT'   DHA DHA DHINNA

180

7) TIRIKIT' T'K TA   KIT'T'K TIRIKIT'   T'K T'K TIRIKIT' |

DHA TIRI KIT'DHA   DHINNA TIRIKIT' | DHINNA TIRIKIT'   DHA DHA DHINNA
Tihaai:

(TIRIKIT T'K T'K TIRIKIT DHADHA TIN S DHADHA TIN S DHADHA TIN SSS) X 3

Some more Kaidas

1) TAKE NATA   TIRIKIT'TAKE   TINNA KINA | DHAGE NADHA   TIRIKIT'DHIN' |

    DHAGE TIRIKIT'   DHINNA GINA |

2) DHA S TI T' DHA DHA TI T'   DHAGE DHINNA | GINA TI T' TI T' DHADHA |

    TI T' DHAGE   TINNA KINA |

    TA S TI T'   TA TA TI T'   TAKE TINNA | KINA TI T'   TI T' DHADHA |

    TI T' DHAGE   DHINNA GINA |

3) DHA S GI GI   TIT' GIN'   DHINNA GINA | T'K DHIN'   NAT'K GE |

    T'K TIN'   TINNA KINA | —— Khaali
Prastaar of the above Kaidas is to be done on the same lines as explained.

Aad Kaida

4) KINA TIT' KIN' TIN' TAKI NA TIN   NAK' TIN NA KINA | DHAGI NA TIN NA'K'

    DHIN' DHA DHA GIN' | DHA TIRIKIT' DI KIT' | GIN' DHIN NA GINA

5) TA TIRI KIT' TI   KIT' KIN'   TINNA KINA | DHA TIRI KIT' DI   KIT' GIN' |

    DHATI GIN'   DHINNA GINA |

Rela

1) GID'NAG' TIT'GID' NAG' TIT' | GID'NAG' TAGE TIT' | GID'NAG' TIT' TIT'

    KID'NAK' TIT' KID' NAK' TIT' | KID'NAK' TAGE TIT' | GID'NAG' TIT' TIT'

2) TA TIRIKIT' TIRI   TIRITIRI KID'N'K'   TA TIRI KID'N'K' | DHA TIRI KIT' DIRI

    DIRIDIRI GID'N'G' | DHA TIT' GID'N'G'   DHINNA GID'N'G' |

Chalan for Rela

3) TAKE NAT'   KIT'TIN'   NAKE TIN' | DHAGE NAT'   KIT' DHIN N' |

    DHAGE NA DHA   GE TIN N'TIN |

Raon

TA S KID' NAK' T'K   TIRIKIT TIN'TIN'   TATI KIN' TIN' TIN' |

DHA S GID' NAG' T'K   TIRIKIT' DHIN'DHIN' | DHATI GIN' DHIN' DHATI

GIN'DHIN' DHIN'DHIN' |

Tihaai: for 3rd Rela

[DHATI GIN' DHIN'DHATI   GIN'DHIN' DHATI GIN'   (DHATI GIN' DHIN'DHATI

GIN'TIN' TIN'TIN'   DHA S -) *x 3*] *x 3*

Dedhi – Dugun G'th (in Tishra Jaati)

T'th KIT'   TAGE N' TAGE TI | T'K'D DHA   TIT'K'D | DHA TIT'   DHAGE TI

T'DHAGE TIT'K'D DHATI T' | DHA TIRIKIT' DHAGE N' | DHAGE TIN NAKI N'

Tukdas and Mohras

1) DHATI S DHA   TI S DHATI   DHA TIRIKIT'T'K TA TIRIKIT'T'K TIRIKIT'T'K T'K
   TIRIKIT' (DHATI   DHA S) *x 9 times*

2) K'D DHA S N' DHAGE TIT' K'th S DHAGE   N'DHA TIRIKIT   DHA S TA S
   SS TIRIKIT   T'K TAGE N   TIN SSS   SSSS   TIRIKITT'K TA   GE N'TIN S
   SS SS   SS TIRIKIT'   T'K TAGE N'   TIN
                                               0

3) K'D DHA S N' DHAGE TIT' K'th S TIT' K'th SSS SS DHAGE N'DHA TIRIKIT'
   DHAGE N'DHA   TIRIKIT' DHAS TA S DHA S SS [(TIRIKIT' T'K TAGE N') *x 3*
   TIN SSS   SSSS   SS -] *x 3*

4) TIRIKIT'T'K T'K   TIRIKIT' TAKI TIRI   KIT'T'K TIRIKIT'   T'K T'K TIRIKIT'
   (DHA DHA DHA TIRI   KIT' DHA DHA DHA   TIRIKIT' DHA DHA   DHA S—) *x 3*

5) GIN TIRIKIT'T'K   TAGE TIT'   K'th TA S GE   NA S DHA S   TUN S NA S
   GE NA TUNNA   (DHA TUNNA DHA   TUNNA DHA TUN   NA S -) *x 9 times*

6) [DHA TIRIKIT'T'K   TA TIRIKIT'T'K   TIRIKIT'T'K T'K   TIRIKIT'TAKI TIRI
   KIT'T'K TIRIKIT'   T'K T'K TIRIKIT'   DHATI DHA S   S DHATI DHA
   SS DHATI DHA S -] *x 3*

7) DHAGE GE DHA GE GE DING' NANA NANA   NA NA KIT'T'K TIRIKIT'T'K DIRI
   KIT'T'K (DHATI   K'th S DHATI   K'DA S N DHATI   DHA S -) *x 3*

Chakradaar from (7)

8) [DHAGE GE DHA   GEGE DING' NANA NANA   NANA KIT'T'K (TIRIKIT'T'K DIRI
     KIT'T'K DHATI   K'th S DHATI   K'DA S N DHATI   DHA SSS) x 3] x 3

G'th Toda

1) DHA S GIN'   DHA G'S TUN   GIN'NAG' DHIN S TA S   K'th S TIT'   K'D DHA TIT'
     DHAGE N'DHA   G'TUN GIN'   NAG'TIT'   K'th TA K'th TA   K'th TIT' TA
     GE N'DHIT   T'GE S N'   DHA SSS
     [DIRIDIRI KIT'T'K   (TA S KIT'T'K) x 3   TA SSS] x 3

2) DHA G'S TUN   G'N'NAG'   TIT'K'th T'   K'D DHA S N'   DHA S K'D DHA
     S N'DHAGE   TIRIKIT'T'K TA   (K'th S TIT'   K'thT'th G'DI   G'N'NAG'
     SS DIRIDIRI   KIT'T'K TA S   SS TIRIKIT'   T'K TA K'th S   SS DIRIDIRI
     K'th S SS   SS DIRIDIRI   KIT'T'K T'th KIT'   DHA SSS) x 3

The above *G'th Toda (2)* can be played as a *Chakradaar* , playing the
bracketed portion only once each of the three times that the *G'th Toda*
is played.

<u>Mohra</u> (Nauhakka – 9 TINS)

DHA S TUN S   TA S K'th T'th   (*K'th S DIRIDIRI   KIT'T'K T'th KIT'   TIN SSS
SS DIRIDIRI   KIT'T'K T'th KIT'   TIN SSS   SS DIRIDIRI   KIT'T'K T'th KIT'
TIN SSS) x 3 * Not to play K'th the 2nd and 3rd time but leave the gap.

- ## K'maali Chakradaar

[DIT' TIT'   DHAGE TIT'   K'D DHA TIT'   K'th S TIT'   G'DIN GIN'
TAGE TIRIKIT'   TUNNA K'th T'th   DHA SSS   K'D GE   S SS N G'D
GE SSS N   K'th SSS   SS DIRIDIRI   KIT'T'K T'th KIT'
(DHA S DIRIDIRI   KIT'T'K T'th KIT') x 2   DHA SSS] x 3

- K'D GE SSS N – play with forefingers of both hands on the *Chanti*.
- G'D GE SS N – play with both palms on the Baayaan
- K'th :- clap with both hands in the form of a "*Namaskar*" (which is a
form of Greeting)

183

Tukda (1 , 2 , 3 TINS)

DHIT S DHIT S   DIT 'TIT'   DHAGI TIT'   K'D DHATIT'

DIRIDIRI KIT'T'K TAKI TIRIKIT'T'K TAKI TIRIKIT'T'K T'th K'DA SN   TIN SSS

DIRIDIRI KIT'T'K TAKI TIRIKIT'T'K TAKI TIRIKIT'T'K T'th K'DA SN (TIN SSS) x 2

DIRIDIRI KIT'T'K TAKI TIRIKIT'T'K TAKI TIRIKIT'T'K T'th K'DA SN (TIN SSS) x 3

Tukda

DIT' TIT'   DHAGI TIT'   K'D DHA TIT'   K'th S TIT'   K'th TA K'th TA

K'th TIT'TA   GE N'DHIT   (DIRIDIRI KIT'T'K   TA S K'th T'th   TIN S -) x 3

Anaaghaat

K'D DHIN S NA   GID'N'G   TIRIKIT'TINNA   KID'N'K   T'th KIT'DHA

S D'DHA S   (DIRIDIRI K'th S   DIRIDIRI K'th S   SSSS) x 2

DIRIDIRI K'th S   DIRIDIRI K'th S   S (Sum on S)
                                     0

Sum

K'th S TIT'   TAGE TIT'   K'thS TIRIKIT'T'K   TAGE TIT'   TUN TUN K'th TA

G'DI GIN'   (DIRIDIRI K'th S   SS TIRITIRI   K'th SSS) x 3   (Sum on K'th)

Ateet

DHAGE TIT'   TAGE TIT'   K'D DHA TIT'   DHAGE TIT' G'DIN GIN'

NAGE TIT'   K'th S TIT'   K'th S DIRIDIRI   KIT'T'K TAKI TIRI

KIT'T'K DHA S DIRIDIRI KIT'T'K   TAKI TIRIKIT'T'K   DHA S DIRIDIRI

KIT'T'K TAKA TIRI   KIT'T'K DHA   (DHA falls after Sum)
                     0

Paran:

DIT' TIT'   DHAGE TIT'   K'D DHA TIT'   DHAGE TIT'   (K'D DHA TIT') x 3

DHAGE TIT'   K'D DHA TIT'   DHAGE TIT'   K'D DHA TIT'   DHAGE TIT'

(K'D DHA TIT') x 3   DHAGE TIT'   DHA S K'D DHA   TIT' DHA S

K'D DHATIT'   DHAGE TIT'   DHA G'S T'   KIT' DHAGE   TIT'K'th TA

K'th TA K'th TA   K'th TIT' TA   GE N'DHIT S   T'GE S N'   DHA SSS

[{ DIRIDIRI KIT'T'K   (TAKI TIRIKIT'T'K) x 2 } x 2

DIRIDIRI KIT'T'K   T'th K'DA S N   TINS SS   SSSS] x 3

184

Taal Jhaptaal

Matras :- 10 , Taali on 1 , 3 , 8 Khaali on 6

1	2		3	4	5
DHIN x 1	NA	I	DHIN 2	DHIN	NA I

6	7		8	9	10
TIN 0	NA	I	DHIN 3	DHIN	NA I

Dugun

DHINNA x 1	DHIN DHIN	I	NA TIN 2	NA DHIN	DHINNA I
DHINNA 0	DHIN DHIN	I	NA TIN 3	NA DHIN	DHINNA I

Chougun

DHINNA DHINDHIN   NATINNADHIN I DHINNA DHINNA   DHINDHIN NA TIN
x
1

NADHIN DHINNA I

DHINNA DHINDHIN   NATINNADHIN I DHINNA DHINNA   DHINDHIN NA TIN
0   3

NA DHIN DHINNA I

Tihaai:

DHINNA DHIN DHIN   NA TINNA DHIN I DHINNA DHA DHA   DHA S DHINNA
DHIN DHINNA TIN   I NA DHIN DHINNA   DHA DHA DHA S I DHINNA DHIN DHIN
NA TINNA DHIN   DHINNA DHA DHA   DHIN
                                        x

185

Theka for Solo and Accompaniment :-

1	**2**	**3**	**4**	**5**
DHIN SSS	DHA S GE S I	DHIN SS K'D	DHIN S DHIN S	DHA S GE S I
x		2		
1				

6	**7**	**8**	**9**	**10**
TIN SSS	TA S T'th S I	DHIN SS K'D	DHIN S DHIN S	DHA S GE S I
0		3		

Paran:

DIT'TIT'   DHAGE TIT'   K'D DHA TIT'   DHAGE TIT'   K'D DHA TIT'

K'D DHA TIT'   K'D DHA TIT'   DHAGE TIT'   DHA S K'D DHA   TIT' DHA S

K'D DHA TIT'   DHAGE TIT'   DHAGE DINGE   NAGE TIT'   K'th S TIRIKIT'T'K

TAGE TIT'   GIN'S TA   S D'DHIT S   TAGE'S N'   DHIT S TA S   KIT'DHITS

DHITS DHITS   TAGESN'   DHITS TAS   (K'th TIT'TA   GEN'TAGE

TIT'GE DHIT   S TA S N'   DHA SSS   K'thTA K'th TA) x 2

K'th TIT'TA   GEN'TAGE   TIT'GE DHIT   S TA S N'   DHIN

Peshkaar

1)	DHE S K'D DHINDHA	S DHA DHINDHA	KIT'DHA DHINDHA
	x		2
	1		
	DHINDHIN DHADHIN	DHADHA TINTA	
	TE S K'D TINTA	S TA TINTA	KIT'DHA DHINDHA
	0		3
	DHINDHIN DHA DHIN	DHADHA DHINDHA	
2)	(DHE S K'D DHINDHA	S DHA DHINDHA) x 2	KIT'DHA DHINDHA
	DHE S K'D DHINDHA	S DHA DHINDHA	KIT'DHA DHINDHA
	DHINDHIN DHADHIN	DHADHA TINTA	——Khaali
3)	(DHE S K'D DHINDHA) x 3	S DHA DHINDHA	KIT' DHA DHINDHA
	DHE S K'D DHINDHA	S DHA DHINDHA	KIT'DHA DHINDHA
	DHINDHIN DHADHIN	DHADHA TINTA	——Khaali

4) DHE S K'D DHE S K'D   DHINDHA DHE S K'D   DHE S K'D DHINDHA

    DHINDHIN DHADHIN   DHADHA TINTA   ————Khaali

5) DHE S K'D DHINDHA   K'D DHINDHA S K'D DHIN   DHATIRIKIT DHINDHA

    DHIN DHIN DHA DHIN   DHA DHATINTA   ————Khaali

6) KID'N'K TIRIKIT'T'K T'K TIRIKIT'   DHIN SS DHA S K'D DHA

    KIT'DHA DHINDHA   DHINDHIN DHA DHIN   DHADHA TINTA ————Khaali

7) (KID'N'K TIRIKIT' T'K T'K TIRIKIT'   DHIN SS DHA S K'D DHA) x 3

    S DHA DHIN DHA   KIT DHA DHIN DHA   DHIN DHIN DHA DHIN

    DHA DHA TINTA   ————Khaali

8) (KID'N'K TIRIKIT' T'K T'K TIRIKIT'   DHIN DHA -) x 2

    DHIN DHIN DHA DHIN   DHA DHA TIN TA   ———— Khaali

9) (KID'N'K TIRIKIT' T'K T'K TIRIKIT') x 3   DHINDHIN DHADHIN   DHADHA TINTA
    ————Khali

Tihaai:

    [KID'N'K TIRIKIT' T'K T'K TIRIKIT'   DHINDHIN DHADHIN

    DHADHA TINTA   DHIN S -] x 3

Kaida:

1) DHA S GID'NAG' TIRIKITT'K T'K TIRIKIT' DHATI. GINA DHAGE TINNA KINA

    TA S KID'NAK'   TIRIKITT'K T'K TIRIKIT' DHATI GINA DHAGE DHINNA GINA

2) (DHA S GID'NAG'   TIRIKIT'T'K T'K   TIRIKIT'—) x 3 —DHATI

    GINA DHAGE   TINNA KINA   ———— Khaali

3) DHA S GID'NAG' TIRIKIT'T'K T'K TIRIKIT' DHA S SS TIRIKIT' T'K T'K TIRIKIT'

    DHA S GID'N'G TIRIKIT'T'K T'K TIRIKIT' DHATI GINA DHAGE TINNA KINA
    ———— Khaali

4) (DHA S GID'NAG'   TIRIKIT' —) x 3 – DHA S followed by theme (first line of Kaida)
    ———— Khaali

5) (DHA S GID'NAG') x 3   TIRIKIT'T'K TIRI   KIT'T'K TIRIKIT' followed by theme
    ———— Khaali

6) DHA S GID'NAG'   TIRIKIT'T'K T'K TIRIKIT' DHA TIRI KIT'T'K TIRIKIT'

    T'K T'K TIRIKIT'   followed by theme———— Khaali

7) (DHA TIRIKIT'T'K   TIRIKIT'T'K T'K   TIRIKIT' –) x 2

DHA TIRIKIT'T'K   TIRIKIT'T'K T'K TIRIKIT' DHATI   GINA DHAGE   TINNA KINA
——— Khaali

8) TIRIKIT'T'K T'K   TIRIKIT' TAKI TIRI   KIT'T'K TIRIKIT' (T'K T'K TIRIKIT') x 2

followed by theme——— Khaali

9) [(TIRIKIT'T'K T'K) x 2   TIRIKIT' –] x 3 DHATI   GINA DHAGE   TINNA KINA
——— Khaali

10) (DHATI GINA   DHAGE TINNA   KINA TATI   KINA DHAGE   DHINNA GINA) x 2

Tihaai :

[DHA TIRIKIT'T'K   TIRIKIT'T'K T'K   TIRIKIT' (DHATI   GINA DHAGE   TINNA KINA
DHA SSS) x 3   SSSS] x 3

More Kaidas in Jhaptaal

1)   DHA S GIGI   TIT' KIT'   DHA S GIGI   TIT' GIN'   TINNA KINA
      TA S KIKI   TIT' KIT'   DHA S GIGI   TIT' GIN'   DHINNA GINA

2)   DHATI T'DHA   TIT'DHADHA   TIT'DHADHA   TIT'DHAGE   TINNA KINA
      TATI T'TA   TIT'DHA DHA   TIT'DHA DHA   TIT'DHAGE   DHINNA GINA

3)   DHATIRIKIT'DHI KIT'GINA   DHATI GINA   DHATI GIN'   TINNA KINA
      TA TIRIKIT' TI KIT' KINA   DHATI GINA   DHATI GIN'   DHINNA GINA

Aad

4)   DHA TIRIKIT'   T'K TIRIKIT'   DHATI GE   TIN GINA   DHA TIRIKIT'
      T'K TIRIKIT'   DHATI GE   NA DHATI   DHATI GE   TIN KINA——Khaali

Relas

1) (based on above Kaida no : 3)

DHATIRIKIT'DIRI   DIRIDIRI GID'N'G   DHATIRI GID'N'G   DHATIRI GID'N'G
TINNA KID'N'K

TATIRIKIT' TIRI   TIRITIRI KID'N'K   DHATIRI GID'N'G   DHATIRI GID'N'G
DHINNA GID'N'G

2) GID'N'G   TIT'GID'   N'G TIT'   GID'N'G   TAGE TIT'
    GID'N'G   TIT'TIT'   GID'N'G   TIT'GID'   N'G TIT' ——— Khaali

188

3) DHAS GID'   NAG' TIRI   KIT'T'K   DHATI   DHAS GID'

NAG' DHAS   GID'NAG'   TIRIKIT'   T'KT'K   TIRIKIT'——Khaali

Challan

DHAGE NATI   T' T'th KIT'   DHIN'DHAGE   N'DHA GEDHA   GE TIN'TIN

TAKE NATI   T' T'th KIT'   DHIN'DHAGE   N'DHAGEDHA   GE DHIN'DHIN

Raon for above Challan

DHAGID'NAG'TIRI   KIT'T'KTIRIKIT'   DHIN'DHIN' DHATI GIN'

DHIN'DHATI GIN'DHATI   GIN'TIN' TIN'TIN' ——— Khaali

Tukdas

1) K'th S TIT'   GIGI TIT'   DHATIRIKIT'DHI   KIT'K'thT'th   G'DI GIN'

DHA SSS   (DHA TIRIKIT'T'K   TAS KES   SS GEN S   SS T'S   DHA SSS) x 3

2) DHA TIRIKIT' DHI   KIT' K'th T'th   GIN'ST'RA   SN DHATI   K'thS TIT'

DHA SSS   [(TI S T'S) x 2   SS DHATIRI   KIT'T'K TA SN   DHA SSS] x 3

3) DHA TIRIKIT'T'K   TA S K'th S   SS DHA S   TUN S TA S   KIT'DHA S

TUN S TA S   [(DHA TIRIKIT'T'K   TA S -) x 2   DHA TIRIKIT'T'K   TA SSS] x 3

4) DHAGE TIT'   G'DA S N S   DHA S DIRIDIRI   KIT'T'K TA S   TIT'TIT'

GIGI TIT'   K'th TIRIKIT'T'K   TA S GIGI   TIT' DIRIDIRI   KIT'T'K DHAGE

TIT' KIT'   DHAGE TIT'   T'th S DIRIDIRI   KIT'T'K TAKI TIRI

KIT'T'K (TIRIKIT'   T'K DIRIDIRI KIT   DHA S -) x 3

5) DHIT SSS   SS DIRIDIRI   KIT'T'K T'th KIT'   DHA SSS   DIRIDIRI KIT'T'K

TAKI TIRIKIT'T'K   T'th SSS   (DIRIDIRI KIT'T'K   TAKI TIRIKIT'T'K

T'th S DIRIDIRI   KIT'T'K T'th KIT'   DHA S -) x 3

6) (DHITS DHITS) x 2   (DIT' TIT') x 2   (DHAGE TIT'   K'D DHA TIT') x 2

K'th TIT' TA   S N'DHA S   TIT' K'th TA   G'DIN GIN'   DHA TIRIKIT'T'K

TA S TA S   TA S K'D DHIN   NA S DHA S   DHA S K'D TIN   NA S TA S

TA S K'D DHIN   NA S DHA S   DHA
                                     x

189

Be d'm Chakradaars

1) [DHIT S DHIT S   DIT' TIT'   DHAGE TIT'   **K'D DHA TIT'**   DHA TIRIKIT'T'K
TA S TA S   (TA S K'D DHIN   NA S DHA S   DHA S)—*x 3*]—*x 3*

2) [GIN TIRIKIT'T'K   TAGE TIT'   K'th TA S GI   NA S DHA S   TUN S NA S
GENA TUNNA   DHA TUNNA DHA   **TUNNA DHA TUN**   NA S DHA TUN
NA DHA TUNNA   DHA TUNNA S   **DHA TUNNA DHA**   TUNNA DHA TUN
NA S -] *x 3*

3) [DIRIDIRI KIT'T'K   T'th KIT' DHA S   K'th S TI S   T'S GE S   GE S TI S
T'S DHA S   TUN S TA S   K'th S DIRIDIRI   KIT'T'K T'th KIT'   DHA S DIRIDIRI
KIT'T'K T'th KIT'   DHA S DIRIDIRI   KIT'T'K T'th KIT'   DHA S -] *x 3*

4) [DIT'TIT'   DHAGE TIT'   K'D DHA TIT'   K'th S TIT'   K'th T'th G'DIN
G'N'DHA S   TA S K'th S   TIT' K'th T'th   G'DIN G'N'A   DHA S TA
K'th S TIT'   K'th T'th G'DI   G'N'DHA S   TA S -] *x 3*

G'th's

1) DIT'TIT'   DHAGE TIT'   K'th TA S N'   K'th S TIT'   K'th SSS
(DHAGE N'   DHAGE TIT'   TAGE N'   TAGE TIT')   DHA SSS
SSSS   DHA S TIRI   KIT' DI S   KI S T'S   K'th S TA S
G'S DIN S   G'S N S   (DIRIDIRI KIT'T'K   **TAKI TIRIKIT'T'K**   DHIN S NA S
DHIN S DHIN S   NA S TIN S   NA S DHIN S   DHIN S NA S   DHA SSS) *x 3*

* *Bols in brackets in the second line are in Mishra Jaati ; thereafter all bols are in Chatashra Jaati.*

2) #(DHIN N'T'   K'DHIN N'   T'K'DHIN   N'T'K'   TIRIKIT'T'K
TA K'th S   TIT' K'D   DHA S N')   TIRIKIT'T'K TA   K'th S TIT'
K'D DHA S N   DHIT S TA S   [DIRIDIRI KIT'T'K   (TAKI TIRIKIT'T'K) *x 2*
TUNNA KIT'T'K   TA S K'D DHA   S N'TA S   K'D DHA S N   TA S K'D DHA
S N'TA S   DHA S -] *x 3*

Bols in brackets are in Tishra Jaati

3) DHIT S DHIT S   TIRIKIT' DHIT S   DHAGE TIT'   **TAGE TIT'**   K'D DHIT S TUN
GEN'NAG'   TIT' K'th TA   G'DIN GIN'   (DHA SSS   DHA SSS   DHA SSS

TIRIKIT' DHIT   T'GE S N') x 2   DHA SSS   DHA SSS   DHIN

4) DHA S K'D DHA S N'   (TIRIKIT'T'K TAGEN') x 2   (GINA TIT' DHA) x 2

K'th S TIT'KIT'   (K'th S TIT' KIT' TAGE   TIT' KIT' TAGE T'th

DIRIDIRIKIT'T'K TAGE TIRIKIT'T'K   TAGE TIRIKIT'T'K T'th K'DA S N

DHA SSS SSSS) x 3 (1st six matras in Tishra Jaati and the remaining in Chatushra Jaati.)

5) K'th TA K'th TIT'   K'th TA K'th TIT'   K'th S TIT' K'th   TA S K'th T'th

K'th S TIT'GIGITIT'   DHAGETIT' GIGITIT'   (DIRIDIRIKIT'T'K TAKITIRIKIT'T'K

TAKITIRIKIT'T'K T'th K'DA S N   DHA SSS T'th K'DA S N   DHA SSS T'th K'DA S N

DHASSS SSSS) x 3

NOTE : First four matras are in Khanda Jaati i.e. 1 ¼ speed, rest in Chatushra Jaati.

6) (T'KIT' T'KIT'   DHIN'GID'N'G) x 2   [DHIN'GIN'DHIN'   GIN'T'K T'K

DHIN'GID'N'G   T'K G'DA S N S   DHIN S NA   S DHA S   TIN S NA   S DHA S

DHIN S NA   S DHA S   DIRIDIRIKIT'T'K   TAKI TIRIKIT'T'K] x 3

In the above G'th, only the last two matras are in Chatushra Jaati and the rest in Tishra Jaati.

Chakradaars:

1) (Mishra Jaati)

[DHAGEN'DHAGE TIT'   TAGEN'TAGE TIT'   K'D DHIN S NA S NA S

TIRIKITT'K TUN SSS   TIRIKIT'T'K TUN S NA NA

TIRIKIT'T'K T'K T'K TIRIKIT'T'K   TA SSS GE SS NT'

(DHA SSS DIRIDIRIKIT'T'K   DHA SS GE T'K DHIN) x 3   DHA SSS -] x 3

2) [DHA SS T'KIT'T'K   DHA S DIT'TIT' DHAGE   TIT' K'D DHA TIT' K'th S

DHA TIRIKIT'T'K TA TIRIKIT'T'K   TIRIKIT'T'K T'K TIRIKIT' TAKI TIRI

KIT'T'K TIRIKIT'T'K T'K TIRIKIT'   (DHA TIT' GE S NT'DHA S

GE S NT'DHA S GE S NT'   DHA SSS -) x 3] x 3

Chakradaar Paran

3) [DHAGE TIT'TAGE TIT'   K'D DHA TIT' DHAGE TIT'   G'DINGIN'NAGE TIT'

K'th S TIT' K'th TA K'th TA   K'th TIRIKIT'T'K TAGE TIT'   K'th TIT' TAGEN'DIT'

DHAGE N'DIT' DHAGE N'   (DHA SSS DIRIDIRI K'th S   DIRIDIRI KIT'T'K TA S TA S

TA S K'DHIN NA S DHA S) x 3   DHA (1 matra gap)] x 3

191

Taal Adachoutaal

Matras 14 , Taali on 1 , 3 , 7 , 11. Khaali on 5 , 9 , 13.

1	2	3	4	5	6
DHIN	TIRIKIT' ǀ	DHIN	DHAGE	TUN	NA ǀ
x		2		0	
1					

7	8	9	10	11	12	13	14
T'th	TA	TIRIKIT'	DHIN ǀ	NA	DHIN	DHIN	NA ǀ
3		0		4		0	

Tihaai (81 Dha's)

[DHA TIRIKIT'T'K   TIRIKIT'T'K TA   (TIT'K'T'G'DING'N'
DHADHA DHATIT' K'T'G'DING'N'DHA DHADHA TIT'K'T' G'DINGIN'DHA DHA
DHA S -) *x 3* SSS] *x 3*

Peshkaar (Delhi Gharana)

DHATI	DHA DHA	DHINNA	DHA S K'D	DHATI	DHA DHA	TI S DHA
S K'D DHA	DHINNA	T'K GINA	DHA S K'D	DHATI	DHADHA	TINNA

——— Khaali

Paltas can be made as in a Kaida.

Farrukhabad / Lucknow

1)		
DHE S K'D DHIN DHA	S DHA DHIN DHA	KIT' DHA DHIN DHA
DHIN SS DHA S K'D DHA	DHINNA DHATI	DHA DHA DHINNA
T'K GIDA S N'DHA S	DHINNA DHATI	DHA S K'D DHATI
DHADHA DHINNA	S DHA S K'D DHA	DHINNA DHATI
DHAS K'D DHATI	DHADHA TINNA	

2)		
DHE S K'D DHINDHA	S DHA DHINDHA	KIT'DHA DHINDHA
DHIN SS DHA S K'D DHA	DHINNA DHATI	DHADHA DHINDHA
KIT'T'K TIN SS K'D	TINNA KIT'T'K	TIN'TINNA KINATAKE

TIRIKIT'TIN'TINNAKINA T'KGIDASN'DHAS TINSNAS GIDASN'

DHAS TINSNAS GIDA SN'DHAS TINSNAS DHA
                     x

Kaida

1) GINA TIT' GIN'TINNA TIT'GIN' TINNA K'DDHA TIT'GINA TIT'GIN'

TINNA KINA
——Khali

2) Angushthan Kaida

DHING' DHINNA GINA DHING' DHINNA GINA TIRIKIT' T'KTA

TIRIKIT'DHINNA GIN' DHING' DHINNA GINA ——Khali

3) DHATI T'DI T'DI T'DHA GENA DHINNA GINA

DIT' DHATI T'DI T'DHA GENA TINNA KINA——Khali

4) Aad Kaida

GINA TI T'GIN' TINNA S DHAGEN' DHA TIRIKIT' DIKIT' GINA K'

DHIN G' DHIN NAGIN' DHAGINA DHA TIRIKIT' DIKIT' GIN'TIN

NA KINA——Khali.

Rela

Chalan :

DHA DHE S K'D DHE S K'D DHIN NANA DHINNA GINA

(DHA DHE S K'D DHE S K'D DHIN NANA)—*x 2* ——Khaali

DHA SSS T'th DHIN TIRI KIT'T'K TA DHIN TIRIKIT'T'K DHA TIRIKIT'T'K

DHINTIRIKIT'T'K (DHIN TIRIKIT'T'K DHA TIRIKIT'T'K DHA TIRIKIT'T'K

DHINTIRIKIT'T'K)—*x 2* —Khali

Chakradaar: (Farmaishi in Drut)

[(DIRIDIRI KITT'K T'th KIT DHA S) *x 3* SS T'th KIT DHA SSS

DIRIDIRI KITT'K TAKI TIRIKITT'K (TIRIKITT'K T'K TIRIKIT TAKI TIRI

KITT'K TIRIKIT T'K T'K TIRIKIT DHA S -) *x 3*] *x 3* Bed'm

All the mohras, tukdas, chakradaars, G'ths and Parans as given in Roopak can be played in Drut Adachoutal

Chakradaar

[DIRIDIRI KITT'K   TA SSS   TIRITIRI KITT'K   TA SSS

(DIRIDIRI KITT'K   TAKI TIRIKITT'K   TAKI TIRIKITT'K   T'th K'DA S N

DHA SSS) *x 3*] *x 3*

G'th

DHIT S DHIT S   TIRIKIT DHIT   TAGE S N'   DHA S DHA S   DHA S DHA S

GIN TIRIKITT'K   (DHAGE TIT   TAKE TIT) *x 2*   DHIT TAGE   S N'DHIT S

TAGE S N'   DHA S K'th S   [(TA TIRIKIT DIRI   DIRIDIRI KITT'K

TAKI TIRIKITT'K) *x 2*   TA TIRIKIT DIRI   DIRIDIRI KITT'K   DHA SSS   SS K'th S] *x 3*
No K'th S, the third time.

G'th

T'th SS K'DA   S N'DHA S   KID'NAK   DHIT S TA S   DHA TIRIKIT' DI

KIT'K'th T'th   GIDA S N'   DHIT S TA   *(DHA S G'   DINGIN   DHA TIRIKIT'

DHA S N   K'D DHAN'   K'D DIT'   K'th TIT'   TAGEN   SS GI   D'N'G'

DHAGEN'   DHIN S N')   ** Bols in Brackets are in Dedhi*

DHA S DHA S   G'DING'N'   DHAGE NA DHA   TIRIKIT' DHINN'   DHA S GIN'

DHA S TIT'   K'th SSS   K'th SSS   [(DIRIDIRI KIT'T'K   TA S—) *x 3*   SSS]—*x3*

G'th

(DHA TIT'   DHA K'DA S N   S TIT'   DHA K'DA S N   DHA TIT'   DHA K'DA S N

DHA S DHA S GID'   N'G'TIRIKIT'   GID'N'G'T'K   T'KDHIN'GIN')—in Dedhi

DIRIDIRI KIT'T'K   TAKI TIRIKIT'T'K   TAKI TIRIKIT'T'K   TUNNA KIT'T'K

(DIRIDIRI KIT'T'KTAKI TIRI   KIT'T'K TAKI TIRIKIT'T'K

DIRIDIRI KIT'T'KTAKI TIRI   KIT'T'K T'th K'DA S N   DHA SSS) *x 3*—in double Dedhi

G'th

(DIRIDIRI KIT'T'K   T'th KIT'DHA) *x 3*   SS T'th KIT'   DHA SSS

TI S   T'K'   S TA   GE S   DI NG'   S N'   DHA S DIRIDIRI   KIT'T'K T'th KIT'

DHA S   TIT'   K'th TA   GE DIN   G' N'   DHA S DIRIDIRI   KIT'T'K T'th KIT'

DHA S   TIT' K'th TA   GE DIN G' N'   DHA S DIRIDIRI   KIT'T'K T'th KIT'

DHA
x

194

Taal Ektaal

Matras 12 , Taali on 1 , 5 , 9 , 11. Khaali on 3 , 7

1	2	3	4	5	6
DHIN	DHIN	DHAGE	TIRIKIT' I	TUN	NA
x		0		2	
1					

7	8	9	10	11	12
T'th	TIN I	DHAGE	TIRIKIT' I	DHIN	NA
0		3		4	

Dugun and Chougun can be made the same way as illustrated for Roopak and Jhaptaal.

Following Tihaai to be played at the end.

Tihaai :

DHIN DHIN DHAGE TIRIKIT'   TUNNA T'th TIN   DHAGE TIRIKIT' DHINNA

DHA DHA DHA S I   S DHIN DHIN DHAGE   TIRIKIT' TUNNA T'th

TIN DHAGE TIRIKIT' DHIN   NA DHA DHA DHA I   SS DHIN DHIN

DHAGE TIRIKIT' TUNNA I   T'th TIN DHAGE TIRIKIT'   DHINNA DHA DHA   DHA
                                                                      x

G'th

DIRIDIRI KIT'T'K   T'th KIT' DHAS   SS T'th KIT'   DHA SSS

(DHA TIRIKIT'   DI KIT'   K'th TAG'   DIGIN'   DHA SS   SSS

DHA TIRIKIT'   DI KIT'   K'th TAG'   DIGIN') In Dedhi

[GINS T'RA   SN' DHAS   (SS DIRIDIRI   KIT'T'K T'th KIT' DHA SSS) x 3   SSSS] x 3

Peshkaar

1) DHE S K'D DHIN DHA   S DHA DHATI   DHA DHA DHIN DHA

   T'K GIDA S N'DHA   DHIN NA DHATI   DHA DHA TIN TA ———Khaali

2) (DHE S K'D DHIN DHA   S DHA DHATI   DHA DHA DHIN DHA) x 3

   T'K GIDA S N'DHA   DHIN NA DHATI   DHA DHA TIN TA———Khaali

195

3) (DHE S K'D DHIN DHA   S DHA -) x 2

    DHE S K'D DHIN DHA   S DHA DHATI   DHA DHA DHIN DHA

followed by theme and Khaali

4) (DHE S K'D DHIN DHA) x 3 T'K GIDA S N'DHA   DHINNA DHATI DHA DHA TIN NA
    ————Khaali

5) DHE S K'D DHIN DHA   K'D DHIN DHA K'D DHIN   DHA DHA DHIN DHA

    T'K GIDA S N'DHA   DHINNA DHATI   DHA DHA TINNA ————Khaali

6) DHE S K'D DHIN DHA   S DHA DHATI   DHA DHA DHIN DHA

    T'K GIDA S N'DHA   DHIN NA DHATI   DHA DHA TIN NA

    KIT'T'K TIN TA   KIT'T'K TINN'TINNA   KINA TAKE TIT'KIT'

    T'K GIDA S N'DHA   DHINNA DHATI   DHA DHA DHINNA

7) S DHA S DHA   S DHA DHINNA   DHA DHA DHIN NA

    T'K GIDA S N'DHA   DHIN NA DHATI   DHA DHA TINNA

    TIN'TINNA KINA TAKE   TIT'KIT'TAKE TIT' TAKE TIRIKIT'TINNA KINA

    T'K GINA DHATI   DHA SSS DHATI   DHA SSS DHATI

8) SS DHA DHADHIN NA   SS DHA DHADHIN NA   DHATIDHA DHADHINNA

    SS DHA DHADHIN NA   T'K GIDA S N' DHADHIN NA   DHATIDHA DHATINNA

    TIN'TINNA KINA TAKE TIT'KIT'   TAKE TIT'TAKE TIRIKIT'TINNA KINA

    T'K GIDA S N'DHA TINNA   DHA S TIRIKIT' T'K GIDA S N'

    DHA TIN NA DHA S TIRIKIT'   T'K GIDA S N'DHA TINNA

Note :- No. 8 Fully in Dedhi

Chakradaar G'th: (in Dedhi)

    [DHE K'D DHIN DHA GID'N'G   DHIN'GIN'DHAGE TIRIKIT'DHINNA GID'

    NAG'DHING'DHINNA GINA DHAGE TIT'   GIDA S N DHAGE N'K'TING N'K'

    KIT'T'KTIT' K'Tth TA KIT'T'K   (TA S K'D DHIN NAS DHAS DHAS SS) x 3] x 3
                                                  gap of SS

Kaidas

1)	DHATI	S DHA	TI DHA	GENA	DHA TIRI	KIT'T'K
	DHATI	S DHA	TI DHA	GENA	TINNA	KINA – Khaali
2)	DHINNA	S DHA	GENA	DHA TIRI	KIT'DHIN	NA S
	DHA TIRI	KIT'DHA	GENA	DHAGE	TINNA	KINA – Khaali

196

3) DHA S	TIT'	DHATI	T'TI	T'DHA	TIT'
TIT'	DHA DHA	TIT'	DHAGE	TINNA	KINA – Khaali

4) DHA S	K'D DHA	TIT'	DHAGE	TIT'	K'D DHA
TIT'	TAGE TIRI	KIT'T'K	TIRIKIT'	T'K T'K	TIRIKIT'
DHAGE	TIT'	KIT'	DHAGE	TIT'	K'D DHA
TIT'	TAGE TIRI	KIT'T'K	TIRIKIT'	T'K T'K	TIRIKIT

————— Khaali

Aad Kaida:

5) DHAGEN'	DHA TIRIKIT'	DI KIT'	DHAGEN'	DHA TIRIKIT'	DI KIT'
GINA DHA	TI GINA	DHA TIRIKIT'	DI KIT'	GIN'TIN	NA KINA

————— Khaali

Rela:

Chalan:

1) (DHA S   DHIN DHIN   NA S   DHA S   TIN TIN   NA S) x 4

DHA TIRI GID'N'G'   DHIN TIRI GID'N'G'   DHA TIRI GID'N'G'

DHA TIRI GID'N'G'   TIN TIRI KID'N'K   TA TIRI KID'N'K } x 4

Paltas as usual....

Chalan:

2) DHA S	DHIN S	S DHA	S DHA	S TIN	SS
TA S	TIN S	S DHA	S DHA	S DHIN	SS

Rela :

DHA TIRIKIT'T'K	DHIN TIRIKIT'T'K	TIRIKIT' DHA TIRI
KIT'T'K DHA TIRI	KIT'T'K TIN TIRI	KIT'T'K TIRIKIT'—— Khaali

3) GID'N'G	TIT' TIT'	GID'N'G'	NAGE TIT'	GID'N'G'	TIT' GID'
N'G'TIT'	GID'N'G'	TAGE TIT'	GID'N'G'	TIT' GID'	N'G'TIT' —— Khaali

Mohras:

1) K'D DHA S DHA	TUNNA KIT'T'K	(DHA TIRIKIT'T'K	TIRIKIT'T'K T'K
TIRIKIT'DHADHA	DHA S -) x 3		

2) DHA TIRIKIT'T'K	TA TIRIKIT'T'K	TIRIKIT'T'K T'K	TIRIKIT'TAKITIRI
KIT'T'K (TIRIKIT'	T'K T'K TIRIKIT'	DHA DHA DHA S	S -) x 3

3) DHA TIT' DHA   TIT' DHA DHA   TIT' K'D DHA   TIT' (DHATI
T'DHA S N'   TIT' K'T'G'DIG'N'   DHA S -) x 3

4) DIRIDIRI K'th S   DIRIDIRI K'th S   DIRIDIRI K'th S   DIRIDIRI KIT'T'K
TAKI TIRIKIT'T'K   T'th S DIRIDIRI   KIT'T'K T'th KIT'   DHA S T'th S
DIRIDIRI KIT'T'K   T'th KIT' DHA S   T'th S DIRIDIRI   KIT'T'K T'th KIT'   DHA

Tukdas

1) DHIT S DHIT S   TIRIKIT' DHIT   DHAGE TIT'   TAGE TIT'   K'D DHIT S TUN
GEN'NAG'   TIT' K'th TA   G'DING'N'   (TIRIKIT' DHIT S   TAGE S N'
DHIT S TAGE   SN'DHIT S   TAGE S N'   DHA S -) x 3

2) (DHIT S DHIT S) x 2   (DIT' TIT') x 2   (DHAGE TIT'   K'D DHA TIT') x 2
(DIRIDIRI KIT'T'K   TA S TA S   TA S K'D DHIN   NA S DHA S
DHA SSS   SSSS) x 3

3) DHA SSS   DHIT S TA S   KIT' DHA S   DHIT S TA S   DHIT S DHIT S
TIRIKIT' DHIT S   DHA S K'D DHA   S N'DHA S   (TIRIKIT' DHIT S   T'DA S N'
DHA S T'DA S   S N'DHA S   T'DA S N'   DHA S -) x 3

4) GIN TIRIKIT'T'K   TAGE TIT'   K'th TA S GE   NA S DHA S   TUN S NA S
[GENA TUNNA   DHATUNNADHA   TUNNADHATUN   NADHATUNNA
DHA SS T'th   DHA SSS   SSSS] x 3

5) DIT' TIT'   DHAGE TIT'   K'D DHA TIT'   DHAGE TIT'   (K'D DHA TIT') x 3
DHAGE TIT'   K'D DHIT S DI   KIT'DHAGE   TIT' K'T'   G'DING'N' DHIT S TAGE
S N'DHA S   (K'th S DIRIDIRI   KIT'T'K T'th KIT'   DHA SS Th'   DHA S -) x 3

G'th's

1) (DIT' K'D   DHA TIT'   DIT' K'D   DHA TIT'   DHA TIRIKIT'   DI KIT'
K'th S DI   T' TIT') *All Bols in Brackets above are in Dedhi.*
DHA TIRIKIT' DI   KIT'K'th T'th   K'th S TIT'   K'D DHA TIT'   K'th TIT' TA
GEN'DHIT S   TAGE S N'   DHA SSS   DIRIDIRI   DIRIDIRI
TIRITIRI   TIRITIRI   (DIRIDIRI KIT'T'K   TAKI TIRIKIT'T'K
TAKI TIRIKIT'T'K   T'th S K'DA S N   NA DHIN DHIN NA   NA DHIN DHIN NA
NA TIN TIN NA   NA DHIN DHIN NA   DHA SSS   SSSS) x 3

198

2) K'th S DIRIDIRI   KIT'T'K T'th KIT'   DHA SSS   KIT'T'K DHA S   SS KIT'T'K

TA SSS   KIT'T'K DHA S   SS KIT'T'K   TA SSS   SSSS

[DHIT S DIRIDIRI   KIT'T'K TAKI TIRI   KIT'T'K TIRIKIT'   T'KT'K TIRIKIT

DHA SSS   SS (GE S   GE S GE S   DHA SSS) x 3] x 3

3) KIT'T'K TUN S   SS KIT'T'K   TUN SSS   NA NA KIT'T'K   T'th KIT' DHA S

SS TUN S   S GE S N T'   DHA SSS   DIRIDIRI KIT'T'K   T'th KIT' DHA

TUN S KIT'T'K   TIRIKIT'T'K TA   K'th TIRIKIT' DI   KIT' GIN S   T'RA S N'

(DHA S KIT'T'K   DHA SS TUN   S GE S N T') x 3   DHIN
                                                          x

4) (DHIN N' DHIN   NA GIN') x 2   (T'K DHIN   N'T'K   DHIN N'DHIN   NA GIN')
— Bols in both the brackets are in Dedhi

(TIT' K'th TA   KIT'T'K) x 2   (DIRIDIRI) x 2   GID'NAG'   TIN N'NAK'

(DHA SSS   SS KIT'   TA SSS   SS KIT') x 2   (DIRIDIRI) x 2   GID'NAG'

TIN N' NAK'   (DIRIDIRI KIT'T'K   TAKI TIRIKIT'T'K   TAKI TIRIKIT'T'K

TUNNA KIT'T'K   DHA SS TUN   S GE S N T'   DHA SSS) x 3

5) GINA S DHA   GIN'DHA TIRI   K'D DI KIT'   DHAGE TIT'   K'D DHIT S DI

KIT'K'th T'th   GIN TIRIKIT'T'K   TAGE TIT'   GIGI TIT'   GIGI TUN S

SS TIRIKIT'   T'K TA GIN'   TA KIT'T'K DIRI   DIRIDIRI KIT'T'K

DIRIDIRI KIT'T'K   TAKI TIRIKIT'T'K   * (DHA TA S N   DHA KIT'T'K

TIRIKIT'T'K   DIRIDIRI KIT'   DHA TUN NA   K'th S TIT')* SSSS

(DIRIDIRI KIT'T'K   TAKI TIRIKIT'T'K   TA S GE GE   DHA S GE GE   DHA S -) x 3

* All Bols in this Bracket are in Dedhi

6) DHAGE TIT'   TAGE TIT'   K'D DHA TIT'   K'th TA K'th S   DIRIDIRI KITT'K

TAKI TIRIKIT'T'K   SS DHA S   K'D DHA S N'   TIRIKIT'T'K TA

S N'TIRIKIT'   T'K TA S N   DHIT S TA S   K'D DHA TIT'   (K'th S TIT'

GE SSS   SS NA S   SSSS   TA SSS   SS DIRIDIRI   KIT'T'K T'th KIT'

DHA SSS) x 3

7) DHIT S DHIT S   DIT' TIT'   DHAGE TIT'   K'D DHA TIT'   K'D DHIT S DI

KIT'K'th TA   G'DIN GIN'   DHA S TA S   [DHA TIRIKIT' DI   KIT'K'th TA

G'DIN GIN'   (DHAGE   S N TA') x 3   DHA S -] x 3

199

8) DHA TIRIKIT'   DI KIT'   GIN S T'   RA S N'   T'S K'   DI KIT'
GE GE T'   D'S N'   (DHA GE GE   GE GE GE   TIRIKIT'T'K   DIRIDIRI KIT'
DHA SS   SSS) *x 3* The entire Bol is in Dedhi.

Paran

1) (DHAGE TIT'   K'D DHA TIT') *x 2*   K'th T'th K'D DHA   TIT'K'th T'th
K'D DHA TIT'   GIN'S TA   S D'DHIT S   TAGE S N'   DHIT S TA S
TIRIKIT' DITI   T'TAGE N'   DHIT S TA S   TIRIKIT' DITI   T'TAGE N'
(GIN'S TA   S D'DHIT S   TAGE S N'   DHIT S TA S   TIRIKIT' DIT'   T' TAGE N'
DHIT S TA S   GIGI TIT'   K'th S TIT'   G'DINGIN'   DHA SSS) *x 3*

2) DIRIDIRI KITT'K   T'th S KIT' DHA   DHIN S TA S   K'th S TIT'   K'D DHA S N'
DHAGE TIT'   (SS DI   T'DHAGE   TIT' K'D   DHA TIT'   DHA S K'D
DHA TIT'   K'th TIT   TAGEN') in Dedhi
TIT'K'D DHA   S N'DHA   DHIN S TA   K'th S TIT   DHAGE TIT'
K'D DHATIT'   DIRIDIRIKIT'T'K   T'th KIT'DHA   K'th S TIT'
K'thTAK'thTA   K'thS TIT'   K'D DHA S N   (DHA SSS   K'th TA K'th S
DIRIDIRI KIT'T'K   T'th S KIT'DHA   K'th SDIRIDIRI   KIT'T'KT'th SKIT'
DHA S TIT'   K'D DHAS N) *x 2*   DHA SSS   K'th TA K'th S   DIRIDIRI KITT'K
T'th S KIT DHA   K'th S DIRIDIRI   KITT'K T'th S KIT   DHIN

Chakradaars

1) [DIRIDIRI KITT'K   TA S K'th S   SS DHA S   TUN S TA S   KIT'DHA S
TUN S TA S   (DIRIDIRI KITT'K   TAS SS)—*x 3* SS] *x 3*

2) [GINA TIT   NA TIT'DHA   S TUN S TA   K'th SSS   TUN SSS   S NA SS
SSSS   GE SSS   (NA TIRIKITT'K   TA S K'th TA   K'th S DIRIDIRI
KITT'K T'th S KIT   DHA S DIRIDIRI   KITT'K T'th S KIT   DHA S DIRIDIRI
KITT'K T'th S KIT   DHA SSS) *x 3*   SSSS] *x 3*

3) [DIT DHAGE   TIT K'D DHA   S N'DHA S   K'th S TIT'   (NA DHIN DHIN NA
NA DHIN DHIN NA   NA TIN TIN NA   NA DHIN DHIN NA   DHA S DIRIDIRI
KITT'K T'th S KIT   DHA S -) *x 3*   SS SS] *x 3*

200

Shankh Tal

(Divisions of 4, 4, 2, 3)
Matras:- 13, Taali on 1, 5, 9, 11. Khaali on 3 & 7

1	2	3	4	5	6	7	8
DHIN	TIRIKIT'	DHIN	NA I	DHAGE	NA DHA	TIRIKIT'	TUN I
x		0		2		0	
1							

9	10	11	12	13
NA	TIRIKIT' I	DHIN	DHIN	NA I
3		4		

Chakradaar (Be d'm)

[DHA SST' KIT' T'K   DHA S DIT'   TIT' DHAGE   TIT' K'D DHA   TIT' K'th S

DHATIRIKIT'T'K   TATIRIKIT'T'K   TIRIKIT' T'KT'K   TIRIKIT'TAKITIRI

KIT'T'KTIRIKIT'   T'KT'KTIRIKIT'   DHA (TI T'GE   SNT' DHA S)—x 3]

Peshkaar

1) (FARRUKHABAD / LUCKNOW)

DHE SK'D DHINDHA   SK'D DHA DHINDHIN   DHADHA DHINDHA

KIT'DHA DHINDHA   SK'DDHA DHINDHIN   DHADHIN DHADHA

TINTA TE S K'D   TINTA S K'DTA   TINTIN TATA   TINTA KIT'DHA

DHINDHA SK'DDHA   DHINDHIN DHADHIN   DHADHA DHINDHA

——Paltas to be made as usual.

2) (DELHI)

DHATI DHADHA   DHINNA DHA S K'D   DHATI DHADHA   TI DHA S K'DDHA

T'K GINA DHASK'D   DHATI DHADHA   TINNA——Khaali.

3) (DELHI)

DHA S K'D DHATIRI   KIT'DHA TIRIKIT'   DHATI DHADHIN   NAKIT' DHATIRI

KIT'DHA DHATIRI   KIT'DHA TIDHA   TINNA——Khaali.

Kaidas:

1) DHATI   DHAGE   NADHA   TIRIKIT'   DHATI   DHAGE   DHINNA

   S DHA   TIDHA   GENA   DHAGE   TINNA   KINA——Khaali.

201

2) DHA S   K'D DHA   TIT'   GINA   TIT'   GINA   DHA S   K'D DHA
TIT'   GINA   DHAGE   TINNA   KINA——Khaali.

3) DHINNA   TIRIKIT'   DHINNA   DHES K'D   DHINNA   S DHA   TIRIKIT'
DHINNA   GINA   DHE S K'D   DHINNA   S DHA   TIRIKIT'—Khaali.

Rela:

1) GID'N'G'   TIT'GID'   N'G'TIT'   GID'N'G'   TAGE TIT'   GID'N'G'
TIT'TIT'   GID'N'G'   TIT'GID'   N'G'TIT'   GID'N'G'   TIT'G'D'
N'G'TIT'——Khaali.

2) Chalan :

DHATI   GIN'   DHA T'   K'DHI   KIT'   GIN'   DHATI   GIN'.
DHATI   GIN'   DHATI   GIN'   TIN'——Khaali

Rela:

DHATIRI   GID'N'G'   DHATIRI   KIT'DIRI   DIRIDIRI   GID'N'G'
DHATIRI   GID'N'G'   DHATIRI   GID'N'G'   DHATIRI   GID'N'G'
TIN'NAK'——Khaali

Tukdas :- (in Drut)

1) DIRIDIRIKIT'T'K   (T'th KIT'DHA) x 2   (K'th S DIRIDIRI   KIT'T'K T'thKIT'
DHA SST'   DHAS—) x 3

2) Chakradaar from above Tukda:-

[DIRIDIRIKIT'T'K   (T'th KIT'DHA) x 2   K'th S (DIRIDIRI   KIT'T'K T'thKIT'
DHA SST'   DHAS—) x 3 SS] x 3

3) DIRIDIRIKIT'T'K   T'th KIT'DHA   K'thS TI S   T'S GE S   GE S TI S   T' S DHA S
TUN S TA S   K'th S(DIRIDIRI KIT'T'K T'thKIT'   DHA—) x 3

4) [TIT'K'thTA   G'DING'N'   TI S T'S   K'thTA   G'S DIN S   G' S N'S   TI SSS
T' S K'thS   SS TA S   G' SSS   DIN S G'S   SS N'S   DHA SSS SS—] x 3

5) DHIT S DHIT S   DIT' TIT'   K'D DHA TIT'   (K'th TIRIKIT' DIKIT'   K'T'G'DING'N'
DHA SS T'   DHA S—) x 3 – Tihaai in Dedhi

6) DHA S TUN S   TA S KIT'T'K   TA S K'D DHA   S N'DHA   K'th S DIRIDIRI
KIT'T'K T'th S KIT' DHA SSS   (DHA TIRIKIT'   DIKIT'   K'th TAG'
DIGIN')*—in Dedhi (DHA S GE S   DIRIDIRI KIT'T'K'   TAKI TIRIKIT'T'K'
T'th S DIRIDIRI   KIT'T'K T'th KIT') x 3   DHA

7) GIN TIRIKIT'T'K   TAGE TIT'   K'th TA S GE   NA S DHA S   TUN S NA S
GENA TUNNA   (DHA TUN NA DHA   TUNNA DHA TUN   NA S–) x 3
(The hyphen after S is to show an incomplete Matra)

8) (DIRIDIRI KIT'T'K   T'th S KIT' DHA S) x 3   [DIRIDIRI KIT'T'K (TAKI TIRIKIT'T'K) x 2
T'KDA S N   DHAGE   S NT'   DHA S SS] x 3

G'th's

1) DHAGE TIT   K'D DHA TIT   K'th TIT TA   GEN'DHA S   SS TUN S   SS TA S
SS K'th S   TIT   DHAGE TIT   GID'A S N'   K'th S TI S   T'S DHA S
DIN S GE S   SS NT'   TIRIKITT'K T'K   TIRIKIT TAKI TIRI   KITT'K TIRIKIT
T'K T'K TIRIKIT   DIRIDIRI KITT'K   T'th S KIT DHA   SS GE S   SS NT'
DHA S GE S   SS NT'   DHA S GE S   SS NT'   DHA

2) DIRIDIRI KITT'K   T'th S KIT DHA S   TI S T'S   K'thS TA S   G'S DIN S
GI S N'S   TI SSS   T'S K'S   SS TA S   GE SSS   DIN S G'S
SSN'S   DHA SSS   (DIRIDIRI K'th S   DIRIDIRI KITT'K   TAKI TIRIKITT'K
T'th S K'DA S N   DHA S -) x 3

Chakradaars

1) Farmaishi

[DIRIDIRI KITT'K   T'th S KIT DHA S   SS DIRIDIRI   KITT'K T'th S KIT
DHA SSS   TA SSS   (DHA TIRIKIT   DIKIT   K'th TAGE   DING'N')* Dedhi
(DIRIDIRI KITT'K   TAKI TIRIKITT'K   T'th S K'DA S N   DHA SSS) x 3] x 3

2) [(DHIT S DHIT S) x 2   (DIT TIT) x 2   (DHAGE TIT   K'D DHA TIT) x 2
DIRIDIRI KITT'K   TA S TA S   TA S K'D DHIN   NA S DHA S
DHA S TA S   K'D DHIN NA   DHA S DHA S   TA S K'D DHIN '
NA S DHA S   DHA S -] x 3

203

Taal Pancham Savaari

Matras 15 , Taali on :-1;4;12 Khaali on :-8

1	2	3	4	5	6	7
DHIN	NA	DHIN NA Ι	T'th	DHIN DHIN	NA DHIN	DHINNA Ι
x 1			2			

8	9	10	11	12	13	14
TE S K'D	TINNA	KID'N'K	TINNA Ι	T'th TA	TIRIKIT' DHIN	NA DHIN
0				3		

15
DHINNA Ι

Tihaai:

[(DHA TIRIKIT'T'K   TA TIRIKIT'T'K   TIRIKIT'T'K T'K   TIRIKIT' TAKI TIRI

KIT'T'K TIRIKIT'   T'K T'K TIRIKIT'   DHA S -) x 3 SS SS] x 3

Peshkaar (Farrukhabad)

DHE S K'D DHIN DHA	S DHA DHATI	DHADHA DHINDHA
T'K GIDA S N DHA S	DHINNA DHATI	DHASK'D DHATI
DHA DHA TINNA	KIT'T'K TIN S K'D	TINNA KIT'T'K
TINN'TINNA KINA TAKE	TIRIKIT' TINN' TINNA KINA	T'K GIDA S N'DHA
TINNA S GIDA S N'	DHA TINNA GIDA	SN'DHA TINNA

————Prastaar as usual.

Peshkaar (Delhi)

1) DHATI DHA DHA   DHINNA DHA S K'D   DHATI DHA DHA   TI S DHA S K'D DHA

DHINNA T'K GIN'   DHATI DHA S K'D   DHATI DHA DHA   TINNA - —— Khaali

————Prastaar as usual.

2) DHA S K'D DHA TIRI   KIT' DHA S K'D DHA   TIRIKIT'DHATI

DHADHIN NAKIT'   DHATIRI KIT'DHA   DHATIRI KIT'TIRI

KIT'DHA TIDHA   TINNA - —— Khaali

————Prastaar as usual.

204

Kaidas

1) Aad (Ajrada)

GINA TIT'GIN'   TINNA S DHAGE N'   TINNA S DHAGE N'   GIN'TINNA KIN'
DHAGE N'TINNAK'   DHINN'DHA DHA GIN'   DHATI DHA GEN'TIN
NA KINA - ———Khaali

2) DHA S K'D DHA   TIT' DHAGE   TIT' K'D DHA   TIT'TIRIKIT'
T'KT'K TIRIKIT'   TAKI TIRIKIT'T'K   TIRIKIT'T'K T'K   TIRIKIT' - ——— Khaali

3) Poorab Kaida

(1) DHIN'T'K   DHIN'T'K   T'K DHIN'   T'K T'K   DIN'T'K   TIT'GID'
NAG'TING'   NAK' T'K   T'K DHIN'   T'K T'K   DHIN'T'K   T'K DHIN'
T'K TIT'   GID'NAK'   TING'NAK' —— Khaali

(2) (DHIN'T'K   DHIN'T'K   T'K DHIN'   T'K T'K   DHIN'T'K   TIT'GID'
NAG'TING'   NAK'—) x 3   T'K T'K   DHIN'T'K   T'K DHIN'   T'K T'K
DHIN'T'K   TIT'GID'   NAG'TING'   NAK' - —— Khaali

(3) (DHIN'T'K'   DHIN'T'K   T'K'DHIN'   T'K T'K   DHIN'T'K') x 3 ——
     – followed by(I) and Khaali

(4) (DHIN'T'K'   DHIN'T'K   T'K'DHIN'   T'K—) x 4   T'KT'K   followed by (I) and Khaali

(5) DHIN'T'K'   DHIN'T'K'   (T'K DHIN'   T'K—) x 4   T'KT'K   DHIN'T'K
DHIN'T'K   T'K DHIN'   T'K TIT'   GID'NAG'   TING'NAK' – Khaali

(6) (T'K T'K   DHIN'T'K)x2   T'K DHIN'   T'K T'K   DHIN'T'K   DHIN'T'K
T'K T'K   DHIN'T'K   DHIN'T'K   T'K DHIN'   T'K TIT'   GID'NAG'
TING'NAK' – Khaali

(7) (T'K T'K   DHIN T'K)x4   (T'K DHIN T'K -) x 4   T'K T'K
followed by theme ; i.e. (I) and then Khaali

(8) (T'K T'K   T'K DHIN'   T'K T'K   DHIN'T'K) x 2   T'K T'K
DHIN'T'K   DHIN'T'K   T'K DHIN'   T'K TIT'   GID'NAG'
TING'NAK' – Khaali

(9) (T'K T'K   T'K DHIN'T'K -) x 4   (TIT' GID'   NAG'TING'   NAK' -) x 2 – Khaali

(10)(T'K DHIN   T'K TIT'   GID'NAG'   TING'NAK') x 2   T'K T'K   DHIN'T'K
DHIN'T'K   T'K DHIN'   T'K TIT'   GID'NAG'   TING'NAK'—Khaali.

(11) (TIT'GID'   NAG' TING'   NA'K' -) *x 2*   TIT TIT   GID'NAG'   TING'NAK'
T'K T'K   DHIN'T'K   DHIN'T'K   T'K DHIN'   T'K TIT'   GID'NAG'
TING'NAK' – Khaali

Tihaai

[(T'K DHIN'   T'K -) *x 4*   T'K DHIN   T'K TIT'   GID'NAG'   TING'NAK'
DHAS TIT'   GID'N'G'   TING'NAK'   DHAS TIT'   GID'NAG'   TING'NAK'
DHA SSS   SST'th   DHAS SS   SSSS   SSSS] *x 3*

4) DHA S K'D DHA   TIT'GINA   DHAGE DHINNA   GINA DHA TIRI   KIT'T'K T'KDIT'
TIT'KIT'GINA   DHAGE TINNA   KINA TA S   K'D TATIT'   KINA TAKE
TINNA KINA   DHA TIRIKIT'T'K   T'K DIT'TIT'KIT'   GINA DHAGE
DHINNA GINA   —— Prastaar as usual

5) DHINNA S DHA   TIRIKIT'DHINNA   S DHA TIRIKIT'   DHINN'DHINNA
S DHA TIRIKIT'   DHINNA KID'N'K   TIRIKIT'T'KT'K   TIRIKIT'TINNA
S TA TIRIKIT'   TINNA S TA   TIRIKIT'DHINN'   DHINNA SDHA
TIRIKIT'DHINNA   KID'N'K TIRIKIT   T'K T'K TIRIKIT'

Rela

1) Chalan:

DHADHE   K'DDHE   K'DDHIN   NANA   DHINNA   GINA   DHADHE
K'DDHE   K'DDHIN   NANA   DHINN'   DHADHE   K'DDHE   K'DDHIN
NANA – Khaali

Rela:

DHA SSS | T'th DHIN TIRI | GID'NAG'DHA
DHIN TIRIGID'NAG' | DHATIRIGID'NAG' | DHINTIRIGID'N'G'
DHINTIRIGID'NAG' | DHATIRIGID'NAG' | DHATIRIGID'NAG'
DHINTIRIGID'NAG' | DHINTIRIGID'NAG' | DHATIRIGID'NAG'
DHINTIRIGID'NAG' | DHATIRIGID'NAG' | TINTIRIKID'NAK' – Khaali

2) GID'NAG'   TIT'GID'   NAG'TIT'   GID'NAG'   TAGE TIT'   GID'NAG'
TIT'TIT'   GID'NAG   TITGID'   NAG'TIT'   GID'NAG'   TAGE TIT'
GID'NAG'   TIT'GID'   NAG'TIT' – Khaali

Mohras (in Madhya Laya. Nos. 1,2 & 4——after 7 1/2 matras)

1) DHATIRIKIT'T'K   TATIRIKIT'T'K   TIRIKIT'T'KT'K   TIRIKIT'DHATI
   DHA S T'K TIRI   KIT'DHATI DHA   S T'K TIRIKIT'   DHATI   DHA

2) DHA TIRIKIT'T'K   TIRIKIT'T'K TA   TIT'K'T'G'DING'N'   DHA TIRIKIT'T'K
   TA TIT' K'T'G'DIN   G'N'DHA TIRIKIT'   T'K TA TIT'K'T'   G'DING'N'— DHA

3) DIRIDIRI KIT'T'K   TIRIKIT'T'K(T'K   TIRIKIT'DHADHA   DHA —) x 9 Bed'm

4) TIRIKIT'T'K T'K   TIRIKIT'TAKITIRI   KIT'T'K TIRIKIT'   T'KT'K TIRIKIT'
   S GE S NT'   DHA S GE S   NT'DHA S GE   S NT'— DHA

Tukdas:

1) DHINNA S DHA   GEN'NAGE TIRI   KIT'T'K TIRIKIT'   T'K T'K TIRIKIT'
   DHAGE TIT'   SS KID'NAK'   TIRIKIT'T'K TA   S GE S NT'   DHA S TA S
   KID'NAK' TIRIKIT'   T'K TA S GE   S NT'DHA S   TA S KID'NAK'
   TIRIKIT'T'KTA   SGE ST'   DHA

2) K'D DHA S N'   DHAGE TIT'   K'th S DHAGE   N'DHA TIRIKIT'   DHA S TA S
   (SS TIRIKIT'   T'K TAGEN'   DHAS SS   SS SS) x 3 (No gaps the 3rd time.)

The same Bol can be played by giving a DHA and gap of 1, 2, 3 matras after sum and reducing the gaps) in the Tihaai. The last of the series is as given below:

3) DHAS SS   SS SS   SS SS   SS SS   K'D DHA S N'   DHAGE TIT'
   K'th S DHAGE   N'DHA TIRIKIT'   DHA S TA S   SS TIRIKIT'   T'K TAGEN'
   DHA S TIRIKIT'   T'K TAGEN'   DHA S TIRIKIT'   T'K TAGEN'   DHA SSS
   SS SS (TIRIKIT'T'K TA   GEN'DHA S) x 3   SS SS   SS TIRIKIT'   T'K TAGEN'
   (DHA S TIRIKIT'   T'K TAGEN') x 2   DHA

4) DHA S DHA S   TUN S TUN S   NANA TIT'   KIT' K'th S TIRI   KIT'T'K TA S
   (DIRIDIRI KIT'T'K   TA S K'th T'th   DHA S K'th T'th   DHA S—) x 3

5) T'GE S N'   DHIT S TA   DHIT S DHIT S   (DHA S DIRIDIRI   KIT'T'K TA S
   DIRIDIRI KIT'T'K   DHA S TA S) x 3   DHA

6) DHAGE TIT'   KIT DHAGE   TIT'KIT'   DHAGE TIT'   K'D DHA TIT'
   DHAGE TIT'   K'th TIT' TA   GEN'DHA S   (K'th S DIRIDIRI   KIT'T'K T'th KIT'
   DHA -) x 3 .

Chakradaar from (6)

7) [DHAGE TIT'   KIT'DHAGE   TIT'KIT   DHAGE TIT'   K'D DHATI T'
DHAGE TIT'   K'th TIT' TA   GEN'DHA S   K'th (S DIRIDIRI   KIT'T'K T'th KIT'
DHA -) x 3 SS SS] *x 3*

Nine – Dha   G'th (in Dedhi)

K'th TIRIKIT' DIKIT'   K'T'G'DING'N'   DHA SS   K'T'G'DING'N'
K'th TIRIKIT'DIKIT'   K'T'G'DING'N'   DHA SS K'th SS   K'th S TI S T' S
K'T'K'T'K'T'   K'th TIRIKIT' DIKIT'   K'T G'DING'N'   GIN T'RA S N'
DHA G'S T'th KIT'   (DHA TIRIKIT' DIKIT'   K'T'G'DING'N'   DHA S K'T'G'
DING'N'DHA S,   K'T'G'DING'N'   DHA S SS) *x 3*

Twelve – Dha   G'th

DIRIDIRI KIT'T'K   T'th S KIT' DHA S   DIRIDIRI KIT'T'K   TAKITIRIKIT'T'K
K'th S DIRIDIRI   KIT'T'KT'th S KIT'   DHA SSS   DHAGETIT'   TAKETIT'
K'DDHATIT'   DHAGE TIT'   (DIRIDIRIKIT'T'K   T'th S KIT'DHA S
SS T'th S KIT'   DHA SSS   T'th S KIT' DHA S   SS T'th S KIT'   DHA S -) *x 3*

Fifteen – Dha   G'th

*{DHIT S DHIT   S DIT'   TIT'DHA   GE TIT'   DHA S K'D   DHA S N'
DHA S DHIN   S TA S   DHA TIRIKIT'   DIKIT'   K'th TAGE   DING'N'
(DHAGE TI   T'TAGE   TIT' K'D   DHA TIT') *x 2* } upto here, the G'th is in Dedhi.
[SS GE S   SS NT'   SS (DIRIDIRI   KIT'T'K T'th S KIT'   DHA S -) *x 5*
gap of SS, SS , SS] *x 3*

Chakradaar:

1) [GIN TIRIKIT'T'K   TAGE TIT'   K'th TA S GE   NA S DHA S   TUN S NA S
GENA TUNNA   (DHA TUNNA DHA   TUNNA DHA TUN   NA DHA TUNNA
DHA SS Th'   DHA S -) *x 3*   SS SS] *x 3*

2) [DIT'TIT'   DHAGETIT'   K'DDHATIT'   DHAGETIT'   (K'D DHATIT') *x 3*
DHAGE TIT'   DHA S K'D DHA   TIT' DHA S   K'D DHA TIT'   DIRIDIRI KIT'T'K
(T'th S KIT'DHA   K'Th S DIRIDIRI   KIT'T'K T'th KIT'   DHA S SS   SS -) *x 3*] *x 3*

Farmaishi in Drut

Parans

    DHAGE TIT'   TAGE TIT'   DHAGE DINGE   NAGE TIT'   K'D DHATIT'
    DHAGETIT'   DHAGE DINGE   NAGE TIT'   (K'D DHA TIT'   DHAGE TIT') *x 3*
    G'DINGIN'   NAGE TIT'   [(K'thTAK'thTA   K'thTIRIKIT'T'K   TAGETIT') *x 2*
    (K'th TIRIKIT'T'K   TA S K'thT'th   DHAS SS) *x 3*] *x 3*

2) (DHAGE TIT' TAGE TIT') *x 3* K'D DHATIT' DHAGETIT'   SS SS   DHAGETIT'
    (DHAGE TIT'   TAGE TIT') *x 2* K'D DHATIT'   DHAGETIT'   (K'thTAK'thTA
    K'th TIRIKIT'T'K   TAGE TIT') *x 2*   DHIT S DHIT S   DIT' TIT'   DHAGE TIT'
    K'D DHA TIT'   [K'th TIRIKIT'T'K   TAGE TIT'   K'th S TIT'   K'thTAK'thTA
    (K'th S DIRIDIRI   KIT'T'K T'th KIT'   DHA S -) *x 3*] *x 3* Bed'm

G'th of 5 Layas

3) (DHA S K'D DHA   TIT' K'th TI   T' TAGEN'   TIT' K'th S) ———— Chatushra
    (DHA S K'D DHA S   TIT'K'thTIT'   DHA S TIRIKIT'T'K   TA S K'th SS) —— Khanda
    (DHA S K'DDHATIT' K'thTIT'TAGEN'   DHAGETIT'TAGE TIRIKIT'T'KTAK'thS) ——
                                                        Tishra
    (DHASK'DDHASTIRIKIT'   T'KTASDHAGETIT'   DHAGEN'DHAGETIT'
    TIRIKIT'T'K TA S K'th S) —— Mishra
    [(DHASK'DDHA TIT' K'th TI   T'TAGEN'TIT' K'th S   SS DIRIDIRI KIT'T'K TA S
    TIRIKIT'T'K TA S K'thS T'   DHASS SSSS) *x 3*] Chatushra —— double

4) DIT'TIT'DHAGETIT'   K'DDHATIT' DHAGETIT'   (K'D DHA TIT') *x 2*
    K'D DHA TIT' DHAGE TIT'   (K'D DHA TIT' DHAGE TIT') *x 2*   (K'D DHATIT') *x 2*
    K'D DHATIT' DHAGE TIT' DHA S K'D DHA TIT'DHA S   K'D DHATIT'DHAGE TIT'
    DHAG'ST'th KIT'DHAGE   TIT'K'thTAK'thTAK'thTA   K'th TIT' TAGEN DHIT
    T'GE S N'DHA SSS   (KIT' DHA S N'DHA S N'   DHA S TA S DHA S KIT'
    DHA S N'DHA S N'DHA S   TA S DHA S KIT' DHA S   N'DHA S N DHA S TA
    DHA SSS -) *x 3*

Vasant Taal

Matras 9; Tali on 1,2,3,4,6,8, Khali on 5,7,9

1	2	3	4	5	6	7	8	9
DHIN	TIRIKIT'	DHIN	DHAGE	TUN	NA	DHAGE	NA DHA	TIRIKIT'
x 1	2	3	4	0	5	0	6	0

Tihaai

[DHADHADHATUN   TUNTUNNANA   NA (K'thTIT'KIT'

K'thTIRIKIT'DIKIT'K'thT'th   G'DIG'N'DHADHA   DHAS -) *x 3* S S] *x 3*

Peshkaar

(Farrukhabad)

1) DHE S K'D DHINDHA   S DHA DHINDHA   S K'D DHA DHINDHIN

    DHADHIN DHADHA   TINTA TE S K'D   TINTA S TA   DHINDHA S K'DDHA

    DHINDHIN DHADHIN   DHADHA DHINDHA

2) DHE S K'D DHINDHA   S DHA DHINDHA   S K'D DHA DHINDHIN

    DHADHIN DHADHA   DHINDHA T'KGIDA   S N'DHA DHINNA

    S DHA S K'DDHA   DHINNA DHATI   DHADHA TINNA

    KIT'T'KTIN SS K'D   TINTA KIT'T'K   TIN'TINNA KINATAKE

    TIT KIT TAKE TIRIKIT   TINNAKINA (T'KGIDA   S N'DHA TINNA) *x 3*   DHA

(Delhi)

DHAS K'D	DHA S TIRI	KIT' DHA	S K'D DHA S	TIRIKIT'
DHA S K'D	DHATI	DHA DHA	DHINNA	KITDHA*
TIRIKIT'	DHATIRI	KIT'DHA	TIRIKIT'	DHA S K'D
DHATI	DHA DHA	TINNA – Khaali	——Prastaar as usual.	

Kaida

1) DHA S K'D DHA   TI DHA GENA   DHAGE DHINNA   DHAGE DHINNA

    GINA DHA TIRI   KIT' DHATI DHA   GINA DHAGE   DHINNA DHAGE

    TINNA KINA—Khaali

2) DHA S TIT'   GINA DHATI   T'GINA DHA   **GENA DHINNA**   GINA TIT'
TIT' GINA   DHA TIT'GI   NA DHA GENA   **TINNA KINA** – Khaali

3) DHAGE NA DHA   TIRIKIT'DHIN'   DHAGE TIRIKIT'   **DHIN'DHINNA**
GINA TIRIKIT'   T'K TAS TIRIKIT'   DHIN'DHAGE   TIRIKIT'TINN'
TINNA KINA – Khaali

4) DHATIRI   KIT'DI   KIT'   GINA   DHATI   GIN'   DHAGE
TINNA   KINA   TATIRI   KIT'TI   KIT'   KINA   DHATI
GIN'   DHAGE   DHINNA   GINA

Rela on above Chalan

DHATIRI   KIT'DIRI   DIRIDIRI   KIT'T'K   DHATIRI   KIT'T'K   TIRIKIT'
TINNA   KIT'T'K   TATIRI   KIT'TIRI   TIRITIRI   KIT'T'K   DHATIRI
KIT'T'K   TIRIKIT'   DHINNA   KITT'K

Mohras: (in Drut)

1) DHATIRI KIT'T'K   TATIRI KIT'T'K   (TIRIKIT' T'KT'K   TIRIKIT'DHADHA
DHA S-) x 3

2) K'th TIT'KIT'   (K'thTIRIKIT'DIKIT'   K'T'G'DIG'N'   DHASS) x 3 – in Dedhi

3) DHADHADHATUN   TUNTUNNANA   NAK'thTIT'KIT'   (K'thTIRIKIT'DIKIT'K'T'
G'DIG'N'DHAS SS   SS-) x 3

4) TIRIKIT'T'KT'K   TIRIKITTAKITIRI   KIT'T'KTIRIKIT   T'K T'K(TIRIKIT'
T'KDIT'TIT'KIT'   DHAS-) x 3

Tukdas

1) DHATI S DHA   TI S DHATI   DHA TIRIKIT'T'K   TA TIRIKIT'T'K
(TIRIKIT'T'K T'K   TIRIKIT'DHATI   DHA S DHATI   DHA S DHATI
DHA SSS) x 3

2) (DHIT S DHIT S) x 2   (DIT'TIT') x 2   (DHAGE TIT'   K'D DHA TIT') x 2
DHA TIRIKIT'T'K   TA S TA S   (TA S K'D DHIN   NA S DHA S
DHA S KIT'T'K) x 2   TA S K'D DHIN   NA S DHA S   DHA

3) DHIT S DHIT S   DIT'TIT'   DHAGE TIT'   K'D DHA TIT'   (DHA TIRIKIT'T'K
TA S TA S   TA S K'D DHIN   NA S DHA S   DHA SSS) x 3

4) DHITSDHITS   TIRIKIT'DHIT   DHAGETIT'   TAGETIT'   K'D DHIT S TUN
GEN'NAG'   TIT'K'thTA   G'DIGIN'   (DHA S DHA S   TIRIKIT'DHIT
TAGE S N'   DHA S -) x 3

5) DIRIDIRI KIT'T'K   TA SSS   TIRITIRI KIT'T'K   TA SSS   (DIRIDIRI KIT'T'K
TAKI TIRIKIT'T'K   TAKITIRIKIT'T'K   T'th K'DA S N   DHA SSS) x 3

6) DIT'TIT'   DHAGE TIT'   K'D DHIT S DI   KIT'DHAGE   TIT'K'thTA   G'DIG'N'
DHIT S TAGE   S N'DHA S   (DIRIDIRI KIT'T'K   TA S K'thT'th   DHA S TA S
DHA S -) x 3

7) DIT'TIT'   DHAGETIT'   K'D DHATIT'   K'th S TIT'   [(G'DING'N'   TAGETIRIKIT'
TUNNAK'thT'th   DHA S -) x 3   SS] x 3

G'th

1) * (DHATIRIKIT'   DIKIT'   K'th S DI   T'TIT'   DHATIRIKIT'   DIKIT'
K'th S T'   DHA SS) *   DHATIRIKIT'DI   KIT'K'thT'   K'th S TIT'   K'D DHATIT'
K'thTIT'TA   GEN'DHIT S   T'GE S N'   DHA SSS   (DIRI DIRI) x 2   (TIRI TIRI) x 2
(DIRIDIRI KIT'T'K   TAKITIRIKIT'T'K   T'thK'DA S NT'   DIRIDIRI KIT'T'K
T'th K'DA S NT'   DHA S -) x 3   * Bols in these brackets are in Dedhi.

2) DHATIRIKIT' DI   KIT'K'T'   GIN T'RA   S N'DHATI   K'th S TIT'   DHA SSS
TI S T'S   TI S T'S   (SS DHA S   KIT'T'K TA S N   DHA S K'T'   DHA S -) x 3

3) *DHESK'DDHIN   DHAGID'N'G'   DHIN'GIN'DHAGE   TIRIKIT'DHINNAGID'
N'G'DING'DHINNA   GIN'DHAGE TIT'   GIDA S N'DHAGE   NAG'TING'NAK'
KIT'T'K TIT'   K'th TA KIT'T'K   (DHA TIRIKIT'DIKIKIT'   K'T'G'DING'N'
DHA SS K'T'G'   DING'N'DHA SS   K'T'G'DING'N'   DHASS SSS) x 3
* entirely in Dedhi ang.

4) K'th TIT'TA   GEN'K'thTI   T'TAGEN'   K'thTIT'TA   GEN'DHIT S
DHIT S DHIT S   K'th TIT' TA   GEN'DHAS   TUN S TA S   K'th S K'th S
*DIT'TIT'GID'   N'G'TIRIKIT'TUNNA   KID'N'K'DHINTIRI   KIT'T'KTA STA S
KID'N'K'TIN'   KIN'TAKE TIRIKIT'   [TIN'TINNA KINA   K'th S DHATI DHAS
DHATI DHA S DHATI   DHASS SSS] x 3   All in double Dedhi from * onwards

212

5) K'th TA S GI   NA S DIRIDIRI   K'th S DHATIRI   GID'N'G'DIRIDIRI   K'th SSS
DIRIDIRIKIT'DHA   S D'DHADIRIDIRI   KIT' DHAS D'DHA   DHE S K'D DHINDHA
GID'N'GTE S K'D   TINTAKID'N'K   (DIRIDIRI KIT'T'K   DIRIDIRIKITDHA
S D'DHA DHIN NA   GID'N'G'DHE S K'D   DHINNA GID'N'G
DHA S—) *x 3*——Bed'm

Chakradaars

1) [TIT'K'T'G'DING'N'   DHATIT'K'th   TAG'DING'   N'DHATI S   T'K'thSTA
G'SDIG' SN'DHAS   TI ST S   K'thSTAS   G'SDIN'S   G'SN'S
(DHASSS TIT'K'th ST'   G'DING'N'DHA S TIT'   K'th T'G'DING'N'DHA S
TIT'K'th T'G'DING'N') *x 3* DHAS SS   SS] *x 3*

2) [DHA S DHIN S   TA S DIRIDIRI   KIT'T'K T'th S KIT'   DHA S K'th S
(DIRIDIRI KIT'T'K   T'th S KIT' DHA S   SS DIRIDIRI   KIT'T'K T'th S KIT'
DHA S—) *x 3*   SS   SS] *x 3*

Farmaishi:

3) [K'th S TIT'   K'th S TIT'   GIGI TIT'   GIGI TIT'   K'th TIRIKIT' DI   KIT K'th TA
G'DING'N'   DHA SSS   TI S T'S   K'th S TA S   G'S DINS   G'S N'S
DHA TIRIKIT'T'K'   TA TIRIKIT'T'K'   (TIRIKIT'T'K T'K   TIRIKIT' TAKI TIRI
KIT'T'K TIRIKIT'   T'K T'K TIRIKIT'   DHA SSS) *x 3* gap of SSSS   SSSS] *x 3*

Paran

DIT'TIT'   DHAGE TIT'   K'D DHA TIT'   DHAGE TIT'   (K'D DHA TIT') *x 3*
DHAGE TIT'   (K'D DHA TIT'   DHAGE TIT') *x 2*   (K'D DHA TIT') *x 3*   DHAGE TIT'
(DHA S K'D DHA   TIT'DHA S   K'D DHA TIT') *x 2*   DHAGETIT'   K'DDHATIT'
DHAG'ST'   KIT'DHAGE TIT'K'thTA   K'thTAK'thTA   K'thTIT'TA
GEN'DHFTS   T'GESN'   DHITSTAS   KIT'DHITS   DHITSDHITS
TAGESN'   DHITSTAS [DIRIDIRIKIT'T'K   TAKITIRIKIT'T'K   K'th SDIRIDIRI
KIT'T'KT'thSKIT'   DHAS SS   DIRIDIRIKIT'T'K   TAKITIRIKIT'T'K   K'thSDIRIDIRI
KIT'T'KT'thSKIT'   DHAST'thSKIT'   DHAS SS   DIRIDIRIKIT'T'K
TAKITIRIKIT'T'K   K'th SDIRIDIRI   KIT'T'K T'th S KIT'   DHA S T'th S KIT'
DHA S T'th S KIT'   DHA S SS   SS] *x 3*

213

Dedhi Dugun G'th

DHAGEN'   DHA TIRIKIT'   DIKIT'   DHAGEN'   DHA TIRIKIT'   DIKIT'
GIN'TIN   NA GIN'   TINNA S   DHAGEN'   DHA TIRIKIT'   DIKIT'
GINADHA   TIGIN'   DHA TIRIKIT'   DIKIT'   GIN'TIN   NA KINA

Dedhi:

(DHAGEN'DHA   TIRIKIT'DIKI   T'DHAGEN'   DHATIRIKIT'DI   KIT'GIN'
TINNAGIN'   TINNA SDHA   GEN'DHATIRI   KIT'DIKIT'   GINADHATI
GINADHATIRI   KIT'DIKIT'   GIN'TINNA   KINA—) *x 2*

Dugun:

(DHAGEN'DHA TIRIKIT'   DIKIT'DHAGEN'   DHA TIRIKIT'DIKIT'
GIN'TINNA GIN'   TINNA SDHAGEN'   DHA TIRIKIT'DIKIT'
GINADHA TIGIN'   DHA TIRIKIT' DIKIT'   GIN'TIN NA KINA) *x 2*

Tigun:

DHAGEN'DHA TIRIKIT'DIKI   T'DHAGEN'DHATIRIKIT'DI   KIT'GIN' TINNAGIN'
TINNA SDHAGEN'DHATIRI   KIT'DIKIT'GINADHATI   GINADHATIRI KIT'DIKIT'
GIN'TINNAKINA-) *x 4*

Chougun:

(DHAGEN'DHATIRIKIT'DIKIT'DHAGEN'   DHA TIRIKIT'DIKIT'GIN'TINNA GIN'
TINNA SDHAGEN'DHA TIRIKIT'DIKIT'   GINADHATIGIN'DHATIRIKIT'DIKIT'
GIN'TINNAKINA—) *x 4*

Tihaai:

[DHAGEN'DHA TIRIKIT'DIKIT' DHAGEN   DHA TIRIKIT' DIKIT'GIN'TINNA GIN'
TINNA S DHAGEN'DHA TIRIKIT' DIKIT'   GINADHATI GIN'(DHA TIRIKIT' DIKIT'
GIN'TINNA KINA DHASS DHASS   DHASS -) *x 3*   SSS   SSS] *x 3*

214

Taal : Asht'mangal

Matras 11; Taali on 1, 3, 7, 9. Khaali on 5

1	2		3	4		5	6		7	8
DHIN	TIRIKIT'	I	DHIN	DHAGE	I	TUN	NA	I	T'th	TIN
x 1			2			0			3	

9	10	11	
DHAGE	NA DHA	TIRIKIT'	I
4			

Paran

DHAGE TIT' K'D DHA S N'   DHA K'D DHA   TIT'DHAGE   TIT'K'D DHA

TIT'DHAGE   T'th S DIRIDIRI   KIT'T'K TAGE   TIT' K'D DHA   TIT' K'th S

TIRIKIT'T'K TA   SS K'th TA   K'th SSS   (DIT' TIT'   DHAGE TIT'

DHAGE TIT'   K'D DHA TIT'   TUN S DIRIDIRI   KIT'T'K T'th S KIT'

DIRIDIRI KIT'T'K   T'th S KIT' DIRIDIRI   KIT'T'K T'th S KIT'   DHAS SS   SS SS) *x 3*

Peshkaar (Farrukhabad)

1) DHE S K'D   DHIN DHA   S DHA   DHIN DHA   KIT' DHA   DHIN DHA

   SK'D DHA   DHIN DHIN   DHA DHIN   DHA DHA   TIN TA
   – Khaali and Prastaar as usual.

(Delhi)

2) DHA TI   DHA TI   DHA DHA   DHIN NA   TI DHA   DHA TI

   DHA DHA   DHINNA   DHATI   DHA DHA   TINNA – Khaali

3) DHA S K'D   DHA TIRI   KIT' DHA   TI DHA   DHA TIN   NA – Khaali and
   Prastaar as usual.

Kaidas:

1) DHA S K'D DHA   TIT'DHAGE   TIT'K'D DHA   TIT'KID'N'K'

   TIRIKIT'T'KT'K   TIRIKIT' – Khaali

2) DHA S   GIGI   TIT'   KIT'   DHAGE   TIT'   GIGI   TIT'

   GIN'   TINNA   KINA – Khaali

215

3) * DHA S K'D   DIKIT'   GIN'DHIN   NA GINA   DHAGEN'   DHAGE TI   T'KIT'
DHA TIRIKIT'   DIKIT'   GIN'TIN   NA KINA —Khaali

This Kaida is in Tishra Jaati and could be played first as a Dedhi Dugun G'th and in Chougun, as a
Kaida i.e. : make paltas and Tihaai.

4) DHINNA   S DHA   TIRIKIT'   DHINNA   S DHA   TIRIKIT'   DHINNA
KID'N'K'   TIRIKIT'   T'K T'K   TIRIKIT'———Khaali

Mohra: (1 DHA , 2 DHA's & 3 DHA's)

1) (DIRIDIRI KIT'T'K   T'th S KIT' DHA S) x 3   DIRIDIRI KIT'T'K
TAKI TIRIKIT'T'K   T'th S DIRIDIRI   KIT'T'K T'th S KIT'
DHA S DIRIDIRI   KIT'T'K TAKI TIRI   KIT'T'K T'th S
DIRIDIRI KIT'T'K   (T'th S KIT' DHA S) x 2   DIRIDIRI KIT'T'K
TAKI TIRIKIT'T'K   T'th S DIRIDIRI   KIT'T'K T'th S KIT'
(DHA S T'th S KIT') x 2   DHA

G'th of 9 DHA's

2) (DIRIDIRI KITT'K   TAKI TIRIKITT'K   T'th S DIRIDIRI   KITT'K DIRIDIRI
KITT'K T'th S KIT   DHA S T'th S KIT   DHA S T'th S KIT   DHA S -) x 3

G'th of 12 DHA's

3) (DIRIDIRI K'th S   DIRIDIRI KIT'T'K   T'th S KIT' DHA S   SS T'th S KIT'
DHA SSS   T'th S KIT' DHA S   SS T'th S KIT'   DHA S -) x 3

G'th of 15 DHA's

4) [DIRIDIRI KIT'T'K   TAKI TIRIKIT'T'K   (T'th S DIRIDIRI   KIT'T'K T'th S KIT'
DHA S -) x 5   SS] x 3

Poorab G'th's

5) DIT' TIT'   K'D DHA TIT'   SS DHIN S   NA TIRIKIT'T'K   DHIT S TA S
K'D DHA S N'   NA TIRIKIT'T'K   TA S K'D DHA   S N'DHA S   K'th S TIT'
DHAGE TIT'   K'D DHA TIT'   (DIRIDIRI KIT'T'K   TAKI TIRIKIT'T'K
TUN SSS   NA TIRIKIT'T'K   TA S K'D DHA   S N'DHA S   KIT'T'K DHA S
KID'N'K TIRIKIT'   T'K T'K TIRIKIT'   DHA S TA S   DHAS SS) x 3

6) *(DHIN'T'   K'T'K')   T'K DHINN'   T'K T'K   T'K DHINN' T'K TIT'
GID'N'G'   TING'N'K'   T'K T'K   DHIN T'K   TIT' K'th TA   KIT'T'K
TIT' K'th TA   K'th S DHAGE   TIT' K'thTA   G'DING'N' (N'G'TIT'   K'T GIN S
T'RA S N'   DHA SSS   K'th S DHA S   TIT'K'T'G'DING'N'   DHA S TIT'K'T'
G'DIG'N'DHA S   TIT'K'T' G'DING'N'   DHA S -) x 3

*Note:- *These Bols are in Dedhi Rest, all in Chatushra.*

Chakradaar: (Farmaishi)

1) [TIRIKIT' DHIT S   SS TIRIKIT'   DHIT SSS   TAGE S N'   DHAGE TIT'
TAGE TIT'   K'D DHA TIT'   DHAGE TIT'   GE S TIRIKIT'T'K   TAGE TIT'
K'th TIT' TA   GEN'DHA S   K'D DHA S N'   DHA S K'D DHA   S N'DHA S
K'th SSS   DIRIDIRI KIT'T'K   TAKI TIRIKIT'T'K   TAKI TIRIKIT'T'K
TUNNA KIT'T'K   (TA S K'D DHIN   NA S DHA S   DHA S KIT'T'K) x 2
TA S K'D DHIN   NA S DHA S   DHAS SS   SS SS] x 3

2) (DIT' TIT'   DHAGE TIT'   K'D DHA TIT'   K'th S TIT'   G'DING'N'
TAGE TIRIKIT'   TUNNA K'T'   DHA SSS   K'D GE S NG'D   GE S N K'th S
SS DIRIDIRI   KIT'T'K DIRIDIRI   KIT'T'K DIRIDIRI   KIT'T'K T'th S KIT'
DHAS SS) x 3

Paran: (Chakradaar in Mishra Jaati)

1) [DHAGEN'   DHAGE TIT'   TAGEN'   TAGE TIT'   K'D DHIT S   DIT' TIT'
DHAGEN'   TUNNA K'T'   K'th TIT'   TA S K'th T'   K'th TIT'   TAGE TIT'
K'D DHIT S   DIT' TIT'   DHAGEN'   TUNNA K'T,   K'th TIT'   TA S K'th T'
K'th TIT'   TAGE TIT'   DHA SS   SS GIN'   (DHA S GE   T'K DHIN') x 3
DHAS SS   SS SS] x 3

2) [(DHAGE TIT') x 2   K'D DHA TIT'] x 2   [(K'th T'th) x 4   K'D DHA TIT'] x 2
GIN'S TA   S D'DHIT S   SS DHIT S   TAGE S N'   DHIT S TA S   TIRIKIT' DIT'
T'TAGEN'   DHIT S TA S   TIRIKIT' DIT' T'TAGEN'
[GIN'S TA   S D'DHIT S   TAGE S N'   DHIT S TA S   TIRIKIT' DIT'   T'TAGEN'
DHIT S TA S   GIGI TIT'   K'th S TIT'   (G'DIG'N'   DHA S K'T') x 2
G'DIG'N'   DHAS SS] x 3

217

Assortment of less popular and unheard of Taals

An unlimited array of Taals are in existence and more are composed by the day. By definition , a Taal must have at least one *Laghu* and one *Guru*. However if one were to use more *Laghus* , *Gurus* and their *Pluth* and *Chitpluth* , then there is no limit on one's ability to compose new Taals – provided they abide by the dictates of Taal Shastra and most importantly, gain acceptance. There are Taals which do not conform to the classical definition of Taala. These are the smaller Taals of 2 , 3 , 4 matras , which in reality are only Folk rhythms.

1) P'T' Taal: 2 Matras.

1	2
DHA STIT' I	G'DIG'N'
x	0
I	

2) Madan Taal: 3 Matras

1	2	3
DHA S I	DIN NA	GINA
x	0	
I		

3) N'T' Taal: 4 Matras

1	2	3	4
DHA S	TIT'	K'th TA	G'DIG'N'
x	2		
I			

4) Haruba – Leela Taal: 5 Matras.

1	2	3	4	5
DHAGE	TIT' I	K'th TA	G'DI	G'N'
x	2			
I				

5) Garud Taal: 6 Matras

1	2	3	4	5	6
DHA I	DIN I	TA I	K'th TA I	G'DI I	G'N'I
x	0	2	3	4	5
I					

6) Sameer Taal: 7 Matras

1	2	3	4	5	6	7
DHA S	S T'	DHIT S	TA S	K'th TA	K'th S TIT'	G'DIG'N'
x 1	0	2	0	3	0	4

7) Taal Pushto: 7 Matras.

1	2	3		4	5		6	7
TIN S	S S	TIRIKIT'	|	DHIN S	S S	|	NA S	NA S |
0				1			2	

8) Kha T' Taal: 8 Matras.

1	2	3	4	5	6	7	8
DHA S	DHIT S	DIT'	TA S	TIT'	DHAGE	NA DHA	TIRIKIT'
x 1	2	0	3	0	4	5	6

9) Garugi Taal :- 9 Matras.

1	2		3	4		5	6		7	8	9
DHA	TI	|	DHA	DHA	|	DHIN	TIT'	|	K'th TA	G'DI	G'N'
x 1			2			3			4		

10) Aada Panch Taal: 9 Matras.

1	2	3		4	5		6	7		8	9
DHA	TIRI	KIT	|	T'K'	DHA	|	KIT'	T'K'	|	G'DI	G'N'
x 1	2			3			4			5	

11) Shakti Taal: 10 Matras.

1	2	3		4	5	6		7	8
DHA	DIN'	NAK'	|	DHIT S	DINN'	NAK'	|	TIT'	K'th TA
x 1	2	3		0	4			5	6

9	10
G'DI	G'N'
7	0

12) Ik Taal: 11 Matras.

1	2		3	4	5	6		7	8
DHA	TIRIKIT'	|	DHAGE	NADHA	TIRIKIT'	TUN	|	NA	TIRIKIT'
x 1			2		0			3	

9	10	11
DHAGE	NADHA	TIRIKIT'
4		

13) **Jhumar Taal:** 11 Matras.

1	2	3	4		5	6	7	8	9
DHIN	TIRIKIT'	TIN	NA		DHIN	NA	T'th	TIN	DHAGE
x		0			2		0		3
1									

10	11
NADHA	TIRIKIT'

14) **Mohan Taal:** 12 Matras.

1	2	3	4	5	6	7	8	9	10	11	12
DHA	TI	T'	DHA	DHA	DHIN	TA	TIT'	K'thTA	G'DI	S G'	N S
x	2	3		4		5		6	7		
1											

15) **Dwitiya Mantika Taal:** 13 Matras.

1	2	3	4		5	6	7
DHIN	NA	DHINNA	T'th	|	DHINSSKD'	DHINNA	TINNA
x					2		
1							

8		9	10	11		12	13
K'thTA	|	TIRIKIT'	DHINNA	DHINDHIN	|	NADHIN	DHINNA
		3				4	

16) **Hamsa Taal:** 14 Matras.

1	2	3	4		5	6	7	
DHA	DHA	DHIN	TA	|	DHA	DHIN	TA	|
x		0			2			
1								

8	9	10	11		12	13	14	
KIT'	DHA	DHIN	TA	|	K'thTA	G'DI	G'N'	|
3		0			4			

17) **Taal Phirodust:** 14 Matras.

1	2	3		4	5		6	7
DHIN	TIRIKIT'	|DHIN NA		DHA GE	|NA DHA		TIRIKIT'	| TUN
x		0		2				0
1								

8	9	10		11	12		13	14
NA	DHA TIRI	KIT'DHIN	|	NA K'	DHA TIRI	|	KIT'DHIN	NA K'|
	3			4			5	

220

18) <u>Taal Gajajhampa</u>: 15 Matras

1	2		3	4		5	6		7	8	
DHIN	TIRIKIT'	|	TIN	TIN	|	NA	DHIN	|	DHIN	NA	|
x			0			2			3		
1											

9	10		11	12		13	14		15	
DHA	DHA	|	TIT'	KIT'	|	DHA	DHINNA		GINA	|
4			5			6				

19) <u>Taal Savari</u>: 15 Matras Taali on 1, 4, 12 Khaali on 8

1	2	3		4	5	6	
DHIN	DHA S D'	DHA DHA	|	TUNNA	TA TIRIKIT'	TUNNA	|
x				2			
1							

7	8	9	10	11	
TIRIKIT'T'th	TUNNA	T'th TIN	NA S DHIN'	GIN'DHAGE	|
	0				

12	13	14	15	
NA DHA TIRIKIT'	DHI SS DHAS	S D'DHI S	S DHA S D'	|
3				

20) <u>Saraswati</u> <u>Taal</u>: 16 Matras.

1	2		3	4		5	6		7	8	
DHA	DHA	|	DHIN	TA	|	KIT'	DHA	|	DHIN	TA	|
x			0			2			0		
1											

9	10		11	12		13	14		15	16	
DHA	DHIN	|	DHIN	DHA	|	TIT'	K'thTA	|	G'DI	'N'	|
3			0			4			5		

21) <u>Taal PUNJABI</u>: (for Thumri / Tappa) 16 Matras.

1	2	3	4		5	6	7	8	
DHA S	G'DI	S G'	DHA S	|	DHA S GID'	N'K TIS	S K'	TA S	|
x					2				
1									

9	10	11	12		13	14	15	
TA S	T'th TIN	S K	DHA S	|	DHA S GID'	N'G'DHIN	S K'D'DHIN	
0					3			

16	
NA NA	|

221

22) Vishnu Taal :

17 Matras ; Taali on 1, 5, 7, 11, 13, 15 Khaali on 3, 9.

1	2		3	4		5	6		7	8
DHIN	TIRIKIT'	|	TIN	NA	|	K'th	DHAGE	|	N'DHA	GIN' |
x			0			2			3	
1										

9	10		11	12		13	14		15	16	17
TIN	NA	|	DHAGI	TIRIKIT'	|	DHIN	NA	|	DHIN	DHIN	NA |
0			4			5			6		

23) SHIKHAR TAAL:

17 Matras ; Taali on 1 , 4 , 7 , 13 , 15. Khaali on 10

1	2	3		4	5	6	
DHIN	TIRIKIT'	DHIN	|	DHAGE	TUN	NA	|
x				2			
1							

7	8	9		10	11	12	
DHAGE	NA DHA	TIRIKIT'	|	TIN	TIN	NA	|
3				0			

13	14		15	16	17	
DHAGE	TIT'	|	DHAGE	NA DHA	TIRIKIT'	|
4			5			

24) KARUNA TAAL: 18 Matras Taali on 1 , 5 , 9 , 11 , 15 , 17. Khaali on 3 , 7, 13.

1	2		3	4		5	6		7	8	
DHA	TIRIKIT'	|	TIN	NA	|	DHA	DHA	|	TIN	NA	|
x			0			2			0		
1											

9	10		11	12		13	14		15	16	
DHAGE	N'A DHA	|	TIRIKIT	DHA	|	TIN	NA	|	DHIN'	DHAGE	|
3			4			0			5		

17	18	
NA DHA	TIRIKIT'	|
6		

25) **Taal JAGADAMBAA:** 19 Matras Taali on 1 , 6 , 9 , 11 , 15. Khaali on 3 , 13 , 17

1	2	3	4	5		6	7	8
DHIN	TIRIKIT'	DHIN	DHIN	NA	|	DHA	TIN	NA |
x		0				2		
1								

9	10	11	12	13	14		15	16
DHIN	DHIN	DHA	DHA	TUN	NA	|	DHAGE	TIT'
3		4		0			5	

17	18	19	
DHAGE	NA DHA	TIRIKIT'	|
0			

26) **GOURI Taal:** 20 Matras Taali on 1 , 5 , 9 , 13 , 17. Khaali on 3 , 11 , 15 , 19.

1	2		3	4		5	6		7
DHA	TIRIKIT'	|	TIN	NA	|	DHA	DHA	|	TIN
x			0			2			
1									

8		9	10		11	12		13	14	
NA	|	DHAGE	TIRIKIT'	|	TIN	NA	|	DHAGE	NA DHA	|
		3			0			4		

15	16		17	18		19	20	
TIRIKIT'	DHAGE	|	NA DHA	TIRIKIT'	|	TINNA	KINA	|
0			5			0		

27) **GANESH TAAL:** 21 Matras.

Taali on 1 , 5 , 6 , 10 , 11 , 12 , 16 , 17, 18 , 19

Khaali on 3 , 8 , 14.

1	2		3	4		5	6	7
DHIN	TIRIKIT'	|	TIN	NA	|	GINA	DHAGE	NA DHA
x			0			2	3	
1								

8	9		10	11	12		13	14	15
TIRIKIT'	TIN	|	DHAGE	DHIN	NA	|	TIN	TIN	NA
0			4	5	6			0	

16		17		18		19	20	21	
TIRIKIT'	|	DHIN	|	NA	|	DHIN	DHIN	NA	|
7		8		9		10			

Bibliography

1) A tribute to the "Greatest of Gurus" - Late Khapruji Parvatkar by Malbarao Sardesai in the March 1958 issue of "Vidya" Magazine, in Marathi.

2) Taal, Matra and Laya by Ghanshyamdasji in Hindi.

3) Clarification of Ancient languages regarding Taal by Acharya Brahaspati, in Hindi.

4) "Taal Prakash" by Bhagwat Sharan Sharma, in Hindi

5) "Tabla" by Pandit Arvind Mulgaonkar, in Marathi

6) "Pranava Taal Pradnya" by Pandit H. Taranath Rao

7) "Tabla Vaadan Kalaa our Shaastra" by Pandit Sudir Mainkar

8) Sangeet Ratnakar - Vol II by Sharang Dev

Index

231

237